# Race and Racism

For earnest students and their teachers,
May the "color bar" not define the twenty-first century.

# Race and Racism

## An Introduction

Carolyn Fluehr-Lobban

ALTAMIRA
PRESS

A Division of
ROWMAN & LITTLEFIELD PUBLISHERS, INC.
Lanham • New York • Toronto • Oxford

ALTAMIRA PRESS

A division of Rowman & Littlefield Publishers, Inc.
A wholly owned subsidiary of The Rowman & Littlefield Publishing Group, Inc.
4501 Forbes Boulevard, Suite 200
Lanham, MD 20706
www.altamirapress.com

PO Box 317, Oxford, OX2 9RU, UK

British Library Cataloguing in Publication Information Available

Library of Congress Cataloging-in-Publication Data Available

0–7591–0794–7 (cloth : alk. paper)
0–7591–0795–5 (pbk. : alk. paper)

Printed in the United States of America

♾ ™ The paper used in this publication meets the minimum requirements of
American National Standard for Information Sciences—Permanence of Paper for
Printed Library Materials, ANSI/NISO Z39.48–1992.

# Contents

Racial myth versus fact: Athleticism is not a racial trait. A person's height is influenced by heredity and diet. Boston Celtics 6'11" Bill Walton and Washington Bullets 7'6" Manute Bol from South Sudan, in an October 1985 basketball game. Jim Wilson—the *Boston Globe*. Photograph originally published in the October 9, 1985, edition of the *Boston Globe*. Reprinted with permission.

# Acknowledgments

The inspiration for a course entitled Anthropology of Race and Racism came from a neighbor and friend, Edwige Lefebve-Leclercq, who was studying at the University of Montreal in 1975 and was taking a course in French entitled Nineteenth- and Twentieth-Century Biological and Socio-political Theories of Race and History. I was intrigued by a course that combined the study of racist thought with biological theories, as I had not been exposed to the critical study of race in my anthropological training, including my courses in physical anthropology. Indeed, in my 1960s and 1970s anthropological studies from BA through PhD, race had not been a significant subject for study. Inspired, I introduced a course into the Rhode Island College (RIC) general education program in 1975 entitled Race and Racism. The course was so well received that it was adopted by the anthropology department as one of its regular offerings in 1978 as the Anthropology of Race and Racism. At that time I made a pedagogical decision to offer the course at the introductory level that students could opt to take as part of their basic undergraduate education. Indeed, many students who were not anthropology majors did select the course, particularly from elementary and secondary education, communications, theater and the arts, as well as others of the social sciences.

A frequent comment made at the end of the introductory Anthropology of Race and Racism class was "But I feel as though we're just getting started, I wish the course could go on for another semester." In response to student interest, I developed an advanced undergraduate and graduate course for our Program of African and Afro-American Studies entitled Comparative Race Relations, which explored race and racism in our own and in other cultures. In time, this course evolved to one focusing on Critical Race Theory, as advances in fields other than anthropology were taking place in the post–civil rights era in the United States.

Students from the introductory-level courses were recruited not only to the advanced courses but also to involvement in education and civil rights activism. From these courses the RIC Unity Players emerged, a multiracial group of students who perform skits on race and diversity for community, high school, and university audiences, and who are featured in chapter 8. These skits developed by the students to be at the cutting edge of race relations are informed by anthropology and critical race thinking. Other students have become leaders in civil rights organizations such as the National Association for the Advancement of Colored People (NAACP), community leaders in organizations such as the Rhode Island Black Heritage Society, policy makers, and doctoral students. In other words, courses on race, racism, and anthropology have not only been responsive to student demand but have been transformative as well.

The pioneering Haitian anthropologist Anténor Firmin was discovered and then recovered in a 1988 Anthropology of Race and Racism class. He was brought to my attention by a Haitian student, Jacques Raphael Georges, who asked if I had not heard of Firmin's *De l'égalité des Races Humaines: Anthropologie Positive*, published in Paris in 1885 in response to Gobineau's writings on the inequality of races in 1855. This rediscovery of Firmin led to an English translation of the book by Haitian scholar Asselin Charles that appeared in hardcover in 2000 and in paperback in 2002 as *The Equality of the Human Races: Positivist Anthropology*. The first conference on Anténor Firmin was held at RIC in 2001, and since the English translation two new French editions have been published, one to coincide with the bicentennial of Haitian independence from France.

This book is offered as a tribute to the many students in anthropology, African and African American studies on race courses—to their courage to come into a class in which they know that sensitive matters of race and racism will be openly explored and discussed, and to their engagement with the many struggles to end racism, invigorated by a vision of a future multiracial society built on justice and equity. Much of this book has come directly from classroom lectures and discussion over the past three decades. Many of the examples mentioned in the text are derived from the memorable dialogues that have taken place. Practical suggestions for opening dialogue in the classroom, as well as useful visual teaching tools, are offered. From decades of teaching on this subject, I am convinced that the tools of anthropology can be powerfully and successfully applied both to understanding race and the eventual eradication of racism.

This book was also born from a frustration in locating a suitable text for courses in anthropology and race. I searched for an introductory text that would combine a comprehensible, accessible summary of the biology–physical anthropology of race with the social history of the race concept and its applications in society. Excellent books written by physical anthropologists proved difficult to teach, with students complaining about their scientific remoteness. Excellent studies of the history of the race concept lacked the biological information so important to demythologizing race. This book seeks to bridge this gap.

## SPECIAL THANKS

I express my personal thanks to countless students in Anthropology of Race and Racism who are too numerous to recount individually. However, a number stand out whom I would like to thank for their vital part in the dialogue on race and racism and for the many ways in which they have contributed to this volume. Thanks to Joaquina Bela Teixeira (now executive director of the Rhode Island Black Heritage Society), David Soares, Paul Khalil Saucier, Jasmine Mena, Jacqueline Teang, Mary Callahan, James McDermott, Kerry LaRose, Claudia Widdis, Hannah Resseger, Richard Martin, Sengoudone Sengvelay, Josue Rodas, Forrester Safford, Marco McWilliams, Liz Poli, Bridgit Lee Brady, Heather Fisch, Ryan Anas, Cynthia Williams, the Alexander family (Jim, Judy, Malaika), Barbara Burgo, Pamela Phillips, Stephanie Santos, Joyce Stevos, Shavonne Fairweather, Deneia Fairweather, and Beth Bourassa.

Christopher Souza, Courtney Correia, David Gonzalez, Dwayne Clements, Richard B., and Tenika Daponte were all founding members of the Unity Players and established the spirit, form, and content of the mission of the group of improvisational actors devoted to education about race and racism.

Thanks to Paul Khalil Saucier for critiquing and adding to the section on whiteness and hip-hop. Thanks also to Christine Andrade, who read early drafts of the manuscript. Thanks to Hannah Resseger for her excellent work on the graphics and her poem on affirmative action and white privilege.

Finally, I express my thanks to Leonard Leiberman, professor of anthropology at Central Michigan University, and one of the reviewers of the manuscript, for his many helpful suggestions for improving the clarity of the text and adding useful references. The other reviewers also helped to strengthen the text with their constructive suggestions and encouragement. I also thank Mitch Allen and Rosalie Robertson of AltaMira Press for their support of the concept of a volume on anthropology and race that encompasses physical, evolutionary, and social aspects of race and racism.

Finally, loving acknowledgment is extended to my husband, Richard A. Lobban, with gratitude for our four decades' conversation about race; to our eldest daughter, Josina Parks Fluehr-Lobban, whose namesakes Josina Mutemba Machel, Mozambican liberation fighter, and Rosa Parks, civil rights heroine, may have been too heavy a burden to lay on her shoulders; and to our younger daughter, Nichola, a Peace Corps volunteer in Cameroon who now has firsthand knowledge of struggle. You keep my eyes on the future. And to all of the students who are truly the sons and daughters of my heart and mind, I extend a grateful thanks for being in my life.

# 1

# Anthropology, Race, and Racism

## WHAT IS ANTHROPOLOGY? WHAT IS RACE? WHAT IS RACISM?

Anthropology is the science that studies all of humanity throughout all of time and space. It was born in the nineteenth century in Europe after the concept of race, racial difference, and racial superiority and inferiority had been incorporated into Western science. At that time race was seen as derived from permanent, inherited biological difference.

Race is now viewed as a social construction that is primarily recognized by physical appearance, or *phenotype*. In the United States this means that Americans are socialized first to identify a person's race by skin color, and second by hair form, by facial features such as shape of nose and lips, and eye form, along with other physical features like height. In the United States there is a fundamental denial that race is a central feature of life in "color-blind" America. The United States is often paralyzed by race and an inability to discuss it frankly. Periodic crises remind Americans of the persistence of its race problem. During the 1990s, the Rodney King beating in 1992 and the subsequent acquittal of the indicted Los Angeles police by an all-white jury, which concluded that "Rodney King was in charge," precipitated racial rioting. Deep divisions continued in the perception of justice between black and white America from the belated conviction of open Klan members who carried out the Birmingham bombing of 1963, to the dragging death lynching of Robert Byrd in Jasper, Texas. Everyday racial profiling continues from "driving or shopping while black or Latino," to "flying while Arab," to "hot button issues," such as affirmative action or reparations for slavery. These are often so sensitive

1

they cannot be objectively and dispassionately discussed in legislatures or on college campuses.

Anthropology as a discipline was born after the European Enlightenment of the eighteenth century and began to become established as an accepted science in Europe and America during the last quarter of the nineteenth century. As "the study of mankind" during the era when slavery in America had just legally ended and Europe was busily colonizing much of the non-European world, the major founders of anthropology were occupied with the concept of race and its meaning for the unity and equality of human beings, or for their hierarchical ranking and physical and mental difference. Anthropology grew in the twentieth century to reject biological determinations of race, but the idea of an inborn superiority or inferiority of races has lingered long past anthropological pronouncements and has been resistant to scientific objectivity. The persistence of racism is the major reason for such resistance and anthropology, perhaps, failed to recognize its power and persistence.

America remains fundamentally in denial about race and the manifold effects of racism in its history and the legacy of race. Beginning with the ethnic cleansing and genocide of America's indigenous peoples, paving the way for early capitalist development with the international slave trade as a major vehicle, race and racism have been central to the growth and development of the United States. However, America has a difficult time confronting this history. The state of Rhode Island and Providence Plantations and other New England states that made up the original colonies until recently have had difficulty acknowledging their part in the transatlantic slave trade, or the fact that slaves worked plantations in the North as well as the South. As recently as 2002, the seven-hundred-strong group of white descendants of Thomas Jefferson refused to admit to their prestigious Monticello Association the descendants of Jefferson's slave Sally Hemings, who have been shown by DNA analysis since 1998 to be related to the third U.S. president (Gordon-Reed 1997; *Providence Journal* 2002).

American schools remain highly segregated five decades after the landmark *Brown v. the Board of Education* decision in 1954. Many American universities, such as Middlebury College, did not graduate their first African American men and women until late in the nineteenth or the early twentieth century.

Throughout this book a distinction is made between *racialism* and *racism*. Racialism describes, distinguishes, and classifies racial or phenotypic difference among humans. Racialism includes scientific and ideological approaches that take notice and account of race. Racial data counted and recorded in the U.S. Census and in affirmative action profiles is racialist. Biomedical research comparing data on "blacks" and "whites," for example in a study of high blood pressure, is racialist, that is, it uses race as a

Figure 1.1.    1899. First African American woman graduate, Annette Anderson, of Middlebury College, Vermont. Courtesy of the Richard A. Lobban family.

significant variable in science. Racism not only takes note of racial difference but evaluates that difference, ranking it into superior or inferior,
higher or lower types. Racial profiling of black shoppers, Latino drivers,
or Arab airline passengers is both racialist—taking account of race—and
racist, judging black shoppers as potential thieves, Latino drivers as trans-
porting drugs, and Arab passengers as potential hijackers or terrorists.
Racism both takes note of race and makes judgments about good and bad
behavior, better or worse attributes.

Race is not now, nor has it ever been, simply about the physical
description of human variation. Since its origin in Western science in the
eighteenth century, race has been used both to classify and to rank human
beings according to inferior and superior types. Although race as a concept developed in the West during the Enlightenment, it was spread to
many parts of the non-Western world through international commerce,
including the slave trade and, later, colonial conquest and administration—which have used it as an effective tool of social division. Racism can
be easily identified with ideas of white or Aryan supremacy associated
with Nazism or the Ku Klux Klan, but racism may not be so recognizable
in "scientific" works like the 1994 publication *The Bell Curve* by Richard J.
Herrnstein and Charles Murray, in which superior Asian intelligence is
asserted and the lowest position is still occupied by Negro "ethnicity."
Racialist and racist thought may not be recognized in current ideas about
black athletic superiority in basketball, or in jokes that "white men can't
jump" or whites can't dance. The more complex cultural arguments
about basketball being a city game at which Jewish men excelled in the
1920s, or Euro-American musical and rhythmic traditions, are often overlooked in favor of simpler biological explanations of "natural" ability or
rhythm. As an ideology racism belongs to the realm of cultural construction and of power politics, even as it is rooted in an erroneous biological
foundation and a false belief that the determination of behavior can be
reduced to physical, genetic attributes of race.

Anthropology has a complex and often self-contradictory history
regarding race. Investment in the race concept shaped its origins; it then
tried to dismiss race, deny its scientific existence or dependence on biological theories. Faye Harrison has reminded us of the "persistent power
of race"—that race did not go away as a social construct in all of the decades anthropology sought to dismiss it scientifically (1995). Other critical
anthropologists have described the profession as "color-blind" during the
bulk of the twentieth century while neglecting the ethnographic study
and analysis of the power of race in societies both at home and abroad
(Shanklin 1998).

## How Is Race Different from Ethnicity, Religion, Language, and Other Differences? Why Is There So Much Confusion?

Race is a unique concept belonging in the history of ideas, the world of biology, and the realm of social science. In the United States there is confusion about the categories; perhaps Americans try to make less of race, or more of culture. The terms "diversity" and "multiculturalism" tend to mask what is really at the heart of the American dilemma, namely race. Culture is a more complex concept than race, as it must be discerned by actually getting to know a person. With race, it is assumed that all you have to do is look at a person's outward physical appearance. All a policeman has to do to identify suspicious persons is to radio in that he is pursuing "two black males" without reference to their ethnic heritage, language, or religion for further identification. The same is true for identifying "whites"—outward physical characteristics determine race and often privilege. The terms "Hispanic" and "Latino" confuse culture and race, so the same police officer who could with some certainty identify a "black" or "white" suspect, may equivocate by saying "possible Hispanic male" or "Spanish-looking" suspect.

Historically race has been primarily about phenotype, or outward appearance. Unscientific and often contradictory classifications were erected in Euro-American society during the seventeenth through twentieth centuries—primarily, to describe and rank human variation. Those descriptive words or phrases—Caucasian/white; Negro/black; Mongolian/Asian/yellow; red Indian/Native American—and many more constitute a special part of Western history that began to be critically discussed and reconstructed toward the end of the twentieth century. This history is reviewed in chapter 3, but its legacy means that all Americans carry a certain conceptual and emotional baggage from the preceding three centuries into the twenty-first century. The strength and endurance of racialist description and associated stereotypes continue to show the persistence of the race concept and how difficult it is to shed long-held beliefs, myths, and stereotypes. My generation, raised in the 1960s, believed that it had defeated racism through the political and moral strength of the civil rights movement, only to find that changing laws did not necessarily change hearts, and racism could persist and reassert itself in new forms. During the 1980s, with mass political movements dormant, it was difficult to persuade students that racism was still an American problem. "Thanks" to various cases of racial unrest between black and white neighbors in Bensonhurst and Crown Heights, New York; the gunning down of a Senegalese man who was reaching for his wallet, which was mistaken for a gun by New York police officers; or the torture of Haitian Abner Luima by members of the same police force, the gulf between black and white public opinion has reawakened America to the significance of race. In post–September 11, 2001, America, the profiling of phenotypic Arabs and Muslims has been accepted by many as justified for security ends, although cases of mistaken identity—especially involving turban-wearing Indian Sikhs—have resulted in harassment and death. America usually undergoes its basic education about race and racism through negative experiences such as these. America has yet to be able to initiate or sustain constructive dialogues about race that foster honest exchange—often to the point of personal discomfort—in order to process the history of race relations and achieve racial healing. Most Americans probably want to transcend race and move beyond it to the fulfillment of Dr. King's dream, to a society in which people are judged by the content of their character, not the color of their skin. However, few in the majority white population understand the extent of work to be done.

South Africa undertook a multiyear process of "Truth and Reconciliation" in the period immediately following the end of apartheid whereby racially designated whites, colored, "blacks" or Africans, and Asians testified before a commission. This wisely constructed policy allowed the divided nation to bear its soul and begin the process of racial healing. The United States has yet to engage in such a process or extended conversation.

This book offers a basic education about race and racism for fulfilling the dream of American democracy and enabling the next generation to move beyond its fundamental contradictions regarding race. Education to demythologize race is vital, while an understanding of the roots of racism can change minds and hearts. Although the task may be daunting, it is nonetheless the central work of the twenty-first century. There is often occasion for optimism. The current generation is eager to "move beyond race," yet they lack the analytical tools to change the society they inherited. I was making a presentation recently about race and racism at a local elementary school, and when I told the fifth- and sixth-graders that Asian people used to be referred to as "yellow" they laughed out loud, saying that was silly, nobody's yellow! One fifth-grader wrote to me after this presentation saying that when he thinks of yellow people he thinks of the Simpsons! A generation ago virtually every child would have known that the "yellow race" means Chinese. Optimism is a choice.

## IS THERE A SCIENCE OF RACE?

### How Anthropologists Have Constructed Race

There was little hesitation or discomfort using the term "race" in Western science from the mid-eighteenth century to the middle of the twentieth century. Anthropology is a relatively young science—formally dating from the 1880s in Europe and America. Some argue anthropology's very birth was rooted in the great debate about race (Harris 1968). Anthropologists wrote with ease about the Indian or African races, while "race" was used interchangeably with "culture," assuming a close relationship between biology and society (cf. Knox 1850; Seligman 1930; *Races of Mankind* in Tylor 1881). Edward Burnett Tylor is credited with authoring the first general work in English entitled "Anthropology" in 1881. In this work he accepts racial hierarchy from the darker primitive races to civilized Europeans as a natural condition of humanity. Tylor's view of race is accepted as normative for its time; however, in 1885 Haitian anthropologist Anténor Firmin wrote in French *De l'égalité des Races Humaines* (*The Equality of the Human Races*), in which he fundamentally challenges racial hierarchies and critiques especially French racialist and racist anthropology.

Race in the ninteenth and twentieth centuries was defined and understood from the following premises:

a) Races constitute distinctive divisions of the human species with identifiable boundaries between them.
b) Races vary according to hierarchies from inferior to superior, with inferior races being the source of social problems.
c) Races are homogeneous by heredity (or genes).
d) Races are fixed or unchanging.
e) Interbreeding leads to inferior offspring.

Franz Boas was the first to treat separately race, language, and culture in his 1920 book *Race, Language, and Culture*. Boas devoted much of his scholarly and public life to dispelling myths of racial or cultural superiority. After Boas, Ashley Montagu wrote a bold and pioneering critique of the race concept in 1942, *Man's Most Dangerous Myth: The Fallacy of Race*, at the height of Nazism in Europe.

After World War II race in anthropology lost most of its legitimacy, and few anthropologists, physical or cultural, treated race uncritically. Instead their efforts were directed toward debunking racial myths and finding alternative ways of scientifically describing and analyzing human variation. Certainly, after the world experienced Nazi ideology and Aryan supremacy in practice as well as in theory, any scientific justification for the notion of the purity or innate superiority of races was rejected. It is worth noting that it took the European Holocaust to fundamentally challenge the race concept, while the historically prior cases of the near genocide of American Indians and the four centuries of the Atlantic slave trade, amounting to an African holocaust, served more to preserve racial categories and theories of racial inferiority.

Perhaps the last attempt to use the old race concept seriously in anthropology was Carleton Coon's *The Origin of Races* in 1962, which was sharply criticized because of its arguments supporting polygenesis (the separate origin of races) and its apparent defense of continued segregation in America. Yet Coon was a highly regarded anthropologist, a former president of the American Association of Physical Anthropologists, and a professor at the University of Pennsylvania in Philadelphia, where he hosted his own television show, *What in the World?* Some of America's "finest" scholars at its most pedigreed institutions have been closely associated with racialist or racist ideas as well as practice.

As mentioned earlier the term "racialist" is used to describe ideas that apply the concept of race in its biological and fixed sense to carry out research or analysis. The term "racist" is used to refer to an ideology that asserts the inferiority or superiority of races. Racist ideas almost always rely on biological interpretations of race, but add to their racialist framework a rank ordering of lower and higher races of humans. Thus, early anthropology in Europe and the United States was both racialist and racist.

Anthropology—like other academic fields—has had its racists and antiracists, and it would be less than honest and a disservice to future generations not to acknowledge this complex history. Of the post–World War II generation of anthropologists who worked critically and scientifically with the race concept, C. Loring Brace, Stanley Garn, J. B. Birdsell, F. B. Livingstone, and Ashley Montagu stand out. A growing discomfort with racial classification characterized this postwar generation; anthropologists were especially uncomfortable with the theory of "three great races"—Caucasoid, Mongoloid, Negroid—that had worked its way into public education and the American mind-set as part of the science of race. These anthropologists viewed race as more complex than this. Stanley Garn tried to encourage thinking about race at the local, geographical, and microlevel to move away from the "three great races" idea.

There was also dissatisfaction with the fundamental scientific validity of race. F. B. Livingstone published a paper in 1962 that summarized what many anthropologists had come to think, "On the Non-existence of Human Races." Other anthropologists experimented with alternative terms, hoping to dislodge the race concept. Ashley Montagu offered "genotype" and "ethnic group" as substitutes, asserting that races— defined as groups that individually and collectively are distinguished from other groups—do not exist. The substitute "breeding population," offered by Garn (1961, 7), achieved some consensus, with the acknowledgment that human populations breeding in relative geographical isolation for long periods of time would develop a higher frequency of similar traits. Also the notion of "cline," a regular variation in a physical trait or the frequency of that trait over a geographical area, became widely used in physical anthropology as developed by C. Loring Brace.

By the late 1960s, the civil rights movement and the fundamental moral and scientific questions that it raised had caused many anthropologists to abandon the race concept. For the next generation they would try, in vain, to discard the term and put it once and for all into the realm of historical *pseudoscience* (a false science). Why abandon the race concept? Because, they argued, race has no scientific validity; human variation is more complex than race; and "race" is a loaded, subjective term. The only thing that remained for study was the sociological meaning of race, for race has no biological meaning or scientific status.

Over the years the American Anthropological Association (AAA) has been called on to comment on the idea of race in America. There is a history of resolutions passed by the AAA that parallels the social history of the second half of the twentieth century. The AAA weighed in on the national debate regarding what to do about race classification in preparation for the 2000 Census. After decades of trying to do away with the race concept, the AAA recommended a combined "race/ethnicity" category for the 2000 Census and the elimination of the term "race" from the 2010 Census.

Physical anthropologist Alan Goodman, citing many of his predecessors, has argued that there is no biological basis for race (Montagu 1942; Garn 1961; Dobzansky 1968; Livingstone 1962; Lewontin, Rose, and Kamin 1984). Yet America's most basic applications of the concept—from race requirements on birth certificates to Supreme Court decisions about affirmative action—reaffirm the nation's continued adherence to biological and social ideas of race. The dogged persistence of the idea of race in the face of overwhelming scientific evidence discrediting it suggests that race is not so easy to dislodge. America needs to rethink and reconfigure race, but will it do so by eliminating this powerful idea? To do so, it will have to eliminate racism, for the two have always been intimately connected. Although anthropologists have been among the leading scientists to take a critical view of race, the discipline has been less cognizant of its potent social meaning and its persistence in the United States and in the world.

To this day many scientific-medical studies uncritically use categories comparing "blacks" and "whites" in epidemiological studies of disease, such as heart attacks and strokes, as though the types were real or scientifically valid. A more anthropological approach might question the basic premise whereby supposedly significantly varying biological populations—called "races"—are compared. Were the studies couched in terms of sociological or class categories there would be fewer methodological problems; however, studies that are conceptualized and funded based on race as a significant biological phenomenon can and should be questioned.

## Race as Phenotype—Outward Physical Appearance

Race has been constructed primarily around *phenotype*, outward physical appearance, from Carolus Linnaeus and Johann Blumenbach in the eighteenth century to the contemporary U.S. Census. Biologists contrast phenotype with *genotype*, which is not outwardly observable but constitutes the genetic makeup of an individual, 50 percent from each biological parent; 25 percent from each grandparent. It is understood that there is no perfect match between genotype and phenotype, and that persons carry multiple genetic traits that they may pass on to their offspring, but do not express phenotypically themselves. A brown-haired mother may give birth to a red-headed daughter (as did I); a father with brown eyes may have a blue-eyed son; a relatively darker-skinned mother or father may be a parent to a relatively light-skinned child.

The origin of the term "race" is not entirely clear, and scholars disagree as to whether it came into English from Italian, Spanish or Portuguese, Arabic, or Latin. It is not found in classical Greek or Latin, and may have appeared in English for the first time in English in 1580 with an obscure reference to the "Prince of Wales of the British race," this drawing on meaning already present in the language when speaking of a breed or stock of animals (Pandian 1985, 76).

In 1735 Carolus Linnaeus published *Systema Naturae*, in which he attempted to classify all life forms, including humans. He classified humans as a separate species, grouping them with the higher primates, and he divided the genus *Homo* into four basic races, *europeus, asiaticus, americanus* (meaning aboriginal peoples of America), and *africanus*. His focus on skin color in outlining the four basic varieties of humans is mostly still with us more than 250 years later:

1) Europeans are described as white.
2) Africans are black.
3) Asians are sallow (yellowish).
4) Americans (Indians) are red.

Moreover, along with physical description, this first racial classification offers some cultural information derived from early European accounts of "natives" that are now recognized as ethnocentric, positing a hierarchy based on the European value of government by law.

1) Europeans are muscular; they have long, flowing hair and blue eyes; they are inventive and are governed by laws.
2) Africans have black, frizzled hair, flat noses, and tumid (swollen or distended) lips; the women are without shame; the men anoint themselves with grease; Africans are governed by caprice (whim).
3) Asians have black hair and dark eyes; they are avaricious and are ruled by opinion.
4) Americans have straight, thick, black hair; they have wide nostrils; the men have scanty beards and paint themselves with fine red lines; Americans are obstinate and free and are ruled by customs.

An implicit ranking of humans occurred in this first European classification, from a higher race governed by laws, to middle-level races governed by opinion and ruled by customs, to lower races governed by whimsy. A fuller discussion of the history of race classification is found in chapter 3, but here it is sufficient to point out that race from its beginning to the present time has been and is about observable physical appearance, phenotype. One of the last of the physical anthropologists to attempt a reasonable definition of race, Alice Brues (1977), drew on the persistent power of phenotype: "A race is a division of a species differing from other divisions by certain hereditary traits, among these being features of external appearance that make it possible to recognize members of different populations visually with greater or lesser accuracy" (1–2).

In the United States and elsewhere skin color is the most noticed of the phenotypic features of humans, although there is no logical necessity for this. Nose or ear shape, bushy or sparse eyebrows may have been arbitrarily selected as significant, but what we have inherited and what we teach our children to recognize is skin color. The second great European classifier of humans, Johann Blumenbach, organized humans into five "varieties" between 1770 and 1781 (Smedley 1993, 166) based on geography with associated colors of skin. These five included

Caucasian—white;
Mongolian—yellow;
Ethiopian—black;
American—red;
Malay—brown.

Blumenbach's varieties readily became the accepted science of the day and were widely adopted and taught in Euro-American education. This was the standard science of its day, and its powerful legacy remains with us. Blumenbach's types will be discussed in greater detail in chapter 3 (the illustrations there are taken from a Warren's Geography series, in this case on physical geography, used in American high schools during the late nineteenth and early twentieth centuries.

## America's One-Drop Rule

The notorious "one-drop" rule in the peculiar American history of race is tied to the slave system, which held that "a single drop" of black blood, or "a single ancestor" who was African, constituted "blackness." The one-drop rule is unique in world history as is discussed in chapter 6 in comparative studies of race and racism; its unique history is presently under critical review (Davis 1991). In the history of American race relations it is a relatively obscure fact that Homer Plessy was an "octoroon" (a person with one-eighth black ancestry) who claimed his right to sit in the white-designated seats on Louisiana trains because he could pass for white. The Supreme Court's "separate but equal" decision in *Plessy v. Ferguson* denied Mr. Plessy this right, and thus formally recognized the one-drop rule while legalizing Jim Crow segregation. The "separate but equal" legal doctrine stood until it was challenged in the landmark 1954 school desegregation case *Brown v. the Board of Education*.

As recently as 1982 there was a case in Louisiana that revealed the persistence of the legal legacy of the one-drop rule, filed as *Jane Doe v. State of Louisiana*. Susie Guillory Phipps applied for a birth certificate in 1977 with the state's Bureau of Vital Statistics and discovered that the state had her listed as "colored." Raised as "white" and self-identifying as "white," Susie was "flabbergasted," in her own words (Jaynes 1982). Susie is the great-great-great-great-granddaughter of an enslaved woman named Margarita; Louisiana held that she is "colored" because her heritage is one-sixty-fourth black. The genealogical history was traced back to 1770, when French planter Jean Guillory took his slave Margarita as his mistress. Two hundred years later, in 1970, the Louisiana legislature had reformed the "trace" rule of black blood, making a person black to one-thirty-second. The eighteenth-century law forbidding marriage between a white and a person with any trace of Negro descent survived until the civil rights period. Mrs. Phipps produced photographs of relatives going back three generations whom she described as white with blue eyes, although the state produced two aunts as witnesses who declared that they were raised "colored." The state's evidence showed Mrs. Phipps to be three-thirty-seconds black, more than enough to prove their case that she is "colored." After much national attention the case was settled in court in 1983, and the considerable controversy and embarrassment led to legislative abolition of the one-thirty-second rule while giving parents the right to designate the race of newborns. This carried with it the right to change a baby's classification to "white" on birth certificates if the baby is shown to be white "by a preponderance of the evidence." However, the state did not abolish the trace rule, and in successive appeals to the Louisiana supreme court and the U.S. Supreme Court both declined to review the lower court decision and failed to strike down the venerable, thoroughly American one-drop rule (Davis 1991, 9–10).

Other stories of discovery of black ancestry have been chronicled in the 1990s in books such as Gregory Williams's *Life on the Color Line: The True Story of a White Boy Who Discovered He Was Black* (1995). Judy Scales-Trent describes coping with being a light-skinned black in America's great divide in her *Notes of a White Black Woman* (1995).

If one drop serves to make a person "black," logic holds that one drop could also serve to convey "whiteness." It is most telling that the one-drop rule has worked only one way in America—however, that is not the case elsewhere. The one-drop rule has perhaps been more used when conveying "white" ancestry. One drop of European blood can make a person "white," or convey the potential to be assimilated to white culture, as with the widely practiced Portuguese *assimilado* system, which has influenced the modern societies of Brazil and the former African colonies of Angola, Mozambique, Guinea Bissau, and the Cape Verde Islands. In Brazil less than a 5 percent minority self-identifies as "black" or *prêto*, although it is a multicolored, multiracial nation enriched by African ancestry. Former Haitian leader "Papa Doc" Duvalier once told a surprised American reporter that 95 percent of his country is white, explaining that in Haiti they used the same procedure for counting whites that America used for counting blacks, namely the one-drop rule (Hirschfield 1996).

In most Caribbean and South American cultures the concept of race is much more flexible than the American black-white binary allows. Elsewhere, racial identity is much more fluid and flexible, and race exists more along a continuum than in dichotomous opposition. Most of the "action" along the Latin American–Caribbean continuum is in the middle, with ideas of being of "Creole," or "mestizo" identity having cultural and class importance, as well as racial significance. This is explored in greater depth in chapter 6, on comparative studies of race and racism, but read what Hispanic or Latino students have to say in the section on student reflections about race below in this chapter.

America is locked in a narrow phenotypic range known as the "black-white binary." In America one is either "black" or "white." Historically it has not been possible to be both black and white; or, if you were, you were a pitiful creature known as a "mulatto," the product of miscegenation. The one-drop rule has constructed a large social group of American colored, or black, people comprising such phenotypically diverse persons as James Brown, Colin Powell, Rosa Parks, and Tracey Chapman. Only recently has there been a movement of "biracials" (children of black-white marriages) who have actively campaigned to get America to think beyond the black-white dichotomy by offering the term "multiracial" to reflect their heritage. About the same time the movement appeared, Tiger Woods became an American and world sensation for his talent and because he became the first black Professional Golf Association (PGA) title holder—or was he the first Asian PGA title holder, or was he the first American Indian PGA title holder? Tiger Woods publicly and proudly declared his multiracialism, describing himself as a "Cablindasian," with European, African, American Indian, and Asian blood all combining to make him the best. Tiger Woods became symbolic for the multiracial movement. Some whites with newfound pride and interest in their previously hidden American Indian, Jewish, or Latino heritage indicated that they too would check the "multiracial" category if it were offered. In the 2000 U.S. Census, although neither the term "biracial" nor the term "multiracial" was available, for the first time individuals could check more than one racial category.

Multiracialism quickly became politicized, with opponents from the NAACP and other national black and Hispanic organizations arguing that it would cause confusion, with a potentially large number of new "multiracials" who couldn't be identified as either "black or Hispanic," or "white." The organizations feared, perhaps, that they might lose numbers and influence, which could translate into loss of political power; the 2000 U.S. Census bowed to the pressure they exerted. This reveals that there is still a vested interest in race and racial politics in America that is above science and beyond the simple goodwill of many people who seek to move beyond race, or beyond the black-white dichotomy.

The American linguistic terminology regarding race, amounting to our *folk categories of race*, has been dynamic and reflects a complex, contradictory history regarding race. The terms "Negro," "colored," "black," and "African American" all have their time and context in the history of American race relations, which is also locked into the black-white dichotomy. Ask a darker-skinned American if being referred to as "colored" in 1920 or "black" in 1968 has made any difference in the basic American experience of race relations. Why hasn't "Euro-American"—instead of "white"—developed as a term parallel to "African American"? To a large extent today our folk categories are driven by the most recent established federal system of classification, in place since 1977. That basic and well-known classification is as follows:

black/African American ("Negro" on the 2000 Census form)
white/Caucasian
Asian or Pacific Islander

American Indian or Alaskan native
Hispanic as a separate "ethnic" category
"other" (my personal favorite)

Until 2000 Americans could check only one of these categories on college or job applications.

### Race in Contemporary America = Phenotype + Culture

Racial construction is dynamic and ever changing. Cubans are rapidly becoming "white" as their privileged political status elevates them over other Caribbean immigrants. Other Latinos discover the black-white binary as they are confronted with racial construction in the United States and are treated as "black" or "white" according to their respective phenotypes. In large American cities, minorities, black and Latino, have a common dress style that adds culture to race and is identifiable as "inner city," hip-hop culture. The exclusive use of Spanish, or a Latino-Anglo style of speech, also adds a linguistic marker to race that identifies a person as "Hispanic." Native American dress and ways of being often do not match phenotype, as American Indians constitute a multiracial mélange, especially among Eastern nations. The phenomenon of white imitators of black cultural styles, symbolized by the popular white rapper Eminem, has attracted attention from specialists not only in race but in cultural studies. The offensive term "whigger" has been used to describe such white rappers or hip-hop artists.

## RACE AND ETHNICITY DISTINGUISHED

In the first quarter of the twentieth century Franz Boas, founder of modern American anthropology, cautioned about keeping separate the concepts of *race*, *language*, and *culture*. It is a simple idea, but apparently it has been very difficult for this basic anthropological idea to affect public understanding of race. If race is about phenotype, and language is about speech and communication, and culture is about common heritage and shared identity through distinct customs, dress, food, and more, why are these three so often confused? The answer may be that each is a convenient referent for "others" different from "ourselves" (whoever "we" may be), and the normative race in America is "white."

Those in denial in America about race are fond of citing the "melting pot" idea, according to which the United States is a place where hard work and consistent effort pay off, irrespective of one's race or ethnic origin. This idea has been criticized by sociologists referring to it as "the

myth of the melting pot," for if the melting pot existed at all, the homoge-
nization of the American "soup" happened only for European ethnic
groups who became "white." That is, they became differentiated from
"colored" people, or, to use the current politically correct jargon, "people
of color." Other recent metaphors developed for racial-cultural mixing
that move beyond the melting pot have included the "mosaic" or "salad
bowl" metaphors—colors mix but do not blend. The idea of ethnic
"sauces," not "stews," has been used to describe cultures and races that
keep their distinctive flavors and do not lose their unique character. The
power of race to thwart blending into American culture, thus becoming a
"real American," has made "others" of racial minorities who have been
in this country for centuries.

Black people have certainly been left out of the melting pot. However,
the idea that "blacks" constitute a unique people simply by virtue of their
skin color is absurd. First of all, what about the multiple cultures and linguistic groups from which "blacks" originate, from the great African continent to a host of New World nations and cultures? And what is meant
by "black"? Where is the line between black and white drawn? The reality
of "blackness" in America is that it lies along a continuum from light
skin, to tan, to brown, to black, using the folk categories discernible in
American English. Because of racism "blacks" are not socially, economically, or politically differentiated along a normal, full range of human
experience but are stereotyped as poor people living in inner city ghettos,
and likely not to vote at all or to be solidly Democratic. Thus, the idea of
a middle-class, suburban-dwelling, intact, and Republican black family is
odd, lacking in credibility because it does not fit the stereotype.

Yet, also because of racism "blacks" have a strong sense of common
identity expressed through phenotype that permits African Americans
who are strangers to greet one another among the anonymous masses of
U.S. cities, towns, and college campuses. The one-drop rule, steeped in
racist ideology of "contamination" by Negro blood, nonetheless created
a diverse, multiracial population of African Americans who are bound to
one another and to a group identity by common history, experience,
struggle, and destiny within a racialized America.

Since being "white" in American racial thinking is construed as "normal" or mainstream, whites—though also phenotypically differentiated—are permitted that full range of humanity. Thus, whites are not
stereotyped as being poor, but are acknowledged as representing the full
range of economic strata. Whites can be poor, middle class, or rich.
Whites do not live in ghettos (although America is highly segregated by
neighborhoods), and they can be conservative, liberal, or middle of the
road in matters of politics. Whiteness in America certainly has a phenotypic range as well, with fair to medium to olive skin color being recog-

nized. Darker-skinned whites may be confused with people of other races until other phenotypic variables are noticed, such as hair texture and nose and face shape. The culture of suntanning among whites adds a complexity to the mix of racial phenotyping and ideas of aesthetics and even class that confuse the American black-white binary.

Latino people share a common language and a variety of cultures, but not race. "Hispanic" or "Latino" refers to heritage and cultures, not race. Anyone familiar with Spanish-speaking people from the Caribbean islands of Cuba, Puerto Rico, or the Dominican Republic can recognize the Afro-European or Euro-African appearance of these peoples. Other Spanish or Hispanic/Latino people from Mexico, Guatemala, or other Central and South American countries may appear phenotypically more "Indian" due to the survival of native cultures and the resulting mix of New World groups known as "mestizos," while others may appear more European because ideas of class and race inhibited mixture, while still others may appear more "black," especially where large plantation economies of the post-Columbus era imported enslaved Africans. Along the black-white continuum these folk may fall more in the middle, but individuals may be classed or typed as "black" or "white" strictly by phenotype. If you ask Latinos about race, they have much more flexible and complicated systems than the simple black-white dichotomy. In fact, many Hispanic/Latino immigrants report that they had to learn a new system of racial classification to survive in America, and many report that their first experiences with racism occurred in the United States.

Ethnicity is the sociological expression of culture—it is derived from socially ascribed identity as well as self-identity. Americans recognize a broad range of white ethnic identities, from Irish, Italian, German, and Polish Americans to many others. Americans rarely speak of an English American, although England constitutes a primary source of U.S. heritage. Perhaps this is because the English immigrants were the "first Americans," that is, the first European Americans. The abbreviation "WASP" (White, Anglo-Saxon, Protestant) has become synonymous with the ruling class, because so many U.S. presidents, politicians, and heads of corporations have been and continue to be WASPs. However, WASP can hardly be considered an ethnic group, although the ethnic backgrounds of these prominent Americans are clustered among northern European nations. Being WASP has far more to do with class and privilege than race.

The difference between ethnicity and race may be more clearly understood when Asian Americans are considered. Mainstream America makes little differentiation phenotypically between Chinese Americans, Japanese Americans, Korean Americans, Southeast Asian Americans, or other "Asian Americans." Until the 2000 U.S. Census there was a single

racial category, "Asian American," to encompass all persons whose ethnic origins are in Asia. An essential "Asian" is often thought of as "Chinese," and that designation may be used to describe any Asian. The
strongest phenotypic marker for westerners identifying Asians is eye
shape—an almond shape—resulting from an extra fold of skin above the
eye called the "epicanthic fold." It may be more or less pronounced in
various Asian peoples who, after all, originate in the vast continent of
Asia and presently constitute about two-fifths of humanity, including the
megapopulations of China and India, at about one billion each. In racist
parlance people who have the epicanthic fold are described as "slant-
eyed"; the epicanthic fold has been used in conjunction with other racist
referents to generalize about all Asians. Indians (from the subcontinent)
do not have the epicanthic fold, yet they check the box "Asian American"
on racial identification forms. From an ethnic standpoint Asians are
among the most diverse of the world's people due to the geographical
size of the continent and the antiquity of its peoples and cultures. Marked
differences dot the Asian cultural-linguistic landscape—including tonal
(Chinese and Vietnamese, giving a "sing-song" sound to the Western ear)
and nontonal languages (Japanese and Cambodian); and Hindu, Buddhist, Taoist, Confucian, and Shinto religious cultures, along with the
powerful presence of Islam and Christianity. Yet most Americans are
unable to distinguish spoken Chinese from spoken Vietnamese, nor can
they tell the national dress of Thailand from that of Korea; Philippinos
may be mistaken for Latinos, and the Eastern religions may be viewed as
another part of the "mysterious" Orient. The Japanese kimono has some
recognition, as do the black pants and white shirt of Vietnamese peasants
from the American wartime experience, but for the most part there is little
cultural differentiation made among the nearly three billion people who
make up Asia, nor their relations who have emigrated to the United
States.

Generalizations about Asians have stereotyped them as both ethnic and
racial "others" in American culture. This is reflected in the almost total
absence of an Asian presence in the major media, especially TV shows
and films. A short-lived sitcom about a young Korean American woman
reveals the exotic "other" bias with its title, *All American Girl*, an entertaining idea because the central character is not the blond, blue-eyed,
more traditional girl next-door. The novel and film *The Joy Luck Club* are
viewed as breakthroughs because the story deals with themes of normal,
Asian American, intergenerational family life.

A host of Asian American cultural and political groups reacted to this
simple stereotyping by requesting revision of the U.S. Census Bureau category "Asian American" to the more specific "Chinese American,"
"Korean American," "Philippino American," and so on. These options

**Figure 1.2. Philippino girls, 1996. Courtesy of the author.**

were provided on the 2000 U.S. Census. However, some other government and private agencies declined this request, not out of insensitivity to the issue, but due to a fear that the floodgates of ethnic identity would open and wash away what they believed were more important categories of race.

American Indians prefer to identify themselves as Navajo, Sioux, Iroquois, or Narragansett instead of "Native American," a term invented by the U.S. Office of Budget Management. Due to their near-genocide with the European settlement in America, and the subsequent admixture of indigenous peoples with Europeans and Africans in the eastern third of the Unites States, many American Indians phenotypically resemble Euro- or African Americans. The most physically distinct populations are in the American West, those that survived European contact and were forcibly placed in biological as well as cultural isolation by the reservation system.

It is certainly true that the American icons of Indians—feathers, tomahawks, war bonnets, and war cries—can be used in ways that are offensive to American Indians and are no more authentic ethnic markers than is the racist phenotypic label of "redskins" an accurate physical description of American Indians. Yet American football and baseball teams and many of their fans still find little wrong in the continued use of "Braves," "Chiefs," and other ethnic and racial stereotypes. While race is seemingly fixed by biology and phenotype, culture is more dynamic and flexible. American Indians, who once comprised thousands of different ethnic

**Figure 1.3.   Racially heterogeneous New England Indians, Pequot; Narragansett.
Courtesy of the *Pequot Times*.**

groups and bands, were nearly extinguished biologically and culturally
by the European contact experience. Now, the descendants of those who
survived are forging new cultural identities across ethnic lines, even as
tribal cultural nationalism is revived. Pan-Indian and individual tribal
movements are reinvigorating pride and a sense of Indian-ness that tran-
scends race and culture. This sad story in American history may nonetheless have a great deal to teach us about the irrelevance of race and the
potential of reinventing culture.

### Understanding the Difference between Racism and Ethnocentrism

Race is about outward physical appearance, or phenotype, and racism is
about ranking these differences in humans into inferior and superior
types. Thus, racist ideas can claim that white skin is superior and black
skin is inferior. Racist "science" can use physical measurement of the
skull to show high or low intelligence; it can rank people by racial type,
for example, it can declare Caucasian, Mongolian, and Negro skulls as
holding first, second, and third place on the scale of human capacity. In
popular culture, hair type, nose shape, or skin color can be valued as
"good" or "bad" depending on its approximation of a white, Caucasian
ideal.

Ethnicity, however, is about culture, and it follows that ethnocentrism is the ideology that one's culture or ethnic group is at the center of one's worldview and is viewed as superior or inferior. Americans are socialized to believe in the cultural superiority of the United States in relation to the rest of the world. Ethnocentrism clouds Americans' vision of other cultures and makes them think that their culture is the only way to live, or is the best way to live in comparison with others. In practice, ethnocentrism can be expressed by intolerance of difference and personal judgments of the superiority of one's own culture (or aspects of it) and the inferiority of another's culture (or parts of it). Some well-recognized examples of ethnocentrism can be found in the popular idea of the "ugly American" who is so ignorant of other ways of life that he/she is angered by foreigners' inability to speak English or serve up hamburgers.

Within the great expanse of multicultural America, ethnocentrism may be expressed by, for example, some white Americans who perceive Latino culture bearers as colorful but noisy in contrast to their own standards of peace and decorum; or African Americans who perceive Koreans living or owning businesses nearby as aloof compared to their more friendly, easygoing manner; or geographical northeast Americans who think of themselves as more "cultured" or "civilized" than southerners and carry with them a distinct air of superiority when visiting the South.

Ethnocentrism is about culture, as racism is about race. There can be considerable overlap between race and ethnicity, as when racist remarks are combined with ethnic slurs. Some are obviously offensive and both racist and ethnocentric.

## RACE AND LANGUAGE DISTINGUISHED

Language is a unique form of verbal communication used by humans, characterized by its complexity and its arbitrary use of symbols (Seymour-Smith 1986, 162). Since race is about phenotype and language is about differentiated human speech, they are separate. But, again, we must ask why there is a confusion between race and language? In everyday speech one can hear references to "Spanish people," "Greek people," "Arabs," or "Hebrew people," to mention only a few examples. The United Nations Statement on Race expresses it clearly: "There is no national, religious, geographic, linguistic, or cultural group which constitutes a race ipso facto; the concept of race is purely biological" (UNESCO 1964; IUAES 1998). The UN statement was drafted in the early 1960s, at a time when world events demanded some scientific clarification of race, namely the great wave of independence of African nations and the height of the American civil rights movement. The UN firmly supported the equal capacity of humans for cultural achievement against those who questioned the ability of African nations to succeed on their own without European guidance; it also supported the equal intelligence of all humans against segregationists who argued black and white children could not compete on an equal footing in the classroom. The UNESCO statement was revised and renewed in 1999; the new version restates many of the 1964 principles, including the statement that race is a biological concept having nothing to do with language or nationality. The statement explains that since human beings speaking the same language often tend to intermarry there may be a certain degree of coincidence between physical traits, on the one hand, and linguistic and cultural traits, on the other. The 1999 statement is reprinted in the appendices.

While there may be overlap between language and race, confusing the two plays into generalizations about languages other than American English and the people who speak them. People who appear to be "Spanish" may be assumed to be non–English speakers, or socially pressured not to use the Spanish language in official, public places. Others—for example, Middle Eastern and southwest Asian peoples, or Cape Verdeans—might be addressed in Spanish and respond positively or negatively to having been taken for "Spanish."

Race can be confused with language. Ronald Takaki, who is a third-generation Japanese American, relates a telling story in his *A Different Mirror: A History of Multicultural America* (1993). He describes a ride in a New York City taxi, with the driver interrogating him while glancing in the rearview mirror:

Taxi driver: So, where're you from?
Takaki: California.
Taxi driver: Oh yeah, so how long you been in this country?
Takaki: Three generations.
Taxi driver: You speak English really good.
Takaki: Well, I should, it's my native language.
Taxi driver: So, where'd you say you were from?

Ronald Takaki's visual phenotype overwhelmed the linguistic message he was communicating. His Japanese features signaled "foreigner." The "othering"—from the white, English-speaking norm—that race uniquely shapes is mediated by language, that is, language provides another clue after the racial visual perception has taken place. Because language is such an important source of identity, it is perhaps understandable that it has been confused with race. But, in order for America to reconstruct its own identity language must be treated as the independent and separate factor that it is.

## RACE AND RELIGION DISTINGUISHED

Like language, religion is distinct from race. For example, Judaism is a faith and its practitioners share a common bond of religion, but not race. Jews trace their descent to the Prophet Abraham, but so do Arabs; each descended from one of Abraham's sons, Isaac and Ishmael, providing common descent for the Semites. The Semitic languages include Arabic, Hebrew, Aramaic (the language Jesus spoke), and Amharic, spoken in Ethiopia. The idea of a Semitic race is called into question by the variety of ethnic groups that speak various Semitic languages. Jewish people, since the original Diaspora in the fourth century BCE, have spread throughout the Middle East, North Africa, Europe, and, most recently, North and South America. As a people shaped by religion they have experienced a range of interactions with local groups—from extreme isolation, as in the case of the Ethiopian "Falasha" Jews (*Beita Israel*); to social isolation and ghettos in Europe from medieval to modern times; to acceptance, integration, and intermarriage within other societies, such as in the Spanish Muslim caliphates and twentieth-century America. As a result, phenotypically Jews can vary from "Ethiopian" in appearance, to a European appearance (Ashkenazi Jews), to a Middle Eastern or North African appearance (Sephardic Jews), to American Jews, who are often phenotypically indistinguishable from other Euro-Americans.

In America being Jewish may have as much to do with ethnicity as it does with religion, and no longer very much to do with race, since Jewish people "became white" (Sacks 1994) when they moved from the inner cities to the suburbs and were accepted into the American mainstream. However, anti-Semitism, an ideology of racial inferiority of Jews inherited from European cultural and racial prejudices, has flourished in America as well. It combined ethnic, racial, and religious bias. Jews in America today, and in Israel as well, largely identify themselves in terms of a secular and not a religious identity. Judaism is a faith, the first of the great Abrahamic religions that also include Christianity and Islam. The Jewish people constitute ethnic groups within various nations and the dominant ethnic group in Israel, but they are only partially defined by religion.

Arabs, another of the great family of Semites, may be thought of as all being Muslims, thus stereotyping Arabic language and ancestry with the religion of Islam. Lately that stereotype has linked the Islamic faith with terrorism, so persons who are Arab in appearance may be thought of as violent, aggressive, and anti-American. Although most Arabs are Muslims, most of the world's 1.5 billion Muslims are not Arabs, and significant Christian Arab populations are found in Egypt, Lebanon, and Syria. Muslims no more constitute a racial group than the world's two billion Christians or its eighteen million Jews. Yet, due to American lack of familiarity with Islam, its many ethnically diverse followers from all over Africa, the Middle East, southwest Asia, central Asia, Indonesia, and Malaysia are often lumped into the phenotypic stereotype of a swarthy "A-rab," turban headed, with a Koran in one hand and a gun in the other. The American Muslim may be stereotyped as black, stemming largely from images of the Nation of Islam and a general ignorance of the country's eight to ten million other Muslims, who are mostly from Asia and Africa, as well as being American born. Islam is now the second most practiced faith in America. Islam is probably the most racially and ethnically diverse religion practiced in America today; people of every hue of skin can be found worshipping together in the same mosque.

Another example of the confusion of religion and race is the use of the term "Hindu" to describe people of the Indian subcontinent. Hinduism is one of the world's great faiths that emerged in India, along with Buddhism, Jainism, and Sikhism. Hinduism is a religion, not a race, and it is practiced by an ethnically and phenotypically diverse group of people inhabiting the vast Indian subcontinent with its over one billion people.

It would be absurd to speak of Christian people as being of a single ethnic or racial composition—it is unthinkable because the distinction between religion, race, and ethnicity is understood and not oversimplified as in the preceding, less well-known cases.

## WHAT IS PREJUDICE?

"Prejudice" means literally to "pre-judge" on the basis of superficial information, such as the color of a person's skin; it is making a judgment with insufficient knowledge of the content of a person's character. Prejudice creates in the mind of the observer a negative judgment or opinion without knowledge of the facts. Prejudice is always subjective and operates at the level of human emotion. A person is seen and evaluated phenotypically, and an opinion is formed—consciously or subconsciously—about the person before the observer gets to know the person. Prejudice, in fact, keeps many of us from coming to know many others.

With respect to racial prejudice the phenotypic triggers are obvious, from skin color, to hair type, to facial structure, to body shape and body language, such as style of walking, as well as style of dress. The overwhelming importance of skin color may be modified by dress that suggests middle-class or higher social status. However, the conventional rules of the socially learned triggers of outward appearance can at times play tricks on us. There is a great deal to be learned in the cultural realm of phenotypic triggers. I suggest discussing in class the many ways of sizing up a person—by race, by culture, by dress, by manner of walk, and by so much else that is essentially superficial—before getting to know the person. Consult the exercises at the end of this chapter for in-class projects.

### Forms of Prejudice That Are Not Racial

The American obsession with body size is well known, and from a global perspective Americans are, indeed, overweight people. High-fat and high-protein diets, sedentary lifestyles, and other factors have brought about a steady increase in the size of the average American. In terms of aesthetic ideals and size in the United States, tall is good, but fat is not. Despite the fact that American obesity rates are among the world's highest, there is an ironic obsession with thin bodies, with a resulting prejudice against overweight persons.

A number of sociological and psychological studies have demonstrated that Americans are biased in favor of taller persons. Moreover, Americans perceive taller persons as having greater status; there are minimum height requirements for police in many states, and shorter persons may accentuate their height with lifts or high-heeled shoes. The expression "tall, dark, and handsome" can play with our imagination regarding race, but it is clear about height; "short, dark, and handsome" just doesn't have the same appeal.

Big is perceived by Americans as powerful, while small is seen as weak. Just think of the intimidation felt in the presence of an American football defensive player, irrespective of race. Chauvinistic Americans may feel some kind of biological superiority over smaller peoples, notably some Asian groups. The marked difference in height and body size was mentioned often during the American intervention in the Vietnamese civil war, with more than one world journalist commenting that the big American soldiers still could not defeat the smaller Vietnamese soldiers. Indeed, the famous underground tunnels from which Vietcong launched attacks on foreign enemies had openings only the smaller Vietnamese frame could enter, while the average American or French soldier became an easy target lodged in a tunnel opening too small for his frame.

Apart from nonracial phenotypes having to do with body size, one can be prejudiced about a host of other things that people do or say. Smokers may be disliked as offended persons move away or make a face in their presence; gay and lesbian persons may offend some, or make uncomfortable some in the straight population; some adults just don't like kids; joggers may offend nonexercisers; smart, high-achieving students may offend slackers and may be called derogatory names like "geek" or "dork." The examples of human prejudice unfortunately abound, including major ones such as religious, national, cultural, and linguistic prejudice. And thus far only prejudices recognized in American culture have been mentioned. Imagine compiling a list of all the world's prejudices, culture by culture! This is not to say humanity should be let off the hook because prejudice is a human weakness. Make no mistake, prejudice of whatever variety is learned behavior, and as such it can be unlearned. In fact it must be unlearned, or never taught in the first place. This introductory book is about one human difference—that of race—and one prejudice—racism.

### Breaking the Ice: Class Exercise to Initiate a Dialogue on Race

In this exercise, college students are asked to write about their recollections and reflections about race and racism in their personal backgrounds. Students form racially mixed discussion groups of four to five persons and read or review what they have written and use their experiences to extend the conversation, especially across racial lines. If the class is more racially homogeneous, the reflections can be contrasted with student perceptions of their experiences as compared with dominant white culture.

The questions are as follows.

1) What is your first recollection of race? Of racism?
2) How would you describe the social environment in which you were raised: racially homogeneous, multiracial-multicultural, mix between home/community and school?
3) What patterns of race relations do you recall in high school? How much healthy social interaction was there across racial lines? What about interracial dating?
4) Complete this sentence: The most important thing that America needs to do NOW about race is . . .

In response to the questions students in my classes wrote and shared the following responses.

*Question 1*

My first recollection of race dates back to elementary school. I remember the teachers lining up the children in pairs. I was matched with the other "black" kid in class. Furthermore, when we were allowed to choose our line partners none of the white children seemed to want to hold my hand. So, I always ended up with the same partner, who just happened to be the only other "black" (Cape Verdean) kid in the class. My initial reaction was annoyance (I didn't care that much for Kevin. I thought he smelled funny) and curiosity. Why did I always have to stand in line with smelly old Kevin? It didn't take me long to figure out how Kevin and I differed from the rest. My feelings were hurt, but even at that tender age I felt a sense of indignation more than anything else. How dare they? I was not dirty or contaminated! I did not say anything because I felt powerless to do anything about it. High school was a time of realization. I realized that being Cape Verdean I was not black enough to be ''in'' with the black kids, nor was I white enough to be so with the white kids. My status as an ''other'' became glaringly obvious to me. I felt like a misfit because the way things were set up, I was supposed to fit into one category or the other. I never felt fully accepted in either camp. (Christine Andrade, adult student, used with permission)

After first grade, when I had a black friend, I never had another black friend until junior high-school. My friend Tony was a sports star; Tony became part of our crowd and we all loved him. I can remember as young teenagers playing spin the bottle. The bottle landed between Tony and one of the girls in our group. She would not kiss Tony. Tony was crushed and angry. Some of the group got angry, while the rest of us weren't sure how we felt. An innocent game had rocked our consciousness. Tony struggled with this issue over and over again throughout school. Tony was the best roller skater I knew. I can remember the girls talking about how they loved to roller skate with Tony and hang out with him, but they could never ''go out'' with him. It was OK to be friends but that was it. I often remember thinking that I was glad that I had a steady boyfriend in our group, and I would not be forced into the situation of having to face my own prejudice. Tony also caught grief from other black kids because he hung out with white kids.

I believe that the most important thing we need to do now about race and racism in America is TALK and talk frankly.

My earliest recollection of race was when I was eleven years old and a classmate asked me if my mommy was black and my daddy was white. I told her ''yes'' and she replied to me that she thought that was weird. I didn't really take it negatively because I knew it wasn't weird. My parents taught me well and I was raised to know that it was perfectly natural for my parents to be together. Race wasn't a big issue in my high school, for there were few minorities. Yet if you would go into our lunchroom you would notice the tables were voluntarily segregated.

My earliest recollection of race was that of many of my family members being fair skinned and some with blue or green eyes, therefore different from myself. This was often brought to my attention by my fair-skinned grandfather. It was normal to hear him speak negatively of those individuals with dark complexion. I asked him if he liked me because after all I was dark. Yet he always told me, ''No sweetie, you're different, you're a pretty dark-skinned girl.'' (Jasmine Mena, Dominican student, used with permission)

My first recollection of "race" was in the 7th grade. During this time I befriended a black kid from Brooklyn, New York. From that point on my fellow classmates would constantly point out that I was friends with a black kid. . . . While growing up I became acquainted with two different social environments, suburban and urban life. The suburban life, which mainly consisted of family, was one that did not have much impact on my view of race. The urban side on the other hand had a profound effect on my views. Becoming acquainted with such cultural aspects like graffiti and rap music broadened my narrow-minded views of America. I must also say that the contact I had with so-called minorities was very crucial in developing the person I am today. (Khalil Saucier, white student, used with permission)

The first time I remember that race was a factor in my life was in kindergarten. One of my best friends was called an "oreo" or "zebra." I found this confusing at the time because he did not look like any type of food. Later I came to find out that he was called this because his father was black and his mother was white. I didn't know what to do about it or how to feel because my family is mixed, so what would they call me? Race was apparent in school because my school was predominantly white. All the blacks hung out with the blacks and all of the whites hung out with the whites. There were only a few people who dared cross this line and hang out with both groups. Most of the blacks had good relationships with other minorities, but not with any of the white kids. The most important thing to do in America is to stop the fear associated with race and to educate each other. Once this is accomplished the reality that all races are equal will disperse the fear.

I recall race since I was a little girl because my aunts and one of my cousins are dark skinned. I did not feel uncomfortable around them because I'm Puerto Rican and the people who live there are of different skin colors. It became a problem when I came to this country because everything was if you were not white you were a minority. Then at the age of eight I became aware that there was a difference between black-skinned Puerto Ricans and the new black American. I felt very uncomfortable with the different races since they were being racist toward me. In high school the only bad problems I had was from the Afro-American girls because I was dating an Afro-American guy. They didn't like sharing "their" men.

My earliest recollection of race took place in the first grade. One day I was walking home from school with a kid from school and his mother and I heard the kid's mother telling him not to play with me anymore. The next day I learned that this was because I was black. I felt sort of indifferent at first because I did not fully understand. But later it kind of hurt because I lost a friend. When I went to high school I was one of three African Americans to graduate in my class. I did not really feel fully comfortable in the school, but no one was openly racist to me.

My first recollection of race was in July 1985. I had just come from my country and I used to go out and play in front of my neighbor's house. My aunt told me not to because they were white and didn't like people my color. I really didn't care because I didn't know about racism, but I always kept passing by that house (even though I was a little afraid) to see if they would say something, but they never did. Years later I went to high school and the neighbor I had when I was little was in a class with me. We ended up sitting next to each other. We spoke and since I recognized him I said, "Didn't you used to live on Althea Street?" He said, "Yes, how did you know?" I said, "I was your neighbor back then," and he said that he didn't remember me. I told him I never forget a face. The guy, Jason, ended up having a crush on me; I like him a lot but only as a friend. I've never seen him since. My aunt was wrong.

## Question Two

The social environment that I grew up in was always telling me to be accepting and tolerant, and thus I was. However I grew up in a town that was mostly white and wasn't diverse. Therefore, there was no question of being tolerant and accepting because everyone was the same. I soon saw people only accepting of themselves.

I grew up in Miami. My family lived in a middle-class community that was not diverse. Neither was the private school I went to. However, my mother was a nurse and she was close with a fellow nurse from Trinidad. She had a daughter my age and we used to play together in her neighborhood. One day we were playing outside and a group of African American teenage boys began picking on me and calling me "whitey," and proceeded to try and pull my shorts down. That was when I knew I was white, and race was an issue. I was five years old at the time.

## Question Three

The only thing that I can remember are some of the comments in my school, which had a diverse student body. . . . Those who were black would call the whites "crackers." Those who were white would call the blacks "coons." The Asian group was called "chinks," and those who were of Spanish background were called "Ricans."

I grew up in an area where race was not an issue. It was a small town in Utah where almost everyone was middle-class white Americans. I grew up not knowing or really caring if someone was different from me. Where I grew up we believe that we are all God's children and to judge and look down on someone, we only degrade ourselves.

In high school the blacks would sit in one section of the cafeteria and the Asians in another, the Hispanics and whites in another. My table that I sat at was the most diverse, it was a mixture. . . . The reason for this is that we didn't feel comfortable because of the tables' segregation, so we made our own clique, if you will.

It was in the summer of 1983 when I had just moved from Lincoln, Nebraska, to San Jose, California, that I first encountered racism. I was walking on the sidewalk; there came a group of boys and girls who approached me. They were in front of my face. I was very scared. All of those kids, one by one, said to me, "Why don't you go back to your country? You don't belong here." And then they left. I just stood there. I was numb. I did not know what those kids meant. I thought to myself to which country am I supposed to go back. There was a war in my country. For the first time those kids' words were in my head and embedded in my brain. Those kids made me feel sad and depressed. But I kept my head high and put those words aside to go on with my life. In Nebraska all of my neighbors were American; I did not know the difference between "white" and "black." I just called them American regardless of their skin color. (Jacqueline Tean, Cambodian student, used with permission)

I went to school with all white kids until third grade, when a new black boy, Jeff, enrolled in my school. He was a major discipline problem and the nun was always correcting him for something. I remember wondering if all black kids behave as badly as Jeff because he was the first black I was ever in close contact with.

I went to a rather large suburban public high school with about a thousand students. Probably fifty to a hundred students in the school were nonwhite. We had few, if any, racial incidents, and all seemed to get along pretty well.

I attended a high school that was probably 95 percent white, most of the black friends I made were through football, two of whom I became very close to and still keep in touch with today, kids who I would consider life-long friends. I think the most important thing we need to do about race in America is to strengthen or improve affirmative action programs, and improve relations with police and government agencies across America.

I was in the ninth grade and I was meeting my boyfriend's mother for the first time. She was really nice but she couldn't resist asking about my background. I told her I was West Indian and Portuguese and she said that was interesting. The next day my boyfriend told me that his mother had said that I was exotic looking, while his last girlfriend was pretty.

My freshman and sophomore years in high school I attended a predominantly white school. I felt strange and isolated because I was about the third Hispanic in the school. I hung out with the other minorities that were black. We always stuck to one part of the room in classrooms and in the cafeteria.

Sometimes we interacted with the other white students but not that often. At Hope High (a racially diverse school) I felt more comfortable because I was surrounded by people like me that understood where I came from and did not stare at me like a creature from another planet. I felt I should have been there since the beginning of my high school journey.

Race played a part of my high school experience. We had a huge demonstration because people felt discriminated against. I remember being at my locker and watching this kid fly down the hall and jump on a black kid's back (tenth grade). For a while it was scary because it was a black-versus-white school.

*Question Four*

The most important thing we need to do now about race in America is to *stop the denial*.

## Racial Awareness and Discussions of Diversity in Elementary School

Many educators prefer to discuss diversity as an abstract "rainbow" of humans without specifically addressing issues of race that very young children often confront, as the quotes above show. Or, they teach children how to draw stick figures of five people and ask them to color them "white," "black," "yellow," "red," and "brown" for all of the races of humans, reflecting Johannes Blumenbach's 1776 racial classification. Students report having difficulty finding the "right" colors in their Crayola box, and teachers may labor under the illusion that they have introduced the subject of race. The following are comments from fifth- and sixth-graders after a presentation on race and anthropology by the author.

Thank you for talking to us about race. I found it very interesting. I think that it was a good idea to have that talk because it lets people know that people of a different race are not different.

The truth is that I learned a lot of new things. For example, I have never heard of melanin before.

I learned a lot. . . . I never knew what makes people's skins darker or lighter.

Thank you for coming in and explaining to us what race is and what it isn't. It cleared up a lot of things for me. Since I am multiracial I was curious to know about how to handle things that may happen to me in the future. Previously in my life I've had Jewish people get mad at me because my mother is German. I've also had some people make fun of me because my dad is Middle Eastern. I have no idea why though. I am happy to know more about race and ethnicity.

Thank you for the multicultural lecture. I learned a lot about black, white, and all of the colors in between, and how they get so dark. . . . My favorite thing that I learned was about the melanin. I thought that it was cool!

I didn't know that Chinese people were called "yellow." I thought only Bart Simpson was yellow.

There is a great deal to be learned through discussion of phenotypic triggers. In-class projects can be designed that probe the many ways Americans have of sizing up a person, by race, by culture, by dress, by manner of walk, and by so much else that is superficial. Specific treatment of racial profiling is helpful—for instance, "shopping while black"; driving along a major U.S. highway as a Latino, especially in an expensive car (suspicion of drug transport); "flying as an Arab" (consult Jack Shaheen's *Reel-Bad Arabs* [2001]).

I often ask my students to imagine American reaction to sports teams named the "Chicago Honkies," the "Detroit Blackskins," or the "New York Micks" or "Jewboys"; there would be a great outcry and protests of racism, they say. Discuss why there is not the same sensitivity to team names that depend on stereotyping of American Indians, such as the "Atlanta Braves," or the "Washington Redskins." Are Indians invisible, or do they lack the necessary political clout to change these stereotypes?

## REFERENCES

Boas, Franz. 1920. *Race, Language, and Culture*. New York: Macmillan.

Brues, Alice. 1977. *People and Races*. Repr., Prospect Heights, IL: Waveland, 1990.

Coon, Carleton. 1962. *The Origin of Races*. New York: Knopf.

Coon, C. S., S. M. Garn, and J. B. Birdsell. 1950. *Races: A Study of the Problems of Race Formation in Man*. Springfield, IL: Charles C Thomas.

Darwin, Charles. 1859. *Origin of Species*. London: John Murray.

———. 1871. *The Descent of Man*. New York: D. Appleton.

Davis, F. James. 1991. *Who Is Black: One Nation's Definition*. University Park: Pennsylvania State University Press.

Dobzhansky, T. 1968. *Science and the Concept of Race*. New York: Columbia University Press.

Garn, S. M. 1961. *Human Races*. Springfield, IL: Charles C Thomas.

Gordon-Reed, Annette. 1997. *Thomas Jefferson and Sally Hemings: An American Controversy*. Richmond: University Press of Virginia.

Gould, Steven J. 1981. *The Mismeasure of Man*. New York: Norton.

Harris, Marvin. 1968. *A History of Anthropological Theory*. New York: Thomas Y. Crowell.

Harrison, Faye V. 1995. "The Persistent Power of 'Race' in the Cultural and Political Economy of Racism." *Annual Reviews of Anthropology* 24:47–74.

———, ed. 1998. "Contemporary Issues Forum, Race and Racism." *American Anthropologist* 100, no. 3.

Herrnstein, Richard J., and Charles Murray. 1994. *The Bell Curve: Intelligence and Class Structure in American Life*. New York: Free Press.

Hirschfield, Lawrence A. 1996. *Race in the Making: Cognition, Culture, and the Child's Construction of Human Kinds*. Cambridge, MA: MIT Press.

IUAES (International Union of Anthropological and Ethnological Sciences). 1998. *Proposed Replacement Statement for the UNESCO Documents on Biological Aspects of Race*. Williamsburg, VA: International Union of Anthropological and Ethnological Sciences.

Jaynes, Gregory. 1982. "A Louisiana Lawsuit Asks What It Means to Be Black, White or 'Colored' in America." *Providence Sunday Journal*, October 14, A-19.

Knox, R. 1850. *Races of Men: A Fragment*. Philadelphia: Lea and Blanchard.

Lewontin, R. C., S. Rose, and L. J. Kamin. 1984. *Not in Our Genes*. New York: Pantheon.

Livingstone, F. B. 1962. "On the Non-existence of Human Races." *Current Anthropology* 3:279–81.

Montagu, Ashley. 1942. *Man's Most Dangerous Myth: The Fallacy of Race*. Repr. 6th ed., Walnut Creek, CA: AltaMira, 1997.

Pandian, Jacob. 1985. *Anthropology and the Western Tradition*. Prospect Heights, IL: Waveland.

*Providence Journal*. 2002. "Jefferson Family Votes to Bar Hemmings Kin." May 6, 1.

Sacks, Karen Brodkin. 1994. "How the Jews Became White Folks." In *Race*, edited by Steven Gregory and Roger Sanjek, 78–102. New Brunswick, NJ: Rutgers University Press.

Scales-Trent, Judy. 1995. *Notes of a White Black Woman*. University Park: Penn State Press.

Seligman, C. G. 1930. *Races of Africa*. London: Oxford University Press.

Seymour-Smith, Charlotte. 1986. *Dictionary of Anthropology*. Boston: G. K. Hall.

Shaheen, Jack. 2001. *Reel-Bad Arabs: How Hollywood Vilifies a People*. New York: Olive Branch.

Shanklin, Eugenia. 1994. *Anthropology and Race*. Belmont, CA: Wadsworth.

———. 1998. "The Profession of the Color Blind: Sociocultural Anthropology and Racism in the 21st Century." *American Anthropologist* 100, no. 3:669–79.

Smedley, Audrey. 1993. *Race in North America: Origin and Evolution of a Worldview*. Boulder, CO: Westview.

Takaki, Ronald. 1993. *A Different Mirror: A History of Multicultural America*. New York: Little, Brown.

Tylor, E. B. 1881. *Anthropology: An Introduction to the Study of Man and Civilization*. Repr., New York: D. Appleton, 1902.

UNESCO. 1964. *Proposals on the Biological Aspects of Race*. Moscow: UNESCO.

Williams, Gregory H. 1995. *Life on the Color Line: The True Story of a White Boy Who Discovered He Was Black*. New York: Dutton.

# 2

# Human Evolution, Natural Selection, and Race

## CURIOSITY ABOUT RACIAL DIFFERENCES

Nearly every child and many adults are curious about observable human difference, what is called "race." Children in the United States begin to identify racial difference by age three, and master the adult cultural or folk categories of race by age five. Parents, caregivers, and early childhood teachers often begin the mystification of race by answering children's questions about physical difference with misinformation, legend, and lore about race. An example is the children's story about the Creator making bread loaves of humans, some baked to light perfection, others to a warm brown, some burnt by being left in God's oven too long. Since the civil rights movement, multicultural educators, leaving such stories behind them, have nonetheless invented a new mythology—the "colors of the rainbow"—to solve the problem of presenting race to preschoolers and kindergartners, as if human beings came in bright colors like purple, green, or blue, or the old human colors developed in the eighteenth century by Linnaeus and Blumenbach—white, red, yellow, brown, and black. It may be common for kindergarten or first-grade children to bring home colored stick figures of the human family—one white, one yellow, one red, one black, and one brown. Small wonder that adults, still in discomfort and denial about race, can utter what has become a formulaic denial of the importance of race—"Skin color doesn't matter to me; I don't care if a person is black, white, green or purple."

Because race is not openly addressed or challenged throughout all levels of American education, efforts to undertake national dialogues on race are difficult to initiate. However, children and adults possess a natural curiosity about race: Why is there difference in skin color, hair form? Who is "black," who is "white"? But since silence on the subject of race is the norm, this discussion is avoided in formal educational arenas. Occasionally, Americans are offered a glimpse of the chasm between black and white worldviews, such as the disparate reactions to public events or political candidates. America's racial denial is mirrored in the controversial relationship that Thomas Jefferson had with his slave Sally Hemings. White scholars and citizens were at first reluctant and then amazed to find out what many blacks had known all along—that President Jefferson fathered at least one child, if not many children, from his slave-mistress and that the American Jeffersonian line is a multiracial one.

Learning about race often devolves into oral and folk traditions in families living in segregated American communities in which there is little opportunity to counter racial stereotyping or bias (positive or negative) with real-life experience. Schools, public and private, are largely segregated, reflecting the segregated communities in which they are found. Even multiracial or apparently "racially balanced" schools are frequently largely segregated into racial and ethnic subcommunities—blacks, whites, Latinos, and Asians—that have little social or academic relation to one another. In public high schools honors and advanced placement classes are predominantly white, while college preparation or general education classes are dominated by blacks and other minorities (Ogbu 2003). Learning about race often occurs in either the family or informal settings, in a racial isolation that allows fact and fable to become confused. When a culture of healthy multiracialism is lacking, racialist and racist attitudes flourish unchallenged. In such a world the beliefs that whites and Asians are smart, that blacks make good athletes, and that Latinos are mostly gang members are cloned from school to school and state to state.

Persistent, normative, everyday interaction and exchange among America's racial groups would foster a healthy knowledge of other races and make myths and misinformation about racial difference unsustainable. This chapter is offered as an accessible explanation of the biology of race, in light of our current understanding of human evolution and DNA mapping.

## HUMAN EVOLUTION, THE STORY OF AFRICAN GENESIS, "OUT OF AFRICA"

Twentieth-century paleoanthropology—the study of ancient humans through fossil evidence—and DNA analysis have affirmed that all humans emerged from Africa. This is what some nineteenth-century scholars suspected but most could not prove, and since this analysis is recent not all scientists studying the origins of humans agree. Advanced *hominid* (humanlike) forms that lived exclusively in the African continent from at least 2.5 million years ago coexisted during these ancient times. Most of these hominid forms ultimately became extinct, but one evolved into the human, which dispersed throughout the rest of the world. This probably occurred from between 160,000 and 200,000 years ago to, perhaps, as recently as 52,000 years ago. What began as a hypothesis of humanity's African origins from the fossil finds of the Leakey family in Kenya in the 1960s has become widely accepted science with every new discovery and improvement in the scientific study of human biological history. Prior to this scientific support it had been believed that humans originated separately and at different times across the globe. This was the old idea of *polygenism*, the theory that there were separate (and unequal) origins of humans—and races, by logical extension. The theory was thought to prove that Europeans were the most recent and therefore the most advanced humans, that Mongolians were older and more primitive, and that Africans were the most primitive, least evolved peoples.

The first finds of *protohumans*—those that came before humans—were made in the 1920s in South Africa, where fossils were retrieved from limestone caves and quarries by digging deep into the earth's crust. The protohumans were originally classified as *australopithecines*, "southern apes" —because the size of the cranium (brain case) was only slightly larger than that of a modern chimpanzee, and the ability to walk upright was suggested by the central placement of the spinal cord attachment to the brain, the *foramen magnun* (large opening). The main biological developments toward increasing *hominization*—becoming human—include the following:

1) Movement from semiupright to fully upright posture (beginning around six million years ago)
2) Decreasing size and changing form of teeth (an uneven, but general evolutionary, trend)
3) Increasing brain size reflected in cranial capacity (from around 2.5 million years ago)

The twentieth-century important fossil findings from South African mines and Kenya along the Rift Valley in East Africa were excavated from a natural *stratigraphy*—layering of the earth's subsurface. These were indicative of early humans because the fossil evidence was found in a context with fashioned tools, although they were very crude one-stone hammers, bone chippers, and scrapers made from animal mandibles. These fossil finds were also originally labeled *australopithecine* by South

African paleoanthropologists and later as *Homo habilis* (handy man) by Louis Leakey because the tools—together with the increased brain case (between five hundred and eight hundred cubic centimeters [cc]) and upright posture—made a strong scientific case for the so-called southern apes to be classified as human. The South African and Rift Valley finds unlocked the scientific truth of the great antiquity of an original African human population. This led to further research in other parts of the continent, where fossil finds as old and even older have been found in the Omo River valley of Ethiopia and around Lake Turkana in Kenya, suggesting dates for early humans at 2.5 to 3 million years ago or more.

There quickly emerged a scientific debate as to whether *Homo habilis* was the part of the line leading to modern humans, or if the Omo River finds (also classified as human, or *Homo*) were the ancestors of modern humans, *Homo sapiens*. A recent, dramatic find of an upright, nonprognathic (human facial and jaw profile) skull in Chad dated at six to seven million years old named *Sahelanthropus tchadensis* suggests that the branching model of the human family tree may be the more useful model to explain humankind's origins, rather than the older linear type of one species replacing another. There is still no consensus among paleoanthropologists as to whether this most recent find is ape or "human," that is, an ancient bipedal hominid; however, there is clear consensus that the original humans were Africans.

Before these finds, it was thought that early hominids from Africa—better adapted and more numerous—had migrated out of Africa to Asia where, as advanced hominids, they evolved into *Homo erectus*, considered an intermediate type between ancient and modern humans. *Homo erectus* is thought to have lived about five hundred thousand years ago, was larger brained (averaging 1,000 cc), and was fully upright, with the *foramen magnum* in the modern central cranial position located at the base of the skull. Also *Homo erectus* humans had cultural developments that included the use of fire, advanced hunting techniques, a tool kit that could be used in killing woolly mammoths, and, quite possibly, articulate speech. Because two important discoveries of *Homo erectus* were made in Asia—in China and Java, Beijing Man and Java Man, respectively—it was thought that a separate, later origin of humans occurred there, or at least that the ancestors of modern Asians had a direct link to *Homo erectus*. When *Homo erectus* as well as *Homo sapiens* finds were discovered in Africa and Europe, the idea that ancient, simpler Africans were replaced by more complex Asians was questioned. Current DNA analysis and fossil evidence point to a more recent, common genetic link between African and Asian early humans, suggesting that *Homo erectus* evolved first in Africa and migrated to Asia and Europe probably as recently as two million years ago.

There are no finds of comparable antiquity in the New World, that is, in North or South America. The earliest date for humans in the New World is put at about twenty to thirty thousand years ago, the time of modern humans, *Homo sapiens*, and these original Americans were likely descendants of Asians who crossed the "land bridge" across the frozen Bering Straits during winter, most probably following migratory game.

The evidence has mounted that not only were Africans the original humans, but that evolution of the human line may have taken place exclusively in Africa, with a dispersal of *Homo sapiens*—modern humans—out of the continent as recently as 150,000 to 200,000 years ago. Analysis of DNA genetic material passed from mothers to daughters known as mitochondrial DNA (originating with the so-called African Eve), and genes passed on chromosome 12 (the Y chromosome) from fathers to sons, suggests to current scientists that modern humans arose in Africa and spread throughout the globe, where they replaced older *Homo erectus* populations that had arrived, also from Africa, perhaps two million years before. The DNA pattern on chromosome 12 has its greatest diversity in sub-Saharan Africa, then becomes less diverse in northeast Africa, and is dominated by just one type in the rest of the world. This DNA human blueprint confirms the original African genesis (origin) and maturation in the continent, with the relatively late migration of a population fanning out of Africa through its northeast corridor to southwest Asia. This makes the Asian fossil record more problematic and begs for a fresh interpretation of the place of *Homo erectus* in human evolution. But this is the fun of the science of our human origins, and if we can put the racialist paradigms behind us, then the quest for our shared origins in human evolutionary development becomes a great jigsaw puzzle in which everyone has a piece of the puzzle. The DNA studies also shed new light on "race"—human biological and phenotypic difference—for they suggest late development of so-called racial difference rather than the original prototypes of the three or five races propounded by polygenists and theorists of racial hierarchies.

Further confirmation of human origins in and dispersal from Africa has come from Swedish scientists who analyzed the mitochondrial DNA of fifty-three people from different continents and populations and found all of them to have common ancestry in Africa, from about one hundred thousand years ago.

So, more precisely, when might this African genesis have happened? Using DNA samples of sixteen hundred people from forty-two different populations, geneticists project that the diagnostic hominid "Alu deletion" (a genetic marker on chromosome 12) first occurred within the last five million years, after hominids split off from the other great apes. The deletion is not found in nonhuman primates. Older lineages of Africans south of the Sahara possess the greatest genetic diversity in human populations, implying that their mitochondrial DNA had the longest time to mutate (Powledge and Rose 1996). Calculating a roughly constant mutation rate these researchers argue that people moved beyond the African continent only recently, leaving a relatively short period of time for mutations to occur, perhaps as little as one hundred thousand years (Fischman 1996, 1364).

## Models of the Origin of Races

While the African origin of humanity has gained consensus among scientists, other models have been generated as variations of the "out of Africa" model. These scientists caution against using this new genetic evidence to explain the whole story of human migrations and history. They argue that small, isolated populations tend to lose genetic diversity, and a series of contractions and expansions could produce a picture of similar genetic uniformity.

Some argue for a multiregional approach (Wolpoff and Caspari 1997) that questions the totality of the "out of Africa" interpretation of human origins. Instead of supporting the African genesis hypothesis they argue that regional variations, especially in Asia, Australia, and Europe, flourished as gradual evolution toward modern humans occurred. They are careful to point out that this model is not a replica of nineteenth-century *polygenism* (separate and independent origins of humans), but is polycentric. *Polycentrism* asserts that races reflect regional variations that are nonetheless part of the same general human stream that changed by being infused with different genetic material from the migration of humans (gene flow). These authors think of race not as having been separately and unequally fixed in ancient times, but as dynamic, changing, diverging, and merging channels that are part of the human main stream (Wilford 1997).

The multiregional model has an earlier migration out of Africa of the more primitive *Homo erectus* about a million years ago, migrating into Europe, Asia, and the major island of Australia and nearby landmasses. This model is based on the fossil evidence of *Homo erectus* in Asia, notably in Java and Beijing, that may be ancestral to or bear a genetic relationship to modern Asian populations. This model suggests that the divergence from a common African stock took place much earlier than two hundred thousand years ago and relies more heavily on bones than DNA analysis (Lieberman and Jackson 1995, 236). This model also suggests a multiregional emergence of *Homo sapiens*, making it different from Coon's theory of separate origins of the human races because it emphasizes interbreeding and gene flow between races, making them more similar to one another (Lieberman 2002). The weakness of the multiregional argument is that its last proponent was Carleton S. Coon's *Origin of Races* (1962), whose ideas about separate and unequal origins of the races were used to justify racist policies in the American South advocating continuing segregation.

Scientists do agree that a truly complete story of human origins, development, and migrations isn't going to occur until many more human genetic loci are studied (Fischman 1996, 1,364). And it may be that human history cannot be fully reconstructed through genetic analysis alone (Lieberman 2002; Marks 2002, 209ff.).

Another model of raciation—the development of races or human variation—that employs the African origins theory holds that modern *Homo sapiens* evolved in Africa and then migrated to Europe and southwest Asia, where the more advanced *Sapiens* stock mixed with and eventually replaced existing populations, such as the Neanderthals of the Middle East and Europe (Marks 2002, 209). However, a recent *Homo sapiens* find in Ethiopia dated from 160,000 years ago so closely resembles anatomically modern humans that the idea that Neanderthals preceded modern humans may be resolved (Monastersky 2003).

What is important is that all contemporary models of raciation depend on an African genesis.

## Modern Humans: *Homo sapiens*

Because race is such a problematical concept, the fossil record of human races is equivocal, making it difficult to establish when and how raciation began. The historical movements and migrations of ancient groups are better understood, and it can be determined that certain groups of humans are quite ancient—for example, the peopling of New Guinea took place at least thirty thousand years ago, while Aboriginal Australians have occupied the great island continent for at least forty thousand years. Moreover, climatic changes over the millennia since the development of modern humans occurred would have acted as catalysts to human migration, such as the retreat of the last glacial formations starting some eighteen to twenty thousand years ago, which fostered population movement north above the more temperate zones. Other climatic shifts, such as the relatively recent desiccation that created the Sahara desert—three to four thousand years ago—have acted as a partial barrier to the migration and genetic admixture of northern Africans with sub-Saharan Africa to the south and Europe to the north.

It is likely that from about one hundred thousand years ago humans were spread over much of the globe, except in North and South America.

This modern period saw the emergence of *Homo sapiens* ("man," the wise) and includes the extinct *Homo sapiens* Neanderthal, which has been found in Europe, the Middle East, and Africa. *Homo sapiens*, whether Neanderthal or Cro-Magnon humans, had larger brain cases, with a range of twelve to fifteen hundred cc, had been upright for several hundred thousand years, and evidenced sophisticated tool technology adapted to hunting, fishing, and all types of gathering. Modern humans have a range of one to two thousand cc and are most distinguished by a remarkable cultural development.

With *Homo sapiens* there is also the first evidence of human burials. By thirty thousand years ago modern humans, *Homo sapiens sapiens* (the doubly wise) had created magnificent artwork in caves, bone, ivory, and clay, evidencing a sophisticated consciousness and possible symbolic manipulation of natural forms, including animals, flora, and human figurines, especially female forms. This symbolic revolution, with its expanded scope and geographical range of cultural complexity, strongly suggests to anthropologists that later developments in humans have more to do with culture than biology. Biologically humanity today is little different from the earliest *Homo sapiens*, but culturally there are vast differences, especially since the food-producing revolution turned our species from a relatively rare into an abundant one, and since the industrial revolution set a course for rapid technological development such as the unparalleled growth witnessed in the twentieth century.

The fossil record for the development of raciation in humans is, practically speaking, nonexistent, because racial differences are superficial. Even today when racial type is claimed for early humans, such as the identification of the five-thousand-year-old "Kennewick Man" found on the American northwest coast as "Caucasian," it is controversial and contested. That is because racial differences are not easily identifiable with skeletal remains alone. It is clear that what have been labeled as racial differences are at most minor, superficial ones—literally only skin deep—that developed during the course of the spread of modern humans out of Africa within the past 150,000 to 200,000 years. It has been the received wisdom among geneticists and anthropologists for some time that human races probably evolved at the time of the spread of *Homo sapiens* (Bodmer and Cavalli-Sforza 1976, 562). The development of human variation is most likely the result of the relative isolation of small, dispersed breeding groups occupying environmental niches for long periods of time; in these niches genetic drift (i.e., nonadaptive, random differentiation) and natural selection (adaptation to environmental forces) have interacted to bring about difference, or divergence, from the groups' predecessors (Cavalli-Sforza and Bodmer 1971, 700).

## Human Variation—"Race"—as the Rich History of
*Homo sapiens*

It is important to point out that most human variation is *not* racial. For decades physical anthropologists have been at pains to point out that there is greater physical variation within races than between them. The story of human history written in our genetic and cultural heritage is a very different one from that traced by racialist and racist writers. Human history is the story of the emergence of humanity from a core African population(s), with a past rich in migrations throughout Asia and eventually to the Americas, with a genetic code that is uniform and unified with a single human blueprint. In this story, the color of skin and type of hair are insignificant, though variable, traits.

The peopling of the ancient world is a subject of interest to humans keen to understand their origins. Europeans can see themselves as the biological and social product of earlier human developments in Africa and Asia that blended in Europe and spread dramatically with the diffusion of agriculture after the food-producing revolution about ten thousand years ago. Africans, with the most ancient history of evolution, express the greatest genetic diversity and are highly diverse in physical variation, despite the dominant Euro-American stereotype of them as having common "Negro" characteristics. Asians are likewise physically diverse, reflecting ancient dispersals, migrations, and microadaptations. An understanding of the process of migration is illustrated in the example of the peopling of the Pacific.

The Pacific regions were long a curiosity to the European racial classifiers because of the apparent similarity between dark-skinned peoples of Africa, Aboriginal Australia and New Guinea, and south Asia. The settlement of Indonesia has been clarified by genetic and linguistic analysis, revealing Indonesians' remote ancestors to be from the islands north of Australia and dating from the last Ice Age, about fifty thousand years ago. The land path between New Guinea and Australia was broken only by channels that were narrow and shallow. Rising sea levels and global melting around 10,000 BCE made voyaging more challenging; however, the peopling of the Pacific appears to have been accomplished by remarkable sailors and navigators who sailed against the currents west to east from the Asian mainland over the past several millennia (Stanford 1998). There is archaeological evidence of settlement from New Guinea in the Solomon Islands, the Santa Cruz Islands, Fiji, and Tonga by 1100 BCE. New Zealand was settled by 800 CE; and the Hawaiian Islands, the Marquesas, and Easter Island were settled between 500 and 300 CE. This Polynesian voyaging achieved an unparalleled oceanic breakout over thousands of miles of open sea. The direction seems to have been mainly one way, with little or no contact after the initial voyage, for there are wide variations in culture between eastern and western Polynesia.

Arab and Muslim traders opened the Pacific to commerce and cultural contact centuries before the Portuguese learned navigation from them in the early 1400s, making both Arabs and Europeans contributors to the gene pools of the Pacific islands. When the Portuguese "discovered" the Moluccas, known as the "Spice Islands," they found a developed civilization, a sultanate, with ships that traded east of Malaya and India, and north to China. The oceanic trade to the east, first by Arabs and Muslims and then by Europeans, paralleled the more famous "Silk Road" that conducted trade by land routes from Venice to Xian in western China.

## MECHANISMS FOR BIOLOGICAL
## CHANGE IN HUMANS

All life is comprised of DNA, genes, and chromosomes. According to recent estimates humans have thirty-five thousand to one hundred thousand genes at various loci (positions) on twenty-three pairs of chromosomes. A gene is a segment of a chromosome containing a special linear arrangement of molecules (Brues 1977, 37). The relationship between gene and chromosome occurs at the place—locus—in a chromosome where the gene affecting a particular trait is found. The various molecular patterns occurring at particular loci are called "alleles," and this term is used to describe the variety of gene forms of a trait (Brues 1977, 37; Molnar 1983, 29).

Each individual acquires 50 percent of his or her genetic inheritance from each biological parent, 25 percent from each grandparent, and so on. When humans inherit the same trait from both parents, it is inherited in the *homozygous* form; when a form is inherited from one parent but not the other, it is inherited in *heterozygous* form. Some aspects of inheritance historically considered racial are under the control of a single gene, such as blood type, which comes in three forms or alleles, A, B, and O. These traits are called "monogenic" traits of simple inheritance, that is, from a single gene. Most traits considered racial—such as skin color, body type, hair form—are under the control of several or multiple genes, and are known as "polygenic," or traits of complex inheritance. These traits, with all of human biological evolution, including raciation, fall under the influence of evolutionary forces that have shaped genetic change over time. Evolution has been described as descent with modification, while another useful definition of evolution would be change in gene frequency through time (Molnar 1983, 43).

The forces responsible for change in a population's gene frequency,

# The Myth of Racial Purity

One of the great myths about races is that each is a self-contained and genetically pure entity. Racial purity linked to racism expands this mythology to assert that race mixing—*miscegenation*—is harmful, for it leads to degeneration of the superior race. It is therefore *dysgenic*—producing a negative biological result—and must be stopped by social intimidation, or by law. An example of social intimidation amounting to terrorism was lynching in the American South; it was often employed to allegedly punish or keep black men from raping white women. Antimiscegenation laws were enacted in forty states from the latter part of the nineteenth century to the turn of the twentieth century to prevent race mixing, and most remained lawful until the U.S. Supreme Court declared them invalid in 1967. All were directed toward the preservation of the alleged purity of the white race, and most prohibited black-white marriages; however, others prohibited whites from marrying any non-Caucasian person. Several states in the deep South, notably South Carolina and Alabama, retained these constitutional restrictions on "mixed marriages" until recently. The language was expunged in South Carolina in 1998, and in 2000 Alabama removed Article IV, section 102, of its constitution, dating from 1901: "The legislature shall never pass any law to authorize or legalize any marriage between a white person and a Negro, or descendant of a Negro." Between 1942 and the 1967 Supreme Court decisions repealed antimiscegenation laws in only fourteen of the forty states. In *Loving v. Virginia* (1967) the Court ruled in favor of a white man and a black woman arrested for the crime of being married and banished from the state.

Black state legislator Alvin Holmes sponsored a repeal amendment in the November 2000 ballot in Alabama that was challenged in court by Michael Chappell, leader of the Confederate Heritage (Sengupta 2000). The amendment passed, making Alabama the last state to rescind its miscegenation law. Alabama is a reminder of how deep the prejudice is against interracial marriage. While the more general repeal was a few decades ago, still many interracial couples report today that they have to be cautious in choosing communities, North or South, in which to live.

In the spring of 2002 a high school in Butler, Georgia, held its first ever integrated prom. Taylor County High School, almost equally divided between black and white students, had refused to sponsor a school prom for the fifteen previous years, since the school was belatedly integrated—decades after the *Brown v. Board of Education* Supreme Court decision in 1954 made segregated schools illegal. Since integration, parents of black and white students had organized their own separate events. It was the students who ended the segregated proms, inspired by the slogan "Stand for what is right, or stand alone" (*Providence Journal*, April 21, 2002). The following year the students decided to resume holding segregated proms because of the social comfort of the long-standing practice.

These laws enforced a much older practice of segregated socializing, although there is now enough evidence to show that interracial sexual relations were frequent. The other famous cases in which antimiscegenation laws prohibited racially mixed marriage include Germany and its occupied territories during the Nazi era, and South Africa under apartheid.

and thus for change in the genotype (genetic makeup), which affects phenotype (outward physical appearance), are the following:

1) Mutation
2) Natural Selection
3) Genetic Drift
4) Gene Flow through Migration (Molnar 1983, 46)

"Race" formation results from populations living in relative genetic isolation in varying environments that allow natural selection, and drift to bring about variation and change. Each of the forces listed above is treated as it affects, or may have affected, the development of human variation known as "race."

## Mutation

Genetic mutation provides the only source of new traits, and it occurs as a result of the natural process of cell division, in *meiosis*, that alters a gene or genes. Mutation can result from exposure to external environmental forces, especially ionizing radiation. Mutations also occur naturally at a very low rate in humans, and can be either beneficial or harmful to humans, or they can be neutral. For example, naturally occurring mutations offer advantages to populations undergoing environmental stress when change in the genetic blueprint may be more adaptive to the conditions causing the stress. The genetic change favoring the adaptation of *sickling* in regions where malaria is endemic may have been such a case (see below). Although radiation causes mutation, it cannot be predicted what effects it will have on which genes. A number of legal claims have been made by people exposed to high doses of radiation, or to lower but prolonged doses of radiation, alleging a relationship to birth defects or infertility.

## Natural Selection

Natural selection is the genetic change most closely associated with Charles Darwin, and "survival of the fittest," a phrase coined by Herbert Spencer. Reproductive "fitness," that is, the ability to survive and reproduce in humans or other species, is strongly influenced by natural or environmental factors, such as climate, sunlight, altitude, or geographical locale (e.g., a rainforest or desert). Successful adaptation to varying environments translates into reproductive fitness, thus making natural selection one of the most important mechanisms for biological change. Adaptation to environments may be aided by preexisting mutations through desirable traits useful in particular environments, such as may have occurred for the development of a long, aquiline nose in a dry desert climate, or a broad, flat nose in a tropical one.

Natural selection provides some of the most logical explanations for many traits distributed in gradation, more frequent in some populations, and considered to be racial. Skin color, as already mentioned, probably evolved in close interaction with the selective force of ultraviolet radiation, or environmental pressures of close proximity to the equator. Likewise, hair form may be explained by climatic factors and protection of the head from excessive heat or cold. Likewise, certain body types—short and stocky to tall and lean—may be adaptive to heat or cold, providing that the population has lived for a long time in relative genetic isolation under specific environmental influences, such as the short, stocky Inuit or other circum-Arctic peoples, or the tall, lean pastoral Nilotic peoples of Equatoria and East Africa. Long-term adaptation to higher altitudes may result in greater lung capacity, as exhibited by the "barrel-chested" appearance of Indians of the high Andes.

Sexual selection, that is, the hypothetical cultural preference for a certain phenotype in a mate, has been offered as an explanation for some traits, such as male-female size difference—*sexual dimorphism*—(with average females being about 20 percent smaller than males in certain populations; however, this is not universal).

The adaptation of humans to environmental forces is a slow process of change in frequencies and would not be observed over a few generations.

For example, the body type of tall Nilotic peoples breeding in isolation in an Arctic environment might not change or adapt to the cold for thousands of years. Moreover, cultural adaptation has been a significant variable in evolution, since humans are ever more capable of adapting to environments through technological innovation, from warm clothes to air conditioners.

Perhaps the best modern example of natural selection observable in our own time is the "reproductive fitness" of bacteria and viruses, especially those developing immunity to man-made antibiotics in the thousands of their generations that can be observed in a human lifetime. The changing environment of bacteria causing infectious diseases in humans has been one in which few survive to reproduce under the conditions of the injection of penicillin or sulfa drugs. Continued and extensive use of antibiotics to thwart these microbes, or their overuse or failure to complete a prescribed course of treatment, has created intense environmental pressure for the microbes to adapt. And they have adapted so successfully that older forms of the microbes have become drug resistant (such as staphylococcus), or entirely new forms have emerged through mutations. This poses a serious threat to humanity in the globalized twenty-first century, in which people, bacteria, and viruses move readily across borders and time zones, and in which new microbes, such as the HIV virus or the Ebola bacterium, threaten to plague humans with epidemics that cannot be controlled.

## Genetic Drift

Genetic drift is the random change in gene frequencies from one generation to another. It is related to population size and higher levels of gene frequencies when there is an increased chance of homozygous pairs of genetic traits in the population. In relatively small populations the number of genetic combinations is reduced, resulting in a tendency for the absolute number of genes to become fixed and nondynamic in populations. In larger populations heterozygous, diversifying genetic traits rise, and the gene frequency has a tendency to stabilize. In large diverse populations, such as that of the United States, genetic drift plays a small role.

Isolated island populations or religious sects that restrict mating with outsiders are prone to the effects of genetic drift, whereby high frequencies of genes become concentrated in small populations. Increased gene frequencies can be expressed in the pooling of ABO blood types, although blood type is not distributed in conformity with "races." However, the pooling of genes from close inbreeding can result in a relatively benign effect, or it can increase the risk of harmful genetically transmitted diseases, such as hemophilia. A small breeding isolate, such as that of European royalty who have inbred over centuries, is prone to these effects.

"Founders effect" appears to be like genetic drift because it also occurs in small populations. Founders effect (unlike the internal workings of a small gene pool) results when a small number of founding parents form a new population. Some traits' effects are magnified due to the lack of diversity in the local genetic isolate.

## Gene Flow/Migration

The split of original African into later Asian regional populations was a result of migration and gene flow, and accounts for the peopling of Australia, Melanesia, the Pacific Islands, and pre-Columbian North and South America (Cavalli-Sforza and Bodmer 1971). However, since 1492 the movements of people from the Old World to the new—both voluntary through immigration and involuntary through four centuries of the slave trade—and their impact on the indigenous peoples of the New World have been a major force in human variation and matters of race. In the five centuries since the Columbian encounter an unprecedented migration of populations has constituted the greatest period of gene flow in human history. In this process of the colonization of the Americas, aboriginal populations were devastated to the extent of deracination and near extinction. The result of this near genocide of American Indians is that their genetic contribution in South American nations like Venezuela or Brazil may be less than 2 percent. In the United States, American Indians make up less than 1 percent of the population.

Enslaved Africans forcibly brought to the Americas over four centuries—from the early 1500s to the end of the nineteenth century—constituted an unprecedented involuntary migration of people. Numbering from conservative estimates of fifteen to twenty million people, they provided labor to build the new economies of the New World. Added to this, over the same centuries millions of peasant and poor urban Europeans voluntarily emigrated to North and South America and the Caribbean for new economic opportunities in the New World. The combined effects of these migrations and the depopulation of original Americans fundamentally altered the human gene pool. In remarkable ways it diversified humanity with hybridized New World "races," while the process of human diversification continues today with the flow of migrants from relatively poorer non-Western countries to the West.

*Clinal* distribution—such as the variation in skin color among the world's populations—express traits that vary continuously, often by gradual progression from one geographical region to another. Clines represent genetic distribution over broad areas that reflects a history of gene flow between populations, when the gene represents a selective advantage, such as in the clinal distribution of the genes for sickle cell in malaria endemic regions (Molnar 1983, 141–46).

The overall biological effect of this diversity has been positive for humanity, but the promise of even greater genetic diversity remains to be realized, for racial, ethnic, and class barriers to human mating remain strong in the New World societies.

## Assortative Mating, Inbreeding Effects

Genetic changes multiply faster in a smaller, inbred population. They occur in fewer generations than in larger populations with more diversity in the gene pool. This happened among inbred populations, such as the Ashkenazi Jews of Eastern Europe, the Amish in the United States, and the royal houses of Europe. Closely inbred communities may suffer negative effects of genetic inbreeding. In one community in Ohio where Amish represent 12 percent of the total population, they comprise half of the cases of physical and mental retardation (Clines 2002). The increased chance of coupling negative recessive genes in this closely inbred society is the major cause of the high rates of genetic deformities; however, communities such as the Amish balance these known risks with their greater fear of losing their young to the outside secular world.

First-cousin marriage—strongly preferred and still widely practiced by Arabs and Muslims in the Middle East and North Africa—was thought for some time to be genetically risky; however, these social groups balanced the risk with a preference for keeping wealth and social stability within patrilineally related families. Comprehensive studies in the Middle East and elsewhere have concluded that there is no greater risk of genetic malformations resulting from first-cousin marriages than exists in the general population.

In addition to genes that increase the likelihood of inherited diseases such as hemophilia, alleles for genes that encode physical characteristics such as blue eyes, facial features, and hair color become fewer in small populations, and the people within such a restricted group come to resemble one another.

## Random, Nonrandom Mating

A population in genetic equilibrium is theoretically based on an assumption of random mating, that is, choosing any mate at random with whom to reproduce, with genotype and phenotype randomly selected. However, it is well known that choosing a mate on the basis of phenotype, especially one influenced by skin color or race, is hardly random. High rates of marriage within ethnic and national groups have characterized human mating. For generations America legally forbade sexual relations or marriages between whites and Indians or Negroes. With respect to racial formation after 1492, mating became less random due to racism.

In many cultures, class or kinship are primary criteria for selecting mates. America forbids marriage between first cousins, while in many Arab societies the preferred marriage partner is the first cousin on the father's side. Because of these and other multiple cultural factors, human mating is mostly not random. Marriage (and mating) outside of the local kin group, or exogamy, is frequently cited as a valuable means of extending social ties and alliances through intermarriage.

Through outbreeding humans increase their genetic diversity, which is biologically advantageous, for intermarriage reduces the chances for homozygous mating and the possible deleterious effects of inbreeding. Highly inbred populations are genetically vulnerable to the negative effects of homozygous mating, as well as receiving any perceived benefits, such as preserving "racial purity." An imperfect, but nonetheless useful, analogy is the conscious inbreeding by humans of certain breeds of dog, such as Chihuahuas for their small size, German shepherds or bulldogs for their fierceness, or Labrador retrievers for scent and hunting. Such highly inbred dogs are "pedigreed," but are known for genetic weaknesses, such as nervousness in Chihuahuas or frequent hip problems in retrievers. It is common knowledge and common sense that mongrels, products of diverse genetic intermixtures, are the best all-around dogs.

## RACIAL DIFFERENCE AND NATURAL SELECTION

### Skin Color

Skin color is a genetic trait that developed as a selective response to a number of environmental factors, including the ultraviolet radiation of the sun, which is known to cause skin cancer. Skin color is also linked to Vitamin D synthesis and the prevention of the breakdown of folic acid, vital to avoid possible neural tube defects and sperm reduction (Jablonski and Chaplin 2003). In the course of human evolution early hominids in Africa reduced the amount of hair on the body perhaps as an adaptation for keeping cool, and developed pigmented skins in response to environmental pressures. Protection against cancer-causing ultraviolet radiation was thought to be the primary reason darker skin color evolved, but recent hypotheses added to this the need to synthesize Vitamin D and the necessity of folic acid in human reproduction (Jablonski and Chaplin 2003).

People of all skin tones, from the lightest to the darkest, darken in reaction to the sun's rays—except for albinos, the only truly white people without melanin, who are totally unprotected from potentially harmful ultraviolet radiation. Skin color and the relative proximity of populations to the equator correlates with clinal variations, with darker skin tones being found among aboriginal populations nearer to the equator, medium to dark skin shades found nearer to the Tropics of Cancer and Capricorn, and light to fair skin tones found among peoples of the northern latitudes.

The original skin color of the earliest humans who originated in Africa was probably brown or black, with black hair and dark eyes. The image of dark-skinned ancestors for all of humanity is challenging because we are so conditioned to a Euro-American representation of a light-skinned couple, Adam and Eve, in the Garden of Eden. If we relocate the mythical Garden of Eden to the scientific fact of African origin we can imagine a different picture. It is probable that from humanity's beginnings in Africa the many varieties of humanity have diverged from an original dark skin color, more often by decreasing pigmentation from dark to light, or depigmentation, than by increasing it from light to dark (Brues 1977, 106).

This world distribution of skin color in humans is perhaps most dramatically seen among the distribution of peoples before 1492 and the opening of the New World, leading to massive population movements of peoples mentioned above.

Skin color is a polygenic trait (under the control of a number of separate genes), an expression of the alleles located within these genes, and has been responsive to a number of genetic and environmental factors. Skin color results from the deposits of *melanin* in *melanocytes* in the deeper of the two layers of the epidermis, the germinative layer of the skin. The color of the skin depends on the amount of melanin present in the melanocytes; all humans have the same number of melanocytes. An albino has the same number of melanocytes as a dark-skinned person, but melanin is not produced, while it is abundantly produced in a dark-skinned person.

Melanin is poorly developed in newborns; babies of light-skinned parents are reddish at birth, while babies of dark-skinned persons are born "brick red" and darken as melanin production develops. Male sex hormones may increase melanin production, making males somewhat darker as a rule than females in all skin color groups.

While skin color and exposure to sunlight are linked, it is too simple to conclude that skin color developed solely as a protective response to the risk of damaging DNA resulting in skin cancer. While skin cancer is rare among dark-skinned persons, it is also not common among even light-skinned individuals living near the equator. This leads scientists to doubt that exposure to ultraviolet sunlight was the only selective factor in the

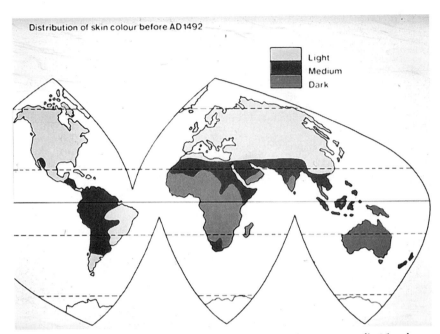

Distribution of skin colour before AD 1492

Light
Medium
Dark

**Figure 2.1.   World distribution of "races" by skin tone before 1492, Audio-Visual Productions.**

evolution of skin color. We know that skin color is controlled genetically by a number of independent genes, which may mean that mutations conducive to the lightening of skin color occurred and became prevalent as human groups moved from southern to northern parts of the Old World. The association of lighter skin color with groups distant from the equator and darker skin color with populations relatively closer to the equator is a tendency, but not a perfect one, if one compares the indigenous peoples at the same latitude across South America to central Africa and the Pacific. It is also possible that some of these indigenous groups have not inhabited these latitudes for a sufficient length of time for darker skin tones to develop in adaptation to the environmental pressure of the equatorial sun. In my own family's melanin-challenged experience a blistering sunburn resulted from my fair-skinned daughter's exposure to less than an hour of midday equatorial sunlight in Sri Lanka when we visited the country with the Semester at Sea program. Having slightly darker skin color than my daughter, but with longer exposure in the Indian Ocean in Kenya, I was severely burned and developed a skin condition, millenaria, from which it took weeks to recover.

Another important factor that has been suggested is the role of skin

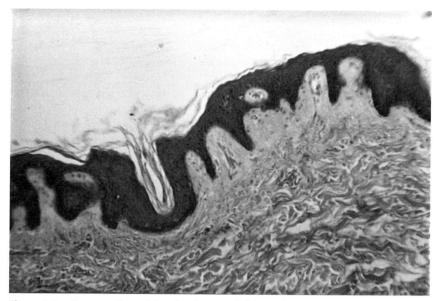

**Figure 2.2.    Cross section of deeply pigmented skin, Audio-Visual Productions.**

color in Vitamin D absorption. Vitamin D synthesis takes place in the skin under the action of ultraviolet light. Dark skin reduces the amount of ultraviolet light that is absorbed and thus reduces the amount of Vitamin D that is formed. Vitamin D insufficiency leads to rickets, a debilitating bone disease, whereas overproduction of Vitamin D can be toxic. Light skin in low sunlight areas, such as northern Europe, would have the selective advantage of admitting more sunlight, needed for Vitamin D production. In crowded urban environments in the United States and Europe during the early years of the industrial revolution, when coal smoke darkened skies and reduced sunlight, rickets was common. Bone deformities resulted, and pelvic deformation in girls made childbirth difficult later in life. Vitamin D–enriched milk has cured this problem. Today year round, overuse of sunblock in sun-deprived regions of North America or Europe can result in Vitamin D deprivation.

Conversely, dark skin in areas of intense sunlight would provide a selective advantage for populations in danger of excessive exposure to sunlight and toxic levels of Vitamin D production. The once mysterious susceptibility of blacks to rickets is now understood as a reduced ability to form Vitamin D due to the screening of sunlight through relatively darker skin color. Thus skin color that is advantageous in one region of the world is disadvantageous in another; too little sunlight results in rickets, too much can cause toxic levels of Vitamin D and tissue damage (Bodmer and Cavalli-Sforza 1976; Brues 1977; Relethford 1997; Jablonski and Chaplin 2003).

Freckling may be a protective response of lighter skin to ultraviolet exposure, as it appears to be stimulated by exposure to the sun. Or it may result from the tanning effect of a natural mixture of pigmentation in the skin, like that seen in persons with what we describe as "red hair" (which is not actually red but made up of a number of pigments) or in men with "red" hair and a dark brown beard. Some physical anthropologists think that this mixture of pigmentation in the melanocytes may also be associated with freckling.

Melanin production protects against the breakdown of folic acid, which is a nutrient essential for fertility and for fetal development in the mother's womb. Ultraviolet radiation penetrates blood vessels in the upper layers of the skin, the *dermis*, where, if unprotected by melanin, folic acid will be destroyed. Light-skinned persons exposed to simulated strong sunlight under laboratory conditions showed abnormally low levels of B vitamin folate in their blood. Research in Australia showed that folate deficiency in pregnant women resulted in higher rates of birth defects, and since this correlation was established, folic acid supplements have become a standard recommendation for pregnant women. Scientists hypothesize that dark skin evolved to protect the body's folate supply from destruction by ultraviolet radiation in the same way as skin color protects against the cancer-causing harmful effects of ultraviolet radiation on DNA (Jablonski and Chaplin 2003, 77).

### "Race" Mixture and Skin Color

Societies that have obsessed about whiteness and light skin color and have devalued dark skin color have likewise developed a hyperawareness of skin tones and the relative advantages and disadvantages of racial mixtures. The one-drop rule in America, which has rendered as black a person with the slightest amount of "black blood," led to obsessions about race mixture and skin color. Lacking the extreme of the one-drop rule, nonetheless some Caribbean or Creole societies have historically been preoccupied with various skin tones that reflect their mixed racial heritage. The social systems in Brazil, the Cape Verde Islands, Haiti, and the Dominican Republic have racialized *mestizo* or *Creole* populations; this will be treated in greater detail in chapter 6. Here the genetics and biology of race mixture are discussed.

Skin color as a polygenic trait (from multiple gene combinations) creates the observable phenotype of different skin tones from light to dark. The folk classifications that developed in the racially heterogeneous

## Skin Color and Standards of Beauty

It is ironic that some whites prefer tanned, brown skin, while some darker-skinned individuals use skin lighteners. These examples stem more from the history of race, racism, and culture than from biology. There exists a cultural norm and preference for whiteness in Euro-American culture, and in the world today whiteness generally dominates culturally and economically, and white standards of beauty prevail. Complex social ramifications result from this fact in what may seem to be irrational and harmful practices that humans nonetheless carry out because they are dissatisfied with the color of their skin.

For example, the popularity of tanning parlors among some Euro-American persons is a peculiar cultural response to congenitally light skin. A tanned complexion in a white person, especially in winter, is perhaps a sign of affluence, indicative of a breakaway vacation to the Caribbean. But tanned skin among whites has not always been a sign of affluence. At the turn of the century tanned white people were common laborers forced to expose their skin to sunlight by working out of doors. "Ladies" carried parasols to protect their fair skin and avoid exposure to the undesirable tanning rays of the sun. The popularity of tanning as an expression of luxury and ease developed especially in the post–World War II suburbanization that favored white, middle-class American dreams and values. Tanning, ironically, became culturally associated with good health and the good life. Only since the medical warning that excessive exposure to ultraviolet radiation is harmful to light-skinned individuals—possibly leading to cancer—has this behavior begun to be modified. Skin cancer screening services have been introduced at health centers, and public awareness campaigns have been introduced at popular beaches in summertime. These campaigns educate especially light-skinned people about the dangers of overexposure to ultraviolet radiation. Yet, so powerful is this cultural preference for tanned skin that tanning parlors are an all-too-common sight in America's white working-class and other neighborhoods.

The cultural preference for golden brown tanned skin among whites has historically coexisted with a cultural disdain for dark to black skin color, which is devalued in white America and in communities across the color spectrum. This "color complex" of America, indeed the Americas, is rooted in racist ideas about "good"/light and "bad"/dark skin color. The preference for fair skin, blond hair, and blue eyes is reflected in multiple cultural expressions, from the popularity of the traditional Barbie and Ken dolls, to beauty pageants and Hollywood stars and starlets, to the many associations of fairness with beauty. There would not have been a need for a "Black Is Beautiful" movement in the 1960s and 1970s if blackness were aesthetically prized, and were not associated even with darkness and evil. There are now many works in cultural studies that analyze Western civilization's historical treatment of "black" as synonymous with evil, with enslavement and inferiority, or with a lack of beauty. Snow White as the "fairest of them all" is a deeply rooted myth.

While skin lightening has declined in the United States, it is still present or undergoing revival in societies where Western white cultural dominance is a fact of life. One such case is contemporary Jamaica, where the harmful practice of skin lightening to achieve the effect of "a brownin'," a term used to describe Jamaican blacks with light skin. The use of skin bleaching creams has been on the rise for the past several years, according to one report (*Providence Journal*, August 8, 1999, A-15). Young Jamaican Latoya Reid comments, "When you are lighter, people pay more attention to you. It makes you more important." Although the use of skin bleaching creams is more common among lower-class women, it is spreading among more affluent women and men as well. In Kenya it is widely believed that lighter skin is equated with wealth, better education, and attractiveness. The old adage from the American civil rights era—"If you're black, get back, if you're brown, stick around, if you're white, you're right"—still has a ring of truth to it. Many persons accepting the natural dignity and beauty of black skin are offended by the revival of skin lightning. Historically, the Jamaican-born "Back to Africa" leader Marcus Garvey, whose movement flourished in the early twentieth century, banned the advertisement of skin lighteners in his publications.

Bleaching has been popular in each of the cultures where white standards of beauty have negatively affected black minority or majority cultures, including the United States, South Africa, or places of white colonialism, like Kenya, the Bahamas, and other Caribbean nations. Yet, despite the known hazards of using skin-bleaching creams, including severe acne, increased risk of skin cancer, stretch marks, and even darkening of the skin, their use has not abated. As long as lighter skin is perceived as a passport to upward mobility and improved social relations its use will continue. As long as racism persists, seemingly illogical practices such as tanning parlors and skin lighteners will also survive.

Some cracks in this facade are evident, with a slight increase in international beauty queens of color and more models of color appearing in the world of high fashion, while literary works such as Nobel laureate writer Toni Morrison's *The Bluest Eye* reveal the depth of these cultural ideals.

Americas after 1492—with perceptible but dwindling native populations—grew with large infusions of European and other immigrants, and great numbers of involuntary African immigrants. They were based exclusively on observable phenotypic differences in skin color. "Black," "white," "mulatto," "yellow" or "high yellow," "brown," "coffee," "café au lait"—these are only a few of the references that have been used in English to describe the skin colors of allegedly pure and mixed peoples. The genetic basis of the inheritance of human traits was not understood until after the turn of the twentieth century. "Mulatto" is poorly understood as a racist designation, for it is derived from "mule," the infertile mixture of the horse and donkey, and reflects the false eighteenth- and nineteenth-century belief that that interbreeding between races leads to degenerate offspring. The term has similar Spanish, French, and Portuguese versions and usage.

Skin color is located on a number of genes with an assortment of alleles. According to the Mendelian law of independent assortment, a mating between a homozygous, "pure" black and "pure" white (that is, indigenous persons of the African and European continents whose ancestors had been breeding in relative isolation for extended periods of time) would result in the following mixture among the descendants of this pair.

In the first generation—the children of the "pure" African and "pure" European—the skin color would be relatively uniform and represent a blend of the parents, resulting in a brown skin tone midway between the darker and lighter skin colors of the parents. However, an independent assortment of alleles would occur in subsequent generations, and skin color would become more varied, with an observable range of skin tones from light to dark noted. African American families have this variety, as does the Cape Verdean family in this picture, whose ancestry combines African and Portuguese genetic heritage.

Race mixture is more the norm in the New World than any fantasies of racial purity, yet racial blinders often prevent people from seeing and appreciating this diverse genetic heritage. Birth records reflect the changing patterns of racial identification in the United States. The birth certificates of Barbara Burgo and her mother, Lorraine Annette Fonseca, recorded in the city of Taunton, Massachusetts, determined the skin color of her mother to be "medium" in 1928 and the skin color of Barbara—under "Color other than white"—to be "mulatto" in 1951.

Compare most African Americans to native-born Africans and the difference in skin color from brown to ebony black is obvious. African American skin color lightened through the centuries of contact and mat-

**Figure 2.3.    Lorraine Annette Fonseca. Courtesy of Barbara Burgo and family, with permission to reprint.**

**Figure 2.4. Barbara Burgo. Courtesy of TR.**

ing, both forced and voluntary, between whites and blacks. Why is it easier to observe the white ancestry of black Americans than the African ancestry of white Americans? The answer may rest in the social fact of the hidden, historically shameful, and unrecognized black ancestry among whites that has been wiped out of social memory and family history. American Indian ancestry among whites was likewise hidden for years before it became "cool" or profitable to claim Indian ancestry.

The notorious case of Mrs. Phipps, involving the one-drop rule in the United States, has already been discussed. Embarrassed by the absurdity of the case the Louisiana courts struck a "compromise" ruling that a person of one-thirty-second black heritage (five generations back) was to be classified as "black." The social history of New Orleans indicates that its residents may have been more concerned with race mixtures than residents of other cities, since the words "Creoles," "mulattoes," "quadroons" (one-quarter "Negro" ancestry), and "octoroons" (one-eighth "Negro" ancestry) were a part of everyday vocabulary. Quadroon balls were popular social occasions at which white men selected their one-quarter black mistresses or concubines for their pleasure and procreation.

### Albinos: The Only People with No Melanin, Found in All Races

Albinos are individuals found in every human population who usually lack the amino acid tyrosine, which is essential for the production of melanin, which is responsible for the degree of skin pigmentation an individual possesses (Molnar 1983, 223–24). Albinos lack skin pigmentation and therefore are utterly unprotected from the damaging effects of ultraviolet solar radiation. Whether Nigerian, New Guinean, or European, albinos are the only humans who are not "people of color," for even the lightest skinned northern European produces some melanin.

Albinism is a recessive trait of simple inheritance (monogenic, located on a single gene), with its particular gene combination occurring more or less frequently in human groups. Albinism occurs more frequently in Nigerians (one in two thousand births), while it occurs less frequently in European populations (one in twenty thousand births) (Molnar 1983, 119).

### Hair Form and Eye Color

Hair and eye color follow a distribution that is similar to that of skin color, suggesting that they may be affected by some of the same forces that create different skin tones. The combination of light eyes and relatively darker skin color visible in many New World persons is the result of a mixture of previously more isolated and homogeneous populations.

Blond and red hair are rare and are concentrated in the same geographic areas of northern Europe. When found in European-derived populations such as in non-Aboriginal Australia and the New World they are the result of gene flow through migration. Red-haired persons appear to be more susceptible to sun damage than blonds, and their protective freckles may be darker.

Hair form and its potentially adaptive value are open to debate. Given the head's critical function of protecting the brain, and the cranium's relationship to the loss of body heat, hair is possibly adapted to a need for protection and insulation. Tightly curled or "woolly" hair (called "kinky" in American colloquial speech) has greater insulating value than straight hair due to trapped air spaces, suggesting it might be more advantageous in cold climates, exactly where it is not found (Brues 1977, 146). The tightly curled hair form of many (but not all) Africans and some aboriginal peoples of Australia and New Guinea may have evolved due to the selective advantage of protecting the head from excessive heat and possible sunstroke. The even more tightly curled "peppercorn" hair of the Khoisan-speaking peoples of the Khalahari (believed by some to be Africa's most ancient extant people) may have evolved to open spaces on the head, allowing rapid evaporation of perspiration in hot or tropical climates.

Straight hair may provide some insulation against colder temperatures and may explain why there is a slight correlation between straight hair and peoples who evolved in temperate zones, in Europe and Asia. European hair is less coarse in texture than that of some Asian populations, yet Europeans are the hairiest of humans in terms of overall body and facial hair. South American Indians living in tropical climes have straight hair like other aboriginal peoples in the Americas. However, they are presumed to have originated in Asia and arrived relatively recently, perhaps only twenty to thirty thousand years ago, while *Homo sapiens* in Africa dates back several hundred thousand years, permitting greater time for breeding in relative isolation and developing the possibly advantageous curlier hair.

The relative amounts of hair on the body may have selective advantages. Among the varieties of humankind, European males appear to be the hairiest. The general absence of hair among East Asians and American Indians may prevent frostbite, while some have suggested that sexual selection may have played a role in the retention of hair on the face and genital areas.

As with other types of obvious human difference, a great deal has been made of hair form in terms of "good" meaning straight hair and "bad" meaning woolly or "kinky" hair. This cultural preference for straight, fine (not coarse) hair has inflicted a poor self-image on many African Americans, and many have purchased hair-straightening creams or undergone painful hair "konking," as described by Malcolm X in his autobiography. Mestizo (Spanish), Creole (French), or "mulatto" mixed populations in the New World may express a cultural concern about the hair type of newborns, wondering whether the child's hair will be "good" or "bad."

### Facial Features

Perhaps the most racialized of facial features has been the relatively broad noses and full lips of blacks, although—to demonstrate the power of normative whiteness and its physical features as the standard of beauty—narrow noses and thin lips might be subjected to the same derision of being viewed as unattractive. Following white aesthetic standards, dark-skinned persons with more aquiline noses and thinner lips may be viewed as more attractive than those with more typically "Negroid" facial features. Ethiopians or Somalis, with their historical mixture with Arabian populations, may be thought of as more beautiful than the people of West Africa, where there is less historical mixture with lighter-skinned peoples.

"What is a good nose?" I ask my students when the subject of noses, race, and stereotypes comes up. Everyone laughs, but each student knows the stereotypes we are about to discuss. "A good nose," they say, "is one that filters the air and doesn't run too much." An attractive nose?—enter the negative stereotypes—is one that is not a "hook" nose like those of the Jews and Arabs, or one that is not too broad and flat, like those of some blacks. How many Jewish or other "Oriental" women have undergone painful and expensive operations to have their noses "fixed" so that their appearance will be more "American," less Semitic, hence more "white"? Black women with more pronounced "Negro" facial features have suffered due to being told they are unattractive and have internalized this harmful, negative self-image.

To offer some possible scientific explanation for differences in nose shape, physical anthropologists have suggested a relationship with relative dryness or humidity in climates. A relatively long aquiline nose would provide a longer channel for moistening and filtering air breathed in a hot, dry, desert climate, such as in the Middle East, home to the so-called Semitic nose, as well as in cold mountain climates (Molnar 1983, 196; Relethford 1997, 421). A broad, flat nose in a hot, moist climate would have the opposite effect of shortening the distance the humid air is breathed, with less need for moistening in the nasal canal.

Full lips may have minimal adaptive value, but they are part of a racial stereotype of blacks that has been exaggerated in cartoon and caricature since the days of slavery and Jim Crow. This has often been part of a package of images that also includes exaggerated *prognathism* (protrusion of the lower jaw), one of the traits that nineteenth-century craniometry claimed proves racial backwardness, since those groups are allegedly closest to apes. There are many ironies in this troubling history of racializing human difference; a contemporary irony is the fashion trend for white females to have collagen injections to create the appearance of fuller lips, giving their faces a more "ethnic" look.

Sometimes environmental factors can produce relatively rapid physical change, such as that discovered by Franz Boas's study of first-generation immigrant children from European populations (Gravelee et al. 2003, 133). Statistically significant changes in head shape, overall height, and other areas of physical growth were recorded after a single generation of life in America, most probably the result of an improved protein diet. Boas's study published in 1912 demonstrated the influence of environmental forces and utterly refuted nineteenth- and early twentieth-century ideas that race is fixed and unchanging. Change at the genetic level is much slower and less likely to reflect responses to environmental factors such as diet, and therefore genes are better indicators of the long-term evolutionary history of humans.

## Body Type

Body types are quite variable, and the old racialist physical anthropology attempted to classify humans according to body type. An ideal *mesomorphic* type was supposed to correlate with an ideal personality. This *somatotyping* was adopted by the behavioral sciences and was taught in

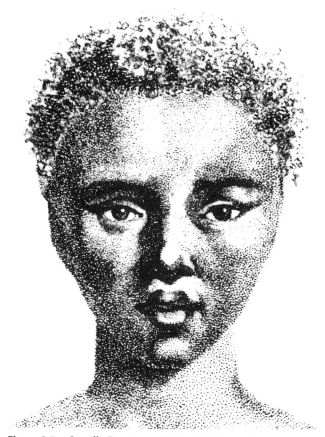

**Figure 2.5.   Saartjie Baartman, "Hottentot Venus."**

basic sociology and psychology as a science of human typology well into the 1960s.

The new physical anthropology has examined human somatic variation and developed hypotheses regarding two extreme opposite types, the short, stocky "Eskimo" type and the tall, lean Nilotic type. Regarding the Nilotic type *Bergmann's Rule* suggests that heat loss is roughly proportional to body surface relative to volume—the more body surface the greater the heat loss. A tall, lean body is thus well adapted to a hot, tropical climate, such as the equatorial part of Africa, where Nilotes are concentrated. *Allen's Rule* hypothesizes that a short, stocky body tends to conserve heat—thus the circumpolar, so-called Eskimo body type. The explanatory value of these oft-cited rules may be limited. The tallest humans, the Nilotic peoples of southern Sudan, Uganda, and Kenya, are the neighbors of some of the world's shortest people, the Mbuti, or so-called Pygmies. The "Pygmies" are hunter-gatherers whose diet is largely vegetarian, with some meat hunted, while the Nilotic people are pastoralists whose subsistence has been based on cattle, an almost entirely protein-based diet. High-protein diets are associated with taller stature. Improvement in the higher-protein American diet has been reflected in increasing average height. Visitors to eighteenth-century homes in New England are frequently struck, literally, by the low doorway entries.

What has been described is classical physical anthropology regarding body type. More recently cultural anthropology has studied body type and self-image among African American women, revealing that American black women do not conform to white standards of the slim, proportionless physical type of white models. There is a greater tolerance for plumpness as being beautiful, and round hips are praised by women and men alike for enhancing sexuality.

Black feminine body typing has also been subjected to racist stereotyping, especially the image of the "Hottentot Venus" extreme of the large hips and buttocks (called "steatopygia") of a small group of genetically isolated southern Africans. The myth of this South African "Venus" was built on a single Khoisan woman, Saartjie Baartman, who was lured to France in 1816 and paraded naked as an example of black inferiority. After Baartman's death her brain, genitalia, and skeleton were displayed as a Musée de l'Homme exhibit until 192 years later, in 2002, when her body was repatriated for burial as an honored "Sister Ancestor" in South Africa (Swarns 2002, 3).

Round hips and full buttocks have been racialized as "black" female traits and are even vocalized as sources of racial pride and envy among my black and white female students. Returning to the example of Jamaica, in addition to the revival of skin lighteners, some women are engaging in an even more dangerous practice. They ingest a chemical used to fatten chickens that is clearly labeled "Poison, not for human use" in order to develop larger breasts and buttocks, which they say Jamaican men prefer. While a problem of both sexism and racism, this example also points to the power of cultural standards of beauty that induce humans to carry out practices that are harmful their health and well-being.

## The Epicanthic Fold, "Asian" Eyes

The epicanthic fold describes a narrowing of the eyes of some Asians, giving the eye an almond shape. The trait is not limited to Asians. The epicanthic fold may have developed in an aboriginal Asian population to protect the eye from extreme cold, wind, or the glare of the sun.

This is purely hypothetical, as is much of what has been suggested about the evolution of racial characteristics, but as inadequate as some of these hypotheses may be they are a better alternative to the racial mythologies and negative stereotypes that have stood in their stead. Surely, as the genetic history of our species unfolds, we will learn more about human variation as a product of human adaptation and migration. To replace racial mythology with a scientific methodology in our thinking is the right step toward a science of human difference.

What is not hypothetical is the practice of surgical "corrections" of so-called Asian eyes, called "blepharoplasty." This was popular among Japanese, Korean, and Vietnamese women living in the United States and other Western countries in the post–World War II and post–Vietnam War periods who considered their eyes too "Oriental." The replacement of almond-shaped "Asian" eyes with "Occidental"—Western—round eyes achieves the desired cultural effect of appearing white and therefore fitting in more comfortably with the phenotypic norm of the dominant society. This eye surgery is often undertaken un-self-consciously and without apology, according to Korean researcher Jin Lee (Neufeld 2003), by as many as 5 percent of South Korean women. Like skin lighteners in African and Caribbean nations, there is a frank recognition that increased opportunities for employment result from the "corrective" surgery.

## BLOOD AND RACE

### Blood Type and Race

Among the many historical but vain attempts to make a science of race, blood type appeared to be a promising differentiator of humans, an inherited trait that was not phenotypic—that is, not based on outward physical appearance—but was genotypic and therefore scientific. Blood type is a trait of simple inheritance, that is, it is carried on a single gene locus with

Figure 2.6. Epicanthic fold, "diagnostic" Asian 'racial' trait; Nuer woman, south Sudan. Courtesy of the author.

Figure 2.7. Epicanthic fold, "diagnostic" Asian 'racial' trait; Asian girls. Courtesy of the author.

three alleles and is therefore traceable from one group to another, perhaps suggesting some historical relationship.

The discovery of the ABO blood groups by Austrian scientist Karl Landsteiner in 1900 was based on patterns of agglutination or clotting of transfused blood between donors and recipients. Different types of human blood were arranged in a system known as the ABO Blood-Group System. Since the original discovery, other major blood types and blood factors have been discovered, such as the Rh and Duffy blood groups. The hope that blood type would cluster by race was quickly overwhelmed by the great diversity of human blood types, suggesting that blood types may be as unique to each individual as are fingerprints.

However, it is the potential racialization of blood type that most interests us. Here the Duffy blood group can be mentioned. This blood group has alleles Fy(a), Fy(b), and Fy(o), which are found in most Caucasians, while a majority of West Africans and many African Americans are negative for these alleles. As a result of this particular clustering, the Duffy blood group is useful as a genetic marker and has been applied in determining Caucasoid admixture in African Americans. However, in the hands of some racist scholars, the Duffy-Fy blood group was used as an indicator of intelligence. These scholars suggested that blacks with lighter skin color, evidenced genotypically by the presence of Duffy Fy, would have higher IQs than darker-skinned blacks as a result of the positive effects of Caucasian blood.

The "Diego" blood factor found in Asian and Asian-derived populations is absent among the Yanomami, a genetically isolated indigenous people of the Amazon River in Brazil and Venezuela. Among other genetic and cultural factors, it was this lack of the Diego factor that attracted geneticist James Neel and anthropologist Napoleon Chagnon to study their sociobiology in the 1960s and thereafter. The research by Neel and Chagnon collected twelve thousand vials of blood from this indigenous population, using prized Western goods to trade with the Indians for their blood. This has raised serious questions of ethics (Fluehr-Lobban 2003) and has led to broader questions involving DNA and human genome research among vulnerable and not fully informed indigenous peoples around the globe.

### Sickle Cell Anemia, Malaria, and Human Evolution

In the United States we think of *sickle cell anemia* being a blood disorder that mainly afflicts African Americans. While it is true that the allele for sickling of the red blood cells does occur in 10 percent of those who identify themselves as of African descent, this does not take into account the numbers of whites carrying African genetic material due to the amount of race mixing that has occurred in America. Also, the trait for sickling of red blood cells is the same as that which occurs in circum-Mediterranean populations, where the resulting anemia is known medically as "thalessemia" and popularly as "Mediterranean anemia." Skeletal remains from early agricultural times in ancient Greece indicate evidence of chronic anemia, which was probably the same as thalessemia or ancestral to it (Molnar 1983, 168). The gene for sickling of the red blood cells, HB, is also found in southern Europe, Turkey, the Middle East, and parts of India. So, the presumed racial trait for sickling is not exclusively African.

What may cause this sickling, and how is it related to processes of human evolution? The sickle cell allelle is found in almost 40 percent of some population groups of West Africa. This is also one of the regions where malaria has been endemic probably from three to four thousand years ago, when the spread of slash-and-burn horticulture cleared the tropical rainforests of animals that otherwise would have been hosts for the bloodthirsty, parasitic mosquitoes that transmit the disease. Mosquitoes breed in stagnant pools of water, which would be abundant after heavy tropical rains, yet the connection between mosquitoes and malaria in humans was not made until the twentieth century. Indeed, untreated malaria was a major problem during the construction of the Panama

Canal. Other areas of the African continent, such as northern Sudan, where I conducted three years of anthropological research, have been subject to malaria epidemics only in the latter part of the twentieth century, as immigrants from endemic regions have carried the disease and the Sudanese government has not exerted sufficient malarial control. I contracted malaria under these circumstances, as did my husband and daughter. The symptoms in the acute phase include high fever, painful joints, severe headache, and pain radiating down the spinal canal. Recovery, even after quinine treatment of the symptoms, takes weeks, leaving the affected person tired and weak from the assault on the red blood cells. I recall being unable to climb stairs for weeks without stopping at each step to catch my breath, and bumpy car rides caused spinal discomfort for a long time. Our young daughter recovered from malaria, but developed pneumonia from a cold due to her weakened immune system. The higher morbidity rates in malarial-endemic regions are often the result of this deadly combination of bouts of malaria and infectious diseases.

Since the genes for abnormally shaped red blood cells are found in some regions where malaria has been endemic for thousands of years, it seemed reasonable to suggest that there may be a relationship between them. Indeed, physical anthropologists were able to show that persons carrying the sickle cell gene in the *heterozygous form* (that is, they inherited the gene from one parent, but not both parents), were less likely to die from malarial infection than noncarriers. It is not that being a carrier of the sickle cell gene immunizes a person against malaria, but the reduced oxygen-carrying capacity of a sickle red blood cell apparently also reduces the virulence of a malarial attack (which assaults human red blood cells) and thus increases chances for survival. Until the connection between mosquitoes and malaria was made, and quinine and quinine-derived drugs proved effective in combating attacks of malaria, humans had little defense against this killer disease. Only the sickle cell afforded some protection from this mortal disease; the sickle cell developed under selective pressure in human evolution in certain malarial-endemic regions, such as West Africa and the Mediterranean.

Evolutionary processes of natural selection are not perfect or fail-safe. Even as the sickle cell gene in the heterozygous form offered a protective advantage against malaria, in the *homozygous form* (that is, when the trait is inherited from both parents) it can be deadly. It can cause the person to suffer from a chronic, debilitating sickle cell anemia, which is nearly always fatal, with few surviving beyond forty years of age. The chronic sufferer is prone to infections since he or she is in a constant weakened condition, while many vital organs are affected by sudden periodic bouts of the disease, which are extremely painful. The only prevention is through genetic counseling if a mating couple knows or suspects they have sickle cell anemia in their background. The sickle cell trait is declining and is estimated to be in perhaps only one in five hundred African Americans. Likewise, with quinine treatment of malaria and mosquito eradication programs, the selective advantage of the sickle cell gene in human populations will also decline. However, malaria is still the world's number one public health problem, and many people in endemic areas view attacks as inevitable, like the common cold is viewed in the United States. Possessing the sickle cell trait may offer some selective advantage in highly polluted environments, where the reduced oxygen-carrying capacity of heterozygous individuals may also mean the reduced introduction of toxins into the human body.

### Lactose Intolerance and PTC Tasting

Intolerance to fresh milk and the ability to taste or not taste phenylthincarbamide (PTC) are inherited traits that may cluster in racial groups but cannot be considered racial traits. Deficiency in the production of the enzyme lactase is responsible for milk intolerance. A majority of Asians and Africans are lactase deficient and are unable to tolerate fresh milk in their diet—even in populations that rely on cattle herding for subsistence. Fermented milk products, such as yogurt and cheese, are tolerated.

The frequency of PTC tasting varies from a high frequency of tasters in India at 40 percent to a low of 5 percent in sub-Saharan Africa. The chemical PTC is present in the cabbage and mustard family of vegetables, which includes cabbage, broccoli, brussels sprouts, kale, and mustard greens.

### Human History through Blood Types: DNA Mapping of the Human Genome

Time and again objective science has shown that race is nonscientific and meaningless at the genetic level, and that the human species comprises one great global family tree. The superficiality and insignificance of skin color, for example, is shown by DNA analysis of the relative closeness or distance of human groups. Africans and Aboriginal Australians, once thought to be genetically related due to similarities in skin color and hair form, have been found to be the most distant from each other in DNA mapping of human groups (Subramian 1995, 54).

There are many other findings that have challenged long-held ideas or myths about races and racial relationships. For example, Africans are closer to Europeans than to Aboriginal Australians, whose closest genetic relatives are Southeast Asians, their geographical neighbors. Moreover, the great genetic distance between all Africans and all non-Africans indicates that the split from the original African continental roots is the oldest of such divergences in the human family. The linguistically unique Khoi-san speakers of southern Africa (known as the !Kung or San—and pejora-tively by the term white South Africans coined, the "Bushmen"—and speaking "click" languages) may be the oldest extant African population, although they show a genetic mix of populations that are both African and West Asian, perhaps from Ethiopian and Middle Eastern genes. The European Basque population of France and Spain, long a mystery to anthropologists because their language bears no relation to any extant European tongue, in Cavalli Sforza's DNA analysis appear to be the best candidates to be the descendants of the Cro-Magnon people, the first example of European *Homo sapiens*, or modern humans, while Europeans and Asians are subsets of earlier groups of Africans (Marks 2002, 211). North and South American Indians appear to be of three distinct genetic types, possibly suggesting separate historical and geographical migra-tions from Old World Asia from as early as twelve thousand years ago.

### The Human Genome Project

Mapping the human genome is one of the great achievements of modern science, especially because genetic analysis confirms our common roots. But the Human Genome Project initially suffered from a weakness com-mon to much of anthropology's history and biomedical research, an inability to confront race and human variation. From the outset of the Human Genome Project physical anthropologists complained that the biological diversity of the world's populations was not being represented. A broad range of scientists and ethicists argued that a preferred process was to collect DNA samples from a cross section of persons from major ethnic and racial groups to construct the human genome map.

Concerns about proprietary control over human genetic materials were also raised. Indigenous groups protested the patenting by the U.S. gov-ernment or Western scientific corporations of their genetic material and future cell lines. This material was derived from blood samples taken often without their full informed consent about what would be done with the biological samples. In one celebrated case the U.S. government issued a patent, despite international protest, of the DNA of a Hagahai man from Papua New Guinea because he was infected by one of the few viruses that causes cancer in humans and had not developed the disease. His DNA could be invaluable if his genetic material is used to develop an immunity vaccine to cancer. Throughout the 1990s many human rights and indigenous rights groups stood not against scientific advance, but against the exploitation of peoples who have already not fared very well in their encounter with Western civilization.

Race was a significant factor yet not allowed to be a part of the scientific or social process; this led scientists to an overreliance on a single individual, or a single corporate process, in the mapping of the human genome.

### DNA: Helping African Americans Trace Their Roots

Research projects have collected DNA from contemporary populations of African Americans, and a skeletal database of the vast African Burial Ground in Manhattan has been assembled by project director Michael Blakey, who also has analyzed the data. These projects may make possible analysis of the origins of enslaved Africans brought to America. However, the DNA analysis may not be conclusive in conjunction with historical and ethnological information. For example, the DNA analysis will show not only African roots but also substantial European lineage, because slave owners and other whites interbred with Africans.

This chapter could also be entitled "a natural history of race," since biological race has been a part of humanity's physical evolution and expansion across the globe. However, it has been the social construction of race and pernicious ideas of racism that have most affected the human condition. Were our species able to dislodge and disown this history, we as a universal human entity could explore more deeply our rich biological heritage in a neutral scientific manner.

### REFERENCES

Boas, Franz. 1912. "Changes in the Bodily Form of Descendants of Immigrants." In *Race, Language and Culture*, 281–89. New York: Macmillan.
Bodmer, W. F., and L. L. Cavalli-Sforza. 1976. *Genetics, Evolution, and Man*. San Francisco: W. H. Freeman.
Brues, Alice M. *People and Races*. 1977. Repr., Prospect Heights, IL: Waveland, 1990.
Cavalli-Sforza, L. L., and W. F. Bodmer. 1971. *The Genetics of Human Populations*. New York: W. H. Freeman.
Cavalli-Sforza, Luigi Luca. 1995. *The History and Geography of Human Genes*. Princeton: Princeton University Press.
Clines, Francis X. 2002. "Research Clinic for Ills That Haunt the Amish." *New York Times*, June 20, A1, A21.
Fischman, Joshua. 1996. "Evidence Mounts for Our African Origins—and Alternatives." *Science* 271 (March 8): 1,364.
Fluehr-Lobban, Carolyn. 2003. "Darkness in El Dorado: Research Ethics Then and Now." In *Ethics and the Profession of Anthropology: Dialogue for Ethcially Conscious Practice*, 85–106. Walnut Creek, CA: AltaMira.
Gravelee, B., and Leonard et al. 2003. "Heredity, Environment, and 'Cranial Form': A Reanalysis of Boas' Immigrant Dream." *American Anthropologist* 105, 125–38.

Jablonski, Nina G., and George Chaplin. 2003. "Skin Deep." *Scientific American*, special edition, "New Look at Human Evolution," August 25, 2003, 72–79.

Lieberman, Leonard. 2002. Personal communication. July 20.

Lieberman, Leonard, and Fatimah Linda C. Jackson. 1995. "Race and Three Models of Human Origin." *American Anthropologist* 97, no. 2:231–42.

Marks, Jonathan. 1995. *Human Biodiversity, Genes, Race and History*. New York: Aldine DeGruyter.

———. 2002. *What It Means to Be 98% Chimpanzee: Apes, People, and Their Genes*. Berkeley: University of California Press.

Molnar, Stephen. 1983. *Human Variation, Races, Types and Ethnic Groups*. 2nd ed. Repr., Englewood Cliffs: Prentice-Hall, 2002.

Monastersky, Richard. 2003. "Scientists Say They Have Found Remains of Humanity's Closest Ancestors." *Chronicle of Higher Education*, June 20, A14.

Neufeld, Jodi. 2003. "Opening Eyes for Beauty, Blinding from Oneself: Blepharoplasty among Young Korean Women." *Colgate Maroon-News*, January 31, 5.

Ogbu, John. 2003. *The Performance of Black Students in an Affluent Suburb: A Study of Academic Disengagement*. Mahwah, NJ: Lawrence Erlbaum Associates.

Powledge, Tabitha M., and Mark Rose. 1996. "The Great DNA Hunt: Genetic Archaeology Zeroes in on the Origins of Modern Humans." *Archaeology*, September–October, 36–44.

*Providence Journal*. 2002. "For Georgia High School Students, Integrated Prom Will Be a First." April 21, A4.

*Providence Sunday Journal*. 1999. "Skin Bleaching Soars in Popularity in Jamaica." August 8, A-15.

Sengupta, Somini. 2000. "Removing a Relic of the Old South." *New York Times*, "Week in Review" section, November 5, 5.

Stanford, Peter. 1998. "How the Races of Mankind Came Together in the Immense Mixing Bowl of the Pacific." *Sea History* 54 (Spring): 10–15.

Subramian, Sribala. 1995. "The Story in Our Genes." *Time*, January 16, 54–55.

Swarns, Rachel L. 2002. "Mocked in Europe of Old, African Is Embraced at Home at Last." *New York Times*, May 4, A3.

Wilford, John Noble. 1997. "Not about Eve." Review of *Race and Human Evolution: A Fatal Attraction*, by Milford Wolpoff and Rachel Caspari. *New York Times on the Web*, February 2, at http://holtz.org/library/tofile/notabouteve.htm.

Wolpoff, Milford, and Rachel Caspari. 1997. *Race and Human Evolution: A Fatal Attraction*. New York: Simon and Schuster.

# 3

# Making a Science
# of Racial Inequality

### RACE AND THE ORIGINS OF ANTHROPOLOGY

P hysical anthropology was constructed on Linnaean science, and in its early years it became the scientific study of racial difference (Marks 2002, 61). In 1749 Count de Buffon introduced six varieties of the human species on the basis of color, body shape, and disposition, making the association of race with physical type. In 1735 Carolus Linnaeus classified four races of humans, and between 1770 and 1781 Johann Blumenbach distinguished five races. Blumenbach's five-part racial system based on color became the accepted science of its time, and was already a century-old, time-honored tradition by the time anthropology made its appearance on the world scientific stage. "Enlightened" Europeans constructed race from a belief that they were at the top of the racial ladders they constructed, and they saw themselves as liberal, scientific, and thoroughly modern. Two hundred and fifty years later we are still trying to undo their work.

No better example of the contradictions and present legacy of race coming from this period is America's Enlightenment president, Thomas Jefferson, who was profoundly committed to democracy and equality as well as an attendant belief in the inferiority of the Negro and Indian races. He had a long-term relationship with his slave Sally Hemings—a daughter of Elizabeth Hemings, who was born in Africa. Sally bore fourteen children from four men, including seven children allegedly fathered by Thomas Jefferson, one of whom, Eston Hemings Jefferson, provided DNA for the current analysis of Jefferson's African American descendents, confirming their relationship to the writer of the Declaration of Independence (Alexander 1998). Jefferson failed to free his several hundred slaves, whose labor made him one of the richest men in Virginia. In this regard he was unlike America's first president, George Washington, who did free his three hundred plus slaves in his last will and testament. Many U.S. presidents owned slaves, including four of the first five presidents, excluding John Adams (#2): George Washington (#1), Thomas Jefferson (#3), James Madison (#4), and James Monroe (#5). The Enlightenment shines less brightly in Euro-American history when the vital concept of race is taken into consideration.

Anthropology, as a new science and a separate discipline within the academy, began to gain acceptance in the mid- to late nineteenth century. In America its scientific debut can be dated from its first seminal work, Lewis Henry Morgan's *League of the Iroquois* (1851), and his theoretical *Ancient Society* (1877). The honor of the first academic position to be held by a scholar calling himself an anthropologist belongs to Franz Boas, a German-Jewish immigrant trained in physics who initially taught anthropology at Clark University and then institutionalized anthropology in the United States from the Department of Anthropology at Columbia University from 1896 until his death in 1942. Boas's students became some of the most famous anthropologists of the twentieth century, including Margaret Mead, Ruth Benedict, Ashley Montagu, and many others.

## ONE OR MANY SPECIES OF HUMANITY: MONOGENISM VERSUS POLYGENISM

The origins of anthropology and its early development are closely tied to a concept of race and ideas about race that were already extant in the nineteenth and early twentieth centuries. Anthropology, as the self-described "study of man," weighed in on the scientific debates of the day regarding human physical and cultural evolution and the single or multiple origins of humans. The main debate about the nature of man that divided nineteenth-century scholars was between the *monogenists* and *polygenists*—those who saw the single or multiple origins of humans. The monogenists prevailed, and the debate shifted in the early twentieth century to the relative ranking of races by degrees of cultural evolution on a scale from "savage" society to "civilized."

The debate between a single versus multiple origins of humans raged into the late nineteenth century. Since American Indians are not mentioned in the Bible at the time of the dispersal of humans after the great flood—only mentioned are Noah's sons: Ham (descendants in Africa), Shem (descendants in Asia), and Japeth (descendants in Europe)— Indians were thought to be nonhuman or protohuman. The issue of mankind belonging to one species was resolved theologically in the wake of criticism of the Spanish and the church for their treatment of Indians of the New World, especially after three million Indians of Hispanola died in less than a decade, from 1493 to 1503. This was "the result of disease, warfare, enslavement, and forced labor," according to Bartolome de las Casas, the Dominican friar who had been the most critical. He argued that the Indians were human and had been cruelly and inhumanely treated by Spaniards, which turned into something of an anti-Spanish, anti-Catholic backlash and one of the many seeds of the Protestant Reformation. So in the early sixteenth century (when Europe was in the throes of the Reformation) the Catholic Church and the pope declared that Indians were fully human. Until that time Spaniards had apparently felt little compunction in killing Native Americans because they were not descendants of Adam and Eve (Pandian 1985, 65). Prior to this acknowledgment of shared humanity scholars had hypothesized that American Indians belonged to some "pre-Adamite" stage, before biblical creation, and were thus not fully human.

However, scholars through the eighteenth-century Enlightenment were still not sure about the unity—much less the equality—of human groups, including the founding fathers of the American Revolution. They remained conflicted between the biblical story of a single creation from a single pair, Adam and Eve, on the one hand, and their own "scientific" observations of real and imagined physical and cultural differences among non-Western peoples, especially American Indians and Africans in their midst. Thus, the controversy between monogenists and polygenists remained scientifically unresolved.

In the nineteenth-century expression of the debate, the monogenists argued for the single origin of all humans without reference to the Bible, but with reference to the science of Darwin and biological evolution, while the polygenists, who disputed this view, continued to assert the separate origins of different races of humans, perhaps at different times in evolutionary history. Theological monogenists and polygenists continued to use the Bible to defend their opposing points of view, with the monogenists having Adam and Eve as a single creation idea. The theological polygenists supported separate and unequal origins of humanity using the story of the Tower of Babel, whereby God dispersed different groups of men with special hereditary characteristics. The debate between monogenists and polygenists continued throughout the nineteenth and early twentieth centuries, and its echoes could still be heard during the American civil rights era of the 1950s, when integrationists and segregationists disputed whether white and colored children could sit in the same classrooms. The single origin thesis was not vindicated scientifically until the Leakey family's discovery of fossil evidence confirming humanity's single origin in Africa.

The "science" of race met the politics of race over the issue of slavery. Some of the most ardent defenders of slavery were dogmatic polygenists, arguing that Negroes and whites belong to different species. A typical polygenist scheme was that of the English physician Charles White, who attempted to prove on anatomical grounds that four separate races exist (*Account of the Regular Gradation of Man*, 1799, in Harris 1968, 89); in descending order they are:

1) Europeans
2) Asians
3) Americans (Indians)
4) Africans

White argued that Negroes occupy a place in the "great chain of being" closer to the apes than to Caucasians (Harris 1968, 89), thus suggesting a demeaning relationship between apes and Negroes that has been difficult to erase from Euro-American consciousness. Racial slurs against blacks using references to monkeys have been all too common.

It was with some relief and amusement that I learned on my second trip around the world with the Semester at Sea (SAS) program that a common Han Chinese view of Europeans is that they look like monkeys because the men are so hairy, with full beards. One blond full-bearded student from SAS who was visiting the Great Wall was pointed at by Chinese children; the words were translated, "Look, monkey!" (See figure 3.1.)

It can be seen that White's ranking of races is similar to ideas embedded in Linnaeus's and Blumenbach's classification of race, with Europeans being most superior and Africans lowest in the grades of humanity. Another speculative classification of the four races, created by Carl Gustav Carus in 1838 compares them to the phases of the planet—day, night, dawn, and dusk—which must be reflected in all life forms, such as animals active in the daytime and at night, and plants that bloom in the daylight, at dusk, or at dawn. So it must be with man: a day race, the Europeans and west Asiatics; a night race, the Negroes; a dawn race, the Mongols; and a dusk race, the American Indians. Making "science" of his four-part racial classification, Carus used Morton's craniology, which demonstrated that the brain of the day race is great, while that of the night race is small, with the dawn and dusk races having intermediate-size brains (Boas 1938, 21).

Both Linnaeus and Blumenbach were monogenists, while White asserted the polygenist, separate origins of races, which shows that monogenism alone was not sufficient to make writers free of racialist thinking. The liberal monogenist position gained more sway in scholarly

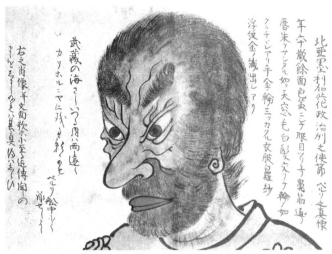

**Figure 3.1.** Japanese portrayal of a hairy Commodore Perry in the *Black Ship Scrolls* depicting initial encounter between him and Japanese at Shimoda, Okinawa, 1854. From Oliver Statler's *The Black Ship Scroll* (Tokyo: John Weatherhill, Inc., 1963).

circles and was held by most early anthropologists, although many accepted the idea of humanity being ordered by different grades of physical and cultural evolution, including Linnaeus, Blumenbach, and de Buffon, who were monogenists; and Paul Broca, head of the Paris Anthropology Society, and Louis Agassiz, professor of zoology at Harvard, who were polygenists.

## RACE AND NINETEENTH-CENTURY EVOLUTION: SAVAGERY, BARBARISM, CIVILIZATION PROGRESSING FROM DARK TO LIGHT RACES

### From "Black" and "Red" Savages, to "Yellow" and "Tan" Barbarians, to "White" Civilized Races

The ideas of Charles Darwin outlined in *Origin of Species* (1859) and *Descent of Man* (1871) had a major impact on the developing science of anthropology. The idea of progressive development or evolution of life from simple to complex, and the dawning recognition of the antiquity of life on earth and of mankind itself, unleashed an inquiry into the science of human progress that Darwin himself did not attempt. However, scholars impressed by Darwin supported a doctrine of the perfectibility of humanity. Were the idea of evolution to have developed in an era free of the race concept the outcome we are about to describe would have been quite different. But the idea of evolution became entangled with the idea of race (which had already established itself as "science"), and hence the notion of "lower" and "higher" races of mankind on the scale of evolution became an unfortunate by-product of the Darwinian revolution.

In early anthropology ideas of evolution were expressed as stages of cultural evolution, particularly in the works of L. H. Morgan, America's first ethnographer and anthropologist. His *Ancient Society* (1877) makes a systematic scheme of evolution from lower to higher stages of culture, described as progressing from savagery to barbarism to civilization. In each major stage Morgan describes lower, middle, and upper levels. Thus, for example, within savagery are levels of upper, middle, and lower savagery. Significantly, civilization, once achieved, does not arrive in lower, middle, and upper stages but as a singular achievement at the apex of cultural evolution. The savage levels, commencing with the infancy of the

Figure 3.2. African with apes. From Robert Wilson Shufeldt, *America's Greatest Problem: The Negro* (Philadelphia: F. A. Davis Company, 1915).

human race and from the knowledge of the use of fire to the acquisition of pottery-making skills, are occupied by Aboriginal Australians, Polynesians, and certain tribes of North and South America. The stages of barbarism begin with pottery making and proceed through the domestication of animals, the cultivation of maize, and the smelting of iron ore to the culmination of the barbaric stages with the invention of the phonetic alphabet; in this stage are the "settled tribes" (i.e., agriculturalists) of North, Central, and South America, and in the uppermost state of barbarism, the Grecian, Italian, and Germanic tribes before the age of empire in Europe. The status of civilization, achieved with the invention of the alphabet, divides into ancient and modern periods; admitted to ancient civilization is Egypt, because of hieroglyphics, and the foundations of Western civilization, with the composition of the Homeric poems in ancient Greece around 850 BCE (Morgan 1877, 10–12).

As a cultural evolutionist, Morgan separates his stages by technological advancement, and as a unilineal evolutionist he saw the stages of savagery, barbarism, and civilization as universal and as a necessary sequence. Thus, savagery was generally confined to what we would call hunters and gatherers today; while barbarism witnessed advances in technology, such as the early stages of farming (known as the Neolithic period in archaeology today) or the Bronze Age in the Middle East and Europe; while civilization came with the rise of full-fledged agriculture, surplus production, private property, and the ancient state, defined by literacy. In the end Morgan is highly critical of the pursuit of property in modern civilization, saying it had become "an unmanageable power" (1877, 552). Social organization and kinship systems evolved through these stages, as did religious and ideological systems. As the first "science of culture" the evolutionary stages of Morgan gained legitimacy, and his materialist approach was infused with the dialectical method by Frederick Engels, who basically rewrote *Ancient Society* as a Marxist work in *The Origin of the Family, Private Property and the State* (1884).

As the astute reader can tell by now, Morgan is a more complex figure than he might appear at first glance. As an ethnographer of the Iroquois he was a scholar, friend, and advocate for the Iroquois nation and for American Indians in general. He was, however, prejudiced against Negroes espousing the cause of abolitionism, in the belief that unprotected by slavery the Negro race would disappear (Harris 1968, 139). Earlier in his career he believed, like many other scholars of his day, that Negroes belonged to a separate species; later he became a committed monogenist, but retained a belief in uneven evolutionary development, with the idea of inferior and superior races. It is worth noting that in his stages of savagery through civilization, African culture and history is not mentioned at all, though he sees human progress as embodied in the growth of intelligence.

Morgan does not address race explicitly, although the categories of human advancement he developed became racialized, especially with the distinction between "civilized" and "uncivilized" races. Embedded in this cultural ranking is the notion of the darkest races being the most inferior, while biocultural evolution proceeded from dark to lighter to white races. Two other major anthropological founding figures, Edward Burnett Tylor and Herbert Spencer in England, paralleled this racial determinism with explicit or implicit renderings of the idea that civilization is a white European achievement.

Edward Burnett Tylor devotes two chapters to race in what is widely regarded as the first anthropology text, titled, appropriately, *Anthropology: An Introduction to the Study of Man and Civilization* (first published in England in 1881, released in America in 1902). In his chapter "Races of Mankind" he accepts the previously generated "great races" of black, brown, yellow, and white even while he acknowledges the difficulty of classifying some races, such as the natives of India, where a variety of complexions and features are found (83). Interestingly, he distinguishes "fair-whites" of Northern Europe from the "dark-whites" of southern Europe, the brownish yellow of the Malays, the full brown of the American tribes, the deep brown of the Australians, and the black brown of Negroes. Tylor, while accepting the basic racial divisions of mankind, nonetheless sees that skin color, from the fairest Englishman to the darkest African, has no hard and fast lines, but varies gradually from one tint to another (67).

Distinctive odors were said to emanate from people of different skin colors, unpleasant to people of other races (69–70). "There seems to be in mankind inbred temperament and inbred capacity of mind" (74); thus for Tylor there are clearly lower and higher races, with the browner or blacker types generally being at the lower end of human intelligence. "Curiously," he adds, "the pure negro in the United States has undergone a change in a few generations which has left him a shade lighter in complexion and altered his features, while the pure white in the same region has become less rosy, with darker and more glossy hair, more prominent cheekbones and massive lower jaw." These he sees as authenticated cases of "race-change," which we might describe differently today as examples of racial hybridization in the context of imposed slave-master conditions. Aboriginal Australians for Tylor are undisputed "savages." Savages rise to the barbaric stage when they take to agriculture, while civilized life begins with writing, recording history, law—underscoring again the vast gulf that exists between nonliterate (or preliterate) peoples and civilized nations, between near-civilized barbaric peoples and the most-evolved white race.

Creating a science of anthropology with this text, Tylor views whites as not a single, uniform race, but as a varied and mixed population with dark and fair varieties. Modern DNA analysis supports this view. However, modern anthropology could hardly support his conclusion that the latest formed and most evolved of races, the white race, remote from its savage ancestry, is "gifted with the powers of knowing and ruling which gives them sway over the world" (113). Tylor's *Anthropology* was written just as Britain launched its full-fledged imperial advance across the continents of darker-skinned "barbarians" and "savages," whose good fortune it was to fall under the influence of civilized society. It should be recalled what Mahatma Gandhi said as the English colonial adventure was coming to its end after World War II. When asked by a Western journalist what he thought of Western civilization, he replied, "Why, I think it would be a very good idea!"

### Savages

Ask a westerner to close his or her eyes and imagine a "savage," and the honest imaginer will reveal a dark-skinned person in his or her mind's eye, living in the tropics wearing few clothes, adorned with feathers and paint. Bare-breasted "savage" women have routinely been featured in natural history or geographic magazines, while bare-breasted white women have been featured in censored or pornographic publications.

The "savage" other was concocted in the racialized tradition of Western thought as the utter antithesis of a civilized person. "Savages" were especially associated with "Red Indians" in the New World, but the lingering usage of the term contemporarily can refer to blacks or Africans as well. For polygenists and those who accepted their ideas, neither Negroes nor Indians were considered as of the same species as Europeans. And in the case of enslaved Africans, they were treated as property, not as human beings, well into the second century of American democracy, with both the *Amistad* slave ship and Dred Scott cases treating slavery as a property issue, not one of human rights. It was not until the post-Reconstruction period that Negroes in the United States were treated legally as a full person, not the property of another or the infamous three-fifths of a person.

American Indians and Africans were both seen as concrete examples of savagery. With ideas of polygenesis, or even liberal monogenism, widely accepted it became simply a matter of determining exactly where in the great chain of being savages fit—separate and unequal creations to be sure—but closer to humans or to beasts?

## A "Noble Savage" Is Still a Savage

But Indians had not been enslaved or "civilized" by their contacts with whites, as had Negroes. Despite the reality that millions of Indians had perished in what we now call the Columbian encounter, which approached genocide, and others who had survived contact had been sold into slavery and were becoming deracinated, a romantic image of the Indian prevailed. Indians were free, the wild indigenous inhabitants of the conquered lands of the New World. The American Indian became the archetypical referent for the savage other from the late Renaissance onward, for he posed the greatest threat to European dominance and expansion in the New World (Pandian 1985, 65–66). The wild, crazy Indian, brandishing his tomahawk, fierce, proud, even noble, became the dominant stereotype, still alive in many ways today. During the French Enlightenment Rousseau pictured and philosophized about "man in a state of nature," free, living in harmony with nature, a "noble savage." Nonetheless, a noble savage is still a savage. Savages were exhibited next to animals to show their close relationship to beasts.

American Indians were constituted as a separate race by Blumenbach and were characterized as: having "red, copper color; black eyes of indolent, passive expression; large aquiline nose; large mouth; coarse, black, straight hair; and lean, muscular figure" (Warren 1873, 90). Indians were viewed as a race that had all but vanished. It was into this context that American anthropology was born, with a strong sense of urgency to gather information about the American Indian before no trace of a bygone life was left.

## Barbarians

Barbarians, according to the nineteenth-century typologies, may have been civilized at one time and lost their capacity for civilization, or they may be half-civilized peoples midway between savagery and fully developed civilization. The dominant image of the barbarian in the West as coarse, uncultured, fierce, brutal was derived from the word's Latin meaning, "foreign country," and probably referred to specific Greek cultural encounters with North African Berbers or people from the Barbary Coast in modern Algeria and Tunisia—*barbaroi*, "stutterers"—whose language and ways they could not understand.

The Middle Eastern "Oriental" barbarian is probably the strongest representative of this stereotype that is both racial and cultural. The "Orient"—the places to the East from the vantage point of the West, from the eastern shores of the Mediterranean to Indochina and Malaya, the "Near East" and the "Far East," respectively—became synonymous with the exotic, with the irrational, with cruel and despotic government, with devolution and degradation from former higher civilizations. Lord Cromer, the architect of British colonialism in Egypt and the Sudan, could say without hesitation, after the English occupied and began to rule Egypt, that "England made Egypt." Three thousand years of Egyptian civilization, more than two thousand of which had preceded ancient Greece and Rome, was reduced to Egypt being an English creation!

Today ideas of cultural backwardness among Middle Eastern peoples, and among Muslims in general, pervade our society. Anti-American villains from the region, whether Saddam Hussein or Osama bin Laden and al-Qaeda, are regarded as "barbaric" or as modern "barbarians."

Historical images of Chinese, Japanese, and other East Asian "barbarians" are also visible on our cultural-racial landscape. The Mongols of Genghis Khan's time, Han Chinese, imperial Japanese, or even communist Vietnamese—each of these "Oriental" societies may have been labeled "barbarian" because of their fierce resistance to Western colonial expansion or foreign domination.

### Civilized Peoples

In the nineteenth and twentieth centuries the colonial powers by definition were the "civilized races," and the colonized people were the "subject races," from Africa to the Near and Far East. The pervasive thinking of the era was the unquestioned assumption that European and European-derived cultures are civilized and have the right, even the responsibility, to rule over the less civilized peoples. Rudyard Kipling, the English bard of imperialism, coined the phrase "the white man's burden," meaning the burden for Europeans to rule and uplift—that is, civilize—the inferior races. He also used phenotypic racist descriptions of those Africans who successfully resisted the first colonial adventure of the British in the Sudan, the "Fuzzy Wuzzies" (referring to the natural "Afros" of the Beja and Hadendowa peoples). These peoples "broke the British square," that is, they defeated the English square infantry formation and kept them from conquering the Sudan from 1884 until 1898.

As mentioned, early anthropology tried to make a science of cultural evolution by acknowledging ancient civilizations outside of Europe that had developed agriculture, cities, states, and writing as having achieved civilized society. Thus ancient Mesopotamian, Egyptian, and the Indus Valley were clearly non-European civilizations, but had declined or lost civilization. This is succinctly put by Tylor (1881, 25): "It seems that civilization has actually grown up in the world through these three stages, so that to look at a savage of the Brazilian forests, a barbarous New Zealander or Dahoman, and a civilized European, may be the student's best guide to understanding the progress of civilization."

## THE THREE GREAT RACES: CAUCASOID, MONGOLOID, NEGROID

Blumenbach's five races were simplified in the nineteenth- and twentieth-century conception of the three great races of mankind—Caucasoid, Mongoloid, and Negroid, still with us to this day. Blumenbach was widely regarded as the father of physical anthropology. His classification of the varieties of humankind emphasized not only the unity of humans but the arbitrary nature of any classification and should have laid the basis for a more skeptical science of race. Instead, by the middle of the nineteenth century a tripartite division of the human species, each race graded in relation to the others, had gained some acceptance. Perhaps the tripartite division was an effort to simplify the increasingly complex reality of race; it cannot be ignored that its proponents were either acknowledged racists or offered their ideas in highly racially charged times.

Arthur Gobineau (about whom we will learn a great deal more in chapter 4) offers "three great and clearly marked types, the black, the yellow and the white" in his *Essay on the Inequality of Races* (1851–1855; original in French), a title requiring no further explanation. The Negroid variety is the lowest, the yellow races clearly superior to the black, and the white race is immensely superior to the lower two (134–37). I can find no other scientific statement of the ranking of the three great races before Gobineau. What astonishes even today is that this three-part ranking was not challenged, and that it survived into the twentieth century, making its way to Germany on the eve of the Nazi takeover in 1931, when the German scientist von Eichstedt proposed the scientific terminology for the three great races, Caucasoid, Mongoloid, and Negroid.

By 1961, as America was in the throes of the civil rights revolution and the race question was revived, many books trying to offer some common sense about race nonetheless still accepted this three-way division of humans: "There would be very general agreement on a broad division of most men into three main streams, Mongolian, Negro, and White or Caucasian" (Mason 1960, 32). This was the anthropology that I was taught as an undergraduate in the late 1960s, and in the first classroom where I taught Anthropology of Race and Racism a world map made in Germany hung with depictions of these three great races of mankind.

That the three great or basic races idea is still alive can be seen in the recent work on race and intelligence *The Bell Curve* (1994), in which Herrnstein and Murray divide "Ethnic Differences in Cognitive Ability" (the title of chapter 13) into three groups: Asian Americans, African Americans, and European Americans—in other words, Mongoloid, Negroid, and Caucasoid.

## Caucasians, the Civilized Race: Where Did the Name Come from and Why Is It Used for All Whites?

Some reflective whites in America may have paused for a moment when checking a census form or filling out a college or job application and asked themselves why they are checking "Caucasian" and from where this term might have come. "Why, they might ask, am I not checking "European American," paralleling the contemporary racial terms "African American" and "Asian American"? Is there a Caucasia, like the continental references to Africa and Asia? What is the geographical or cultural referent? These are good questions that require complex racialist answers.

Anthropologists studying race in America (Smedley 1993, 167) have suggested that Blumenbach, like so many of his contemporaries in the eighteenth century, thought that the original human form was that of European whites. After all, they had probably seen many European paintings of the original humans, Adam and Eve, portrayed with long, straight brown or blond hair. Indeed, images of Jesus Christ painted by Europeans bore a striking resemblance phenotypically to these images of Adam. Whiteness as the original human color was associated with "man in God's image," and therefore the most attractive human beings were Europeans. According to Smedley, Blumenbach selected the term "Caucasian" for his European white classification because he felt that the women of the Caucasus region in Russia were the most beautiful of all the Europeans—sort of like the Snow White story, in which the question is posed to the magic mirror "Who is the fairest of them all"?

The historian Charles Lyons (1975, 27) tells a different and perhaps a more plausible tale, given the scientific rationale that Blumenbach may have been seeking. Blumenbach had already embraced Linnaeus's monogenist ideas in 1775, but when he divided mankind into four broad categories he too established a rank ordering of types:

1) European/white race
2) Mongolian/yellow race
3) Ethiopian/black race
4) Malay/brown race

In 1781 he added a fifth category, the American or red race. When he revised his racial classification in 1795 Blumenbach dropped the word "European" and coined the term "Caucasian," revising the former in favor of a recent discovery he regarded as significant enough to warrant the change. In the 1790s he came across a single skull from the Caucasus region and found that its measurements closely corresponded to those of several German skulls in his collection. He wrongly hypothesized on the basis of this single skull that all European peoples must have their origins in the Caucasus, hence the preference for the term "Caucasian" over the continental designation "European." From Blumenbach's error we derive a racial category for whiteness that is widely misunderstood as "scientific." Even when it is proven false it is emotionally charged when some whites conjure their genetic "purity." We will soon see similar misconceptions and falsifications regarding the other "scientific" categories of "Mongolian" and "Negro," leading to a simple conclusion that most of the history of the science of race is really a history of a pseudoscience using race as its major device.

Caucasians are described according to Blumenbach as:

distinguished by light color of the skin; straight or curling hair; the oval face; vertical position of the teeth; and the well-formed, active and graceful figure. Inhabiting southwest Asia, northern Africa, nearly the whole of Europe and large parts of North and South America and Australia (through European immigration), it is the only true cosmopolitan and historical race. The leading nations of the world who have reached the highest state of civilization belong to this race. It is from this that the Caucasian race has been called the "active race," while the others, embracing the uncivilized or half-civilized peoples, have been termed the "passive races." (Warren 1873, 86)

Using the biblical division of nations in Chronicles, Blumenbach subdivided the Caucasian race into three branches:

1) The descendants of Ham (Hamites) of the Nile Valley and Ethiopian highlands
2) The descendants of Shem, the Semites, embracing Israelites and Arabs
3) Aryans, the most important branch, descended from Japheth, the last to leave the old home of the race, who either drove out or conquered the darker, passive races when they encountered one another (Warren 1873, 87)

In the hands of twentieth-century supporters of Aryan-Nordic supremacy, the "Nordic type" became idealized phenotypically as follows:

The Nordic race is tall, long-legged, slim, with an average height among males, of above 1.74 meters . . . narrow faced, with a cephalic index of around 75 and a facial index above 90. . . . The skin of the Nordic race is roseate-bright and the blood shines through. . . . The hair color is blond; among most of the existing types it can extend from a pink under-tone of light blond up to dark blond. (Hans Gunther, Nazi professor, quoted in Chase 1980, 348–49)

In American phenotypic ideals "Caucasians" have light skin color and blond hair with an ideal of blue eyes, all of which make a person with all or some of these characteristics "beautiful." "Good" hair, eyes, or skin color among darker persons might be judged based on how closely one's physical features match these ideals.

Among the greatest ironies is that in today's post-Soviet Russia one of the groups most discriminated against is residents of the Caucasus, especially Georgians, Chechnyans, and Azerbaijanis. Caucasians, with relatively dark skin color, are described by Russians as *chorniye* (blacks). They are a minority racially discriminated against by the "white" Byelorussians, as a recent apartment advertisement in Moscow demonstrates: "Apartment for Rent, Caucasians need not apply." Such is the logic of race and racism that in today's Russia it is Caucasians who can be blacks.

## Mongoloid Race: The Midpoint in the Hierarchy of Races

Like the great African continent, which gave birth to humans in their original and all subsequent forms, Asia is part of the Old World that nurtured great civilizations equaling, rivaling, and surpassing European culture throughout much of its own history. The great cultural tradition of the Hindu and Buddhist religions in Asia, and the multimillennial imperial civilization of dynastic China, both of which gave so much to world technology and culture, were relegated to inferior folk traditions by nineteenth-century racial evolutionists. The nineteenth-century early anthropologists Morgan and Tylor subscribed to ideas of the social evolutionists that inevitably placed European civilization at the apex of human achievement. Morgan was less sure than Tylor that the development from savagery to barbarism to civilization was an unequivocal success story for Europe and America, but implicit in the writings of both was a certainty about Euro-American (white) superiority. Reading social progress backward, from higher to lower levels, became a method of analyzing the history of culture. Thus, Tylor described the indigenous religions of the "lower races"—those of Africa and Asia—as "savage" or "barbaric." Cultural differences of value and belief, such as ancestor veneration or the religion of the "divine dead," were seen as "barbaric," while comparable European ideas like the Christian All Souls Day (Day of the Dead) were viewed as "survivals" of the more primitive forms of worship found especially among simpler European folk (Tylor 1881, 351). Likewise, spirit possession was seen as common among "savages" as well as "barbarians" in

India or China, but acknowledged only in the European "hysterical-epileptic patient" or "maniac" (Tylor 1881, 354). However, regarding the apparently primitive European custom of priests exorcising devils (Tylor cites Spanish priests here), he notes that the practice "will probably cease in a few years" when "civilized" medicine shows them how to treat epilepsy (Tylor 1881, 355). Likewise, in "barbaric" theology the Great Earth Mother is worshipped, even in classical European times, while by clear implication the male monotheistic God of the Christians is the "civilized" standard of religious belief.

Physically the Mongolian race was characterized by Blumenbach as yellow or olive in color; with straight, coarse black hair; large and projecting ears; small and obliquely set eyes; a narrow forehead; and projecting cheekbones. Mongolians occupy northern and eastern Asia, west to the steppes and plains of the Caspian Sea and Ural Mountains and south to the Himalayas and Malay Peninsula.

For Tylor (in *Anthropology*), the physical description of the Mongolian type of man has its best representatives on the vast steppes of northern Asia. Their skin is brownish yellow; their hair is black, coarse, and long; but their facial hair is scanty. Their skull is characterized by breadth, projection of cheekbones, slight brow ridges, the slanting aperture of the eyes, and the snub nose. The Mongoloid race is immense in range and numbers. In his wide migration over the world, the Mongoloid, through change of climate and intermarriage with other races, gradually loses his special features. It is so in China and Japan, where the characteristic breadth of the skull is lessened (Tylor 1881, 97–98), while "the Tatar and Japanese show the skew-eyelids of the Mongolian race" (Tylor 1881, 63).

## "Mongolian Idiocy," "Mongolism," Down's Syndrome

That the "Mongolian race" occupies the midpoint between the superior Caucasian and inferior African races is most clearly demonstrated in the history of European analysis of "Mongolism," what we call today "Down's Syndrome." The little-known history of scientific thinking about this disorder resulting in "idiocy" or mental deficiency is intimately tied to nineteenth-century racism.

John Langdon Down was an English physician who had observed a condition in certain of his patients that resulted in forms of mental retardation and abnormal physical growth and appearance.

His 1866 publication of a scientific paper, "Observations on an Ethnic Classification of Idiots," described for the first time "Mongolian idiocy." Patients afflicted with the disorder, according to the paper, possess physical characteristics like those of the "real Mongol"—a flat and broad face, obliquely placed eyes, a small nose, and yellowish skin. The scientific

**Figure 3.3.   John Langdon Down,
physician identifying "Mongolism"
later known as Down's Syndrome.**

explanation that Down offers is that the feeble-minded might be classified
according to ethnic standards: the Ethiopian, Malay, Amer-Indian, and
the more frequently observed Mongolian type of idiocy. "A very large
number of congenital idiots are typical Mongols," he writes (Down 1866,
260). After describing an afflicted child he theorizes: "The boy's aspect is
such that it is difficult to realize . . . that he is a child of Europeans, but so
frequently are . . . these characters presented that there can be no doubt
. . . that these ethnic features are the result of . . . degeneration" (Down
1866, 261).

In Down's view the Mongol-like features of Caucasians affected with
the disorder were proof of the degeneration of the superior Caucasian
type to the lower Mongolian type. As a scientific monogenist Down saw
racial divisions not as fixed and definite, but as malleable and flexible, so
that disease is able to break down the barriers and features of one race
and cause them to appear in another. How else to explain the presence of
features characteristic of the Mongolian race in the Caucasian race? He
believed that diseases such as tuberculosis brought about the degeneracy,
resulting in racial reversion, atavism, or what we might call "throwbacks"
to lower races.

With the publication of Down's paper the term "Mongolian idiocy" was introduced into science, and by the turn of the century the term "Mongolism" had become part of medical-scientific vocabulary. The racial referent to Asian or Mongolian people was not questioned as scientists found examples of "Mongolism" among races other than Caucasians; a 1933 report of "Mongolian idiocy" in a Negro infant was hailed, and a great breakthrough heralded when cases of Mongolism were found in China, with the people affected dubbed "Mongol Mongolians." At the height of the "science" of craniometry, in 1904, a group of physicians specializing in the study of "Mongolism" discussed the importance of comparing the brain of a "Chinaman" with that of a Mongol idiot.

Down came to question his own conclusions, writing in 1887 that he was inclined to adopt a classification of idiocy based more on the etiology of the disorder than on race. His son Reginald, continuing Down's work, suggested the disorder resulted from regression to even more primitive races than the Mongolian race. A French scientist, Edward Seguin, was actively investigating the same disorder in 1866 and came to very different, nonracialist conclusions. It was not until after the science of genetics developed that it was understood that "Down's Syndrome" is the result of tripling of the twenty-first chromosome, and the appropriate scientific designation is, or should be, "Trisomy 21." A more recent discovery of a genetic disorder resulting from the tripling of the thirteenth chromosome is medically referred to as "Trisomy 13," so why not "Trisomy 21" as well?

In chapter 4 racist, racialist, and antiracist ideas that have competed for scientific acceptance at various times will be discussed in greater detail. We will discuss the possible reasons for the success of Down's "Mongolism" over other interpretations, and why the scientific community ignored even Down's own revision of his ideas. "Mongolian idiocy," "Mongolism," and "Mongoloid" as scientific and popular descriptions for what was later understood as a genetic disorder lasted well into the 1960s before sensitivities about overt racial reference and interpretation changed the designation to "Down's Syndrome." Likewise the racialist Asian designation of "Siamese twins" has been reconsidered and has been changed to "conjoined twins."

## Negro/African/Ethiopian Race: Constructing a "Science" of Black Inferiority

Before there was color prejudice, as Frank Snowden shows in his now classic study of Greek attitudes toward blacks/Ethiopians (the "burnt-faced people"), there was no association of blackness with inferiority or slavery. In fact, all of the classical states that were the ancient predecessors of Western civilization—whether in Mesopotamia, Egypt, or Greece and

Rome—had slaves. But enslaved peoples were captives, prisoners of war, who became possessions of the state and could be any regional enemy or conquered people.

The Nubians, the true Ethiopians whom the Greeks encountered, were described by Herodotus as handsome," and by Diodorus as "the first of all men," superb in military power, love of freedom and justice, piety, and wisdom (Snowden 1983, 55–56). Nubians were at times despised captives or enemies of the Egyptians, as during the time of King Tutankhamun, but they were also their rulers at other times during the twenty-fifth ("Ethiopian") dynasty, so simple negative or positive stereotypes are useless. There was no clear association of darkness of skin color in antiquity with enslavement, like that of the stereotyped Nubian slave of Ottoman times and European Orientalist images. In fact, Greek descriptions of blacks are full of passion and beauty that can enlighten our own time. Snowden brings to our times the words of men from classical European societies enamored of dark, beautiful women:

> Asclelpiads (c. 290 BCE) on Didyme's beauty: "I melt like wax before the fire as I look on her beauty. And if she is black, what is that? So are coals but when we light them, they shine like rose buds."
> And Philodemus (c. 40–35 BCE) describes his Philaenion as "short, dark, with hair more curled than parsley, who he prefers until he finds another more perfect."
> Ovid's Sappho (43 BCE–17 CE) tells Phaon that she is not "fair but reminds him that Andromeda, dark with the hue of her native Ethiopia, captivated Perseus by her beauty." (Snowden 1970)

The use of color or racial differences to justify slavery did not exist before the West occupied the New World (Pandian 1985, 75). When the Portuguese slave ship the *Jesus* sailed in 1505 it had the tacit blessing of the Catholic Church, which had approved the enslavement of Africans as "infidels" so that their souls might be saved. Thus, the European church contributed to the modern origin of the idea of race. Four centuries of enslavement of Africans provided the economic foundation for the development of Europe, and all the while Europeans justified the exploitation of African peoples by ideas of black inferiority. How else could such a great crime against humanity have been sustained for four hundred years? Black pride movements have covered the New World historical-geographical landscape in which slavery once flourished, from the U.S. "Black Is Beautiful" movement of the 1960s, to the Afrocentric religion of the Rastafarians of Jamaica and the Caribbean, to the current black pride Africanismo of today's Afro-Brazilians. The pride and resistance in the reggae music of Bob Marley have become an international symbol of black-

Figure 3.4.  Second-century BC Hellenistic head of an Ethiopian man, The Brooklyn Museum.

ness from the Caribbean to South America, and in Africa from South Africa to Egyptian Nubia. One of America's great writers and lecturers on race, Cornel West, said in a lecture that I attended in 1998 that he still has lingering moments of black inferiority. Four hundred years of indoctrination and propaganda about slavery, blackness, and inferiority cannot be wiped out with a couple of decades of weak attempts at affirmative action.

Many of America's leading anthropologists at the turn of the century and well into the twentieth century believed in the supremacy of European white civilization and the inability of African peoples to achieve civilization. They had not domesticated any plants or animals, and they learned the skills they possess today from the ancient Egyptians (who Samuel Morton would later claim were Caucasian, based on cranial measurement) or even later under Arab influence. According to Daniel Brinton, Africans were unable to achieve the stage of civilization primarily because of their racially limited intellectual capabilities (*Races and People*, 1890, in Williams 1996, 26). Every trace of civilization—whether the stone tower ruins of ancient Zimbabwe, the kingdoms of the Nile south of Egypt, or the kingdoms of the Sudanic Sahara—was said to be the result of outside influence, of Semites or Hamites, the latter a clever fictional mixture of Asiatic and Caucasian elements.

The great civilization of Egypt in the African continent, of course, could not be denied, but the solution was to make Egypt "white," to artificially cut it out of Africa and lay its glories for three millennia before Christ at the base of Europe rather than the tip of Africa. Thus, Africa, or the Negro race, was relegated to a permanent state of being savage or barbaric, not only without a historic trace of civilization, but without any hope of ever becoming civilized. The racist idea that Africa had no history until Europeans penetrated the continent was a firmly held belief in the West well into the second half of the twentieth century and only began to be debunked with the post–World War II independence of "black" Africa and the emergence of a postcolonial scholarship.

For Blumenbach, the "Ethiopian race" is distinguished by a black or dark brown color; short, black, wooly hair; a broad, flat nose; thick, upturned lips; a receding forehead; flat feet; and an active and muscular body. They occupy tropical and southern Africa, but also are found in America as imported Negroes and their descendants. For Tylor in *Anthropology*, the scientific measure of the "facial angle" is an important point of difference between dark- and light-skinned people. The Australian and African are prognathous or "forward jawed," while the European is orthognathous, "upright jawed." Further, the African and Australian have more retreating foreheads than those of the European "due to the disadvantage of the frontal lobes of their brain as compared with ours"

(Tylor 1881, 62). In short, the cerebral, "thinking" areas of the brain are greater in whites than blacks. *The Bell Curve*, published over a century later, in 1994, basically draws the same conclusion using measurements of the insides of skulls, called IQ and achievement tests.

### Special Case for Lowest Savages: Australian Aborigines, "Hottentot," and "Bushmen"

Australian Aborigines, the so-called Bushmen of the Kalahari Desert, and the Hottentot, seen as the most primitive of the dark-skinned, "woolly" haired Negroes, were given special consideration in the hierarchy of races. Often described as living in cultures barely distinguishable from those of the Stone Age, they were subjected to study and scientific scrutiny as vestigial societies, or marginally human curiosities, in the nineteenth and early twentieth centuries, and as romanticized "noble savages" over the past several decades.

Several notorious cases have come to light in which specimens of these human beings were exhibited by natural history museums in Europe. The case of the "Hottentot Venus" and the repatriation of Saartjie Baartman to South Africa in 2002 were mentioned in chapter 2. Another, less well-known case is that of "El Negro of Banyoles," who was exhibited in the Darder Museum of Natural History in Banyoles, Spain, from 1916 to 1997, and was finally repatriated for reburial in Botswana in 2002. The body, according to contemporary researchers at the University of Botswana, was probably that of a young man from a Batlhaping village near the confluence of the Orange and Vaal rivers who died about 1830 and whose body was stolen from a fresh grave, embalmed, and stuffed by two French taxidermists, the Verreaux brothers. They took it to Paris along with thousands of other specimens of African "wildlife," where it was displayed in their shop until it was purchased by Spaniard Francisco Darder for display at the 1888 Barcelona World Exhibition. After the expo the body went on display at the Darder Museum in Banyoles, Spain, where, painted black, it came to represent all Negro people. This objectification of "El Negro" continued until Dr. Alphonse Arcelin (a Haitian-born naturalized Spaniard) called in 1992 for its removal as an exhibit and repatriation for reburial. Dr. Arcelin sued the city for $1.4 million, arguing that the exhibit was an affront to his honor as a black man (*New York Times International*, March 9, 1997). Senegal and other African nations also pressured Spanish diplomats to get the town to shut down the exhibit. After a six-year legal and moral battle the museum removed the exhibit to place it in storage in 1997. The museum lost the claim to the body upon its repatriation in 2002, but failed to return a spear, bead necklace, and other grave goods associated with "El Negro" on the grounds that the specimen was that of a "Bushman" and not a Negro ("El Negro" 2002).

The legacy of the tripartite division of races into Caucasoid, Mongoloid, and Negroid lingers into contemporary forensic anthropology, that branch of physical anthropology that has practical application in medical, criminal, and legal matters. Forensic anthropologists have been useful in international human rights investigations in which, for example, mass burials may have been part of politically repressive governments or ethnic cleansing campaigns. Forensic anthropologists in recent years have worked in Bosnia-Herzegovina, in Central and South America, and in Rwanda, where massacres occurred. These physical anthropologists rely on generalized craniometric data from past studies to appraise a skull as a probable candidate for one of the classic racial types. However, they admit freely that mixed-race people, especially "Hispanics" in the New World, are problematical due to being of both European and Amerindian descent (Rhine 1993, 64–65). Skulls are assessed by a list of traits and are scored as being more probably "Caucasian," "Negro," "Mongoloid," or "Hispanic." Forensic anthropology provides us with an example of the practical, potentially positive uses to which anthropometry and craniometry can be put. They can be used in the service of humanity rather than for the historical purpose of classifying inferior and superior races.

## AMERICAN RACE CLASSIFICATION

Many younger readers may believe that America has always employed a system of racial classification. Well, in a way it has, since Negroes and Indians were differentiated and segregated from whites starting in colonial times. And the one-drop rule imposed a caste system of relations that dichotomized black and white into polar opposites; people were recognized as either "colored" or "white." Americans of mixed race either were labeled or self-identified as "Negro" or "colored," or they passed as white. Passing became a subject of intense social interest among whites and blacks, the subject of much gossip, while the "tragic mulatto" figure became a staple of American literature, eventually working its way into films.

These are what anthropologists refer to as "emic" categories of race, without science or official status; they are the classifications that people have contrived and used in everyday discourse. There are contemporary emic categories of race that anthropological methods could disclose to show that the official terms may not reflect the social reality. Depending on the region there may be terms differentiating types of whites— "WASPs," "Jews." The term "white bread" carries the meaning of an ordinary white guy. These terms change if used by African Americans, Hispanics, or other groups; the same terms have different contextual meanings depending on the culture of the speaker. The well-known racial epithet for blacks, the "n" word, has been studied in terms of contextual usage. If a white man uses this word in reference to a black man the context is almost certainly racism; if the word is used between black men, or in another context like a rap song, the meaning changes from white-on-black racism to sarcasm or political commentary, or some other meaning. The emic use of "brown" to refer to people of Latin American and Caribbean background has been widely used as a form of self-identification differentiating Latinos phenotypically and also culturally from mainstream white culture. This is a potentially rich area of research, the emics of race in America.

The official face of race classification in America has been the U.S. Census, which has taken account of race since 1900. Racial census taking was no more scientific in 1900 than in 2000. Twenty-six different terms were employed over the course of the last century to describe race, an indication of the evolving, nonscientific nature of the political vocabulary. For example, "colored" or "Negro" were terms employed throughout most of the century until the civil rights era, when "black" pride became a symbol of resistance and antiracism. Today the term "African American" has replaced all of the above as the politically correct usage for the press, the media, educators, and as an important statement of self-identity. The U.S. Census has employed a host of nonracial "racial" terms over the decades to count Americans or resident aliens, from "Hindu" or "Mexican" to the contemporary terms "Hispanic" and "Latino."

The current system of race classification came into existence only in May 1977, when the Office of Management and the Budget (OMB) and its Directive 15 created *Race and Ethnic Standards for Federal Statistics and Administrative Reporting*. The overriding political context was affirmative action and the need to define the categories of protected individuals, women and racial/ethnic minorities. OMB's Directive 15 created four races and a means of standardizing the collection of racial and ethnic information among federal agencies and of including data on persons of Hispanic origin, as required by Congress. The four races that were described included: white, black, American Indian or Alaskan Native, and Asian or Pacific Islander. Two ethnic backgrounds were created: "of Hispanic origin" and "not of Hispanic origin." Directive 15 defined neither race nor ethnicity, and it did not prescribe the method of data collection, that is, self-identification or identification applied by an interviewer. However, the directive did state that the categories should be developed using "appropriate scientific methodologies, including the social sciences," and that the categories were to be thought of as social and cultural as well as biological ancestry (American Anthropological Association 1997). The categories evoked discussion, controversy, and arguments for change from their inception. Many found the categories confusing because the respondent was asked to "select one"; multicultural and multiracial people had difficulty doing this, and some found it offensive to check "Other" when none of the five categories fit their racial/ethnic description. A large Cape Verdean population is found in southeastern New England, where I teach. They are people from the archipelago of islands off the west coast of Africa, settled by the Portuguese, and the only group of African Americans to come to the United States as voluntary immigrants rather than as enslaved persons. Cape Verde remained a colony of Portugal until 1975, so historically the largest number of immigrants came speaking Creole Portuguese and carrying Portuguese documents, the result being that they became known as "black Portuguese." This racialized identity changed dramatically after Cape Verdean independence, as reflected in the immigrants' reaction to the U.S. Census.

Try this exercise. You're Cape Verdean and you're supposed to check one racial identity:

White—(No, but my grandmother was white.)
Black—(No, we're Creole, an Afro-Portuguese mixture.)
Hispanic—(No, but many people think we are and speak Spanish to us.)
Asian/Pacific Islander—(No, not even close.)
American Indian/Alaskan Native—(No, but many mixed Indians in the northeast look like us.)
Other X—(I hate checking this, but there are no other choices.)

Small wonder that Cape Verdeans in New England have campaigned for the addition of the designation "Cape Verdean" to state census forms. So much confusion has reigned that offices of affirmative action have resorted to explaining the categories on the forms to be filled out in order to obtain useful responses. The following questionnaire, from the University of Rhode Island, may be typical:

_____ White: (not of hispanic origin) All persons having origins in any of the original peoples of Europe, North Africa, or the Middle East.
_____ Black: (not of hispanic origin) All persons having origins in any of the Black racial groups of Africa.
_____ Hispanic: All persons of Mexican, Puerto Rican, Cuban, Central or South American, or any other Spanish culture or origin, regardless of race.
_____ Asian/Pacific Islander: All persons having origins in any of the original peoples of the Far East, Southeast Asia, the Indian Subcontinent, or

the Pacific Islands, including, for example, China, Japan, Korea, the Philippine Islands, and Samoa.

———— American Indian/Alaskan Native: All persons having origins in any of the original peoples of North America, and who maintain cultural identification through tribal affiliation or community recognition.

Included on the university form also are questions about gender—male or female—and nonresident alien status and disability, for affirmative action purposes; however, our focus is race. Simple critical analysis reveals that the categories have a great deal of racialized history behind them and are arbitrary in the racial distinctions drawn. For example, the line between white and black Africa is drawn arbitrarily across northern, presumably Arab, Africa, and begins where "black" Africa ends. Admittedly racialized, African studies has conventionally separated North Africa from "black" Africa. But as a specialist on North Africa myself and one who has lived in the Sudan (in North Africa, but the name in Arabic means "the land of the blacks"), Egypt, and Tunisia, I am perplexed as to just where exactly "black" Africa begins. If you travel with the flow of the Nile River, south to north, you will find some of the darkest skinned humans in Equatoria and Sudan (where skin can be what local people call the color of eggplant). Journeying northward, the dark brown color of the central and northern Nile peoples contrasts with that of their southern neighbors, but none of them would check "white" on the American race forms. Nubian peoples straddle the border between northern Sudan and Egypt south of Aswan, and everybody knows that Nubians are black. North of Aswan the lighter brown skin looks Hispanic to the average American, so that, stretching the point, the people living there could be considered white. By the time our Nile journey nears its end in Cairo some light-skinned people, descendants of the Mediterranean groups who have settled here for millennia, are in evidence, but so are millions of darker-skinned people, making Cairo a multiracial society, but nonetheless white according to the U.S. Census.

That Hispanics were singled out in the census as the only nonracial group in categories designed to be racial, and that both whites and blacks are defined as non-Hispanic, illustrates the kinds of problems and contradictions that the pseudoscience of race generates. Presumably Hispanics would either be white or black if it weren't for the fact that they speak Spanish (probably, but not necessarily) and have Spanish surnames. In the 2000 U.S. Census the "Hispanic" category was separated from race and treated as an "ethnicity."

That all Asians are lumped together is absurd, as we have seen, but this reflects the racial view of "Mongoloids" that has persisted. Many northern Indians (Indian subcontinent) are of Aryan descent and could just as well check that they are descended from the original peoples of Europe. Instead their relatively darker skin color and Asian homeland make them categorically the same as Chinese, Koreans, and Japanese.

Native American ancient ancestry is of course Asian, and historically many physical anthropologists created a Mongolian subrace with which to classify American Indians.

Anthropologists who have researched the application of these U.S. government categories have found them often to be unreliable. Self-reported data are more accurate than those estimated by an observer, and reporting by nonwhite racial minorities, such as blacks, Mexicans, and Puerto Ricans, is more accurate than that done by whites. Ethnic reporting by whites is accurate in an inverse relationship to the number of generations their families have been in America (Gordon and Bell 1993, 34) that is, European ethnicity rapidly dissolves into "whiteness," while nonwhite racial groups retain a more distinctive identity. An anthropological study of the application of these categories by the U.S. Army shows widespread misclassification of racial minorities—often the data supplied on Hispanics, American Indians, and mixed-race individuals was over 50 percent inaccurate due to army personnel filling out the forms rather than the recruits (Gordon and Bell 1993, 45).

## American Anthropological Association's Recommendations for 2000 and 2010 U.S. Censuses

Following some intensive discussion in society at large about what to do with the U.S. Census in 2000—how many categories there should be and which ones to include, add, or drop—the OMB recommended that the categories be described as "race/ethnicity" options, and that persons be allowed to identify more than one as a means of reporting diverse ancestry. There was also discussion of adding either "biracial" or "multiracial" as an option for Americans of mixed-race ancestry to check. Interestingly, political opposition came from historically black organizations such as the NAACP and Hispanic groups, which argued that race in America is about identity, not biology, and which perhaps feared that the large number of people who might check a "multiracial" or "biracial" category would dilute the raw numbers and percentages of statistical "blacks" and "Hispanics." In the end the 2000 Census continued to use race as a primary way of counting Americans. However, for the first time respondents could check more than one category as a way of self-identifying mixed racial heritage. Census 2000 retained the primary racial designations— white; black, African American, or Negro; American Indian or Alaskan native; Asian (several new iterations), native Hawaiian, or other Pacific Islander; some other race. Also new in the Census 2000 racial identification form was the dropping of the confusing term "Native American" and (after much criticism of Census 1990) the addition of options for Asian American identities, such as Asian Indian, Chinese, Filipino, Japanese, Korean, Vietnamese, and other Asian. "Spanish/Hispanic/Latino" replaced "Hispanic" based on criticism similar to that of "Asian"—too much diversity is concealed in such lumping terms. The possibilities of checking "Mexican, Mexican American or Chicano"; "Puerto Rican"; "Cuban"; and "other" were included.

The American Anthropological Association also recommended that the term "race" be dropped altogether in planning for the 2010 Census. This step may or may not succeed. Many anthropologists have long desired that the term be dropped because of its lack of scientific meaning or application. Persons of diverse racial backgrounds opposed the elimination of race because of the positive associations and sense of shared identity that race signifies in the United States. Once again, the real problem is racism, not race. If positive racial identification helps us along the road toward racial reconciliation and healing, then perhaps the focus should be on the elimination of racism, not race.

## SUMMARY

Through an exploration of the origin of anthropology in the midst of nineteenth-century debates about the unity and equality of humanity, light can be shed on the importance of the race issue, within which the discipline was founded, and with which it is still wrestling. The nineteenth-century evolutionists who attempted to make a science of the study of humanity and culture had ideas that reflected the already highly racialized system of thinking dominant in the Western world. The debates between the monogenists and polygenists had raged for at least two centuries by the time of the appearance of the first works that used "anthropology" in their titles or analysis. The progression from savagery through barbarism to civilization, which seemed to represent the natural history of the human race, was readily racialized with a phenotypic progression from black, to yellow, to white, or certainly from darker-skinned peoples to light-skinned peoples. This meshed well with the expansionistic, colonial enterprise of European powers, which reached its peak at the time of the birth of anthropology and the cementing in place of the race question. The three stages of cultural development from lower to higher were matched by the three-part classification of mankind into Negroid, Mongoloid, and Caucasiod that became the standardized treatment of race in the twentieth century. Other voices—such as that of the pioneering Haitian anthropologist Anténor Firmin, who asserted that the races are equal—were ignored or marginalized in their time, so that a racialized and racist view of human difference prevailed.

How the racist classification of Gobineau entered the canon of Western thinking on race is a major question that will be dealt with in the next chapter, on racism, racialism, and antiracism in anthropology. Which ideas are accepted and which are ignored is a key question to raise and to answer.

## REFERENCES

Alexander, Daryl Royster. 1998. "Monticello's Other Children." *New York Times,* November 8, B3.

American Anthropological Association. 1997. *Response to OMB Directive 15: Race and Ethnic Standards for Federal Statistics and Administrative Reporting. Executive Summary.* Arlington, VA: American Anthropological Association.

Biddiss, Michael D., ed. 1970. *Gobineau: Selected Political Writings.* Introduction by Biddiss. London: Jonathan Cape.

Blumenbach, J. F. 1795. *On the Natural Variety of Mankind.* 3rd. ed. In *The Anthropological Treatises of Johann Friedrich Blumenbach.* Translated and edited by Thomas Bendyshe. London: Longman, Green, 1895.

Boas, Franz. 1938. *The Mind of Primitive Man.* Rev. ed. New York: Macmillan.

Chase, Allan. 1980. *The Legacy of Malthus: The Social Costs of the New Scientific Racism.* New York: Knopf.

Down, John H. Langdon. 1866. "Observations on an Ethnic Classification of Idiocy." *Clinical Lectures and Reports* (London Hospital) 3:259–62.

"El Negro." 2002. Available at http://ubh.tripod.com/afhist/elnegro/eln0.htm.

Engels, Frederick. 1884. *The Origin of the Family, Private Property, and the State.* Repr., New York: International Publishers, 1972.

Fluehr-Lobban, Carolyn. 1979. "Mongolism, the Scientific History of a Genetic Disorder." Unpublished paper.

Gobineau, Arthur. 1853–1855. *Essai sur l'inegalite des Races Humaines.* 4 vols. Repr., Paris: Belfond, 1967.

Gordon, Claire C., and Nancy A. Bell. 1993. "Problems of Racial and Ethnic Self-Identification and Classification." In *Race, Ethnicity, and Applied Bioanthropology,* NAPA Bulletin no. 13, edited by Claire Gordon, 34–47. Washington, DC: American Anthropological Association.

Harris, Marvin. 1968. *The Rise of Anthropological Theory.* New York: Crowell.

Herrnstein, Richard J., and Charles Murray. 1994. *The Bell Curve: Intelligence and Class Structure in American Life.* New York: Free Press.

Lyons, Charles H. 1975. *To Wash an Aethiop White: British Ideas about Black African Educability, 1530–1960.* New York: Teachers College Press.

Marks, Jonathan. 2002. *What It Means to Be 98% Chimpanzee.* Berkeley: University of California Press.

Mason, Phillip, ed. 1960. *Man, Race, and Darwin.* London: Oxford University Press.

Montagu, Ashley. 1965. *The Idea of Race.* Lincoln: University of Nebraska Press.

Morgan, Lewis Henry. 1877. *Ancient Society.* Foreword by Elisabeth Tooker. Repr., Tuscon: University of Arizona Press, 1985.

Pandian, Jacob. 1985. *Anthropology and the Western Tradition: Toward an Authentic Anthropology.* Prospect Heights, IL: Waveland.

Rhine, Stanley. 1993. "Skeletal Criteria for Racial Attribution." In *Race, Ethnicity, and Applied Bioanthropology,* NAPA Bulletin no. 13, edited by Claire Gordon, 54–67. Washington, DC: American Anthropological Association.

Smedley, Audrey. 1993. *The Idea of Race in North America: Origins and Evolution of a Worldview.* Boulder, CO: Westview.

Snowden, Frank M., Jr. 1970. *Blacks in Antiquity.* Cambridge, MA: Harvard University Press.

———. 1983. *Before Color Prejudice: The Ancient View of Blacks.* Cambridge, MA: Harvard University Press.

"Spanish Museum to Remove Bushmen Exhibit." 1997. *New York Times International,* March 9.

Tylor, E. B. 1881. *Anthropology: An Introduction to the Study of Man and Civilization.* Repr., New York: D. Appleton, 1902.

Warren, D. M. 1873. *Elementary Treatise on Physical Geography.* Philadelphia: Cowperthwait.

Williams, Vernon D. 1996. *Rethinking Race: Franz Boas and His Contemporaries.* Lexington: University of Kentucky Press.

# 4

# Racism and Antiracism in the Nineteenth and Twentieth Centuries

As the title of this chapter suggests, anthropology, like virtually every discipline in Western scholarship, embraces a tradition that contains a broad spectrum of ideas about race. Consider the racially charged environment in which the major first works of anthropology were produced—slavery, the American Civil War and its aftermath, and the great imperialist surge of European powers in the last quarter of the nineteenth century. How could the earliest works of anthropology not have been affected by their times? What is of interest today is the range of ideas that has always existed in the scholarly arena, and how worthwhile it is to examine the ideas that were marginalized or ignored in their time and those that became accepted science. In every era, including our own, there have been writers whom we might classify as clearly racist; that is, they espouse ideas or draw conclusions about the rank-ordered differences among human groups primarily on the basis of physical type, or phenotype. One example of an acknowledged racist writer is the nineteenth-century writer Arthur Gobineau. There are other writers whose works may not be primarily racist in organization or intent, but many of whose ideas and conclusions are framed within a racist context, such as references to "lower" and "higher" races, or references to "subject races" in colonialist texts. E. B. Tylor, who wrote the first acknowledged work of anthropology in English, wrote within a racialist context, although many of his conclusions were liberal for their time.

By contrast, antiracist writers actively confront racist ideas and offer alternative social and historical explanations for human difference while

104

asserting the fundamental equality of races. Too much attention has been paid to the first two types of authors, while far too little attention has been paid to antiracist writers, especially from the early years of the development of anthropology and the scientific study of humanity.

In every era there have been contrasting views of race, as there are today. What follows is a comparison between selected writers along the spectrum of thought from racist to antiracist since the dawn of anthropology. Often the antiracist writer is the more obscure, especially prior to World War II, while the racist writer is a prominent person with high-status academic credentials. Frequently the racist or racialist essence of an idea may be obscured, such as with social Darwinism or the eugenics movement. The fact that we are still challenging racist ideas long known to be unscientific is an important lesson to today's student. It shows that constant study and vigilance are necessary until racist ideology is *only* a matter of history, not a present danger and concern.

## CONTRASTING IDEAS: THE INEQUALITY VERSUS THE EQUALITY OF RACES

### French Author Arthur Gobineau and Haitian Scholar Joseph Anténor Firmin

I can think of no better contrast between a racist and antiracist author than that between "Count" Arthur Gobineau and Joseph Anténor Firmin, both writers in the French language of the mid- to late nineteenth century, one a disillusioned French nobleman, the other a Haitian scholar-activist.

Gobineau was from a French noble line (or so he claimed) and believed that the ideals of the French Revolution—*liberté, égalité,* and *fraternité* (liberty, equality, and universal brotherhood)—had laid the groundwork for the destruction of Western civilization. He outlined this basic thesis in *Essai sur l'inégalité des Races Humaines* (Essay on the Inequality of Human Races), published in France in several volumes between 1853 and 1855. Excerpts of this work were translated almost immediately into English in 1856, 1913, and 1924, and into German in 1911. Gobineau was the subject of a scholarship in France in the nineteenth and twentieth centuries. Interest in him was revived with an annual series begun in 1966, *Etudes Gobiniennes* (Gobineau Studies). As a result of the success of his initial works and the international studies made of his ideology he gained the dubious distinction of being the "father of racism" (Biddiss 1970, 13). Among scholars he also has the notorious reputation of foreshadowing the doctrine of Aryan supremacy. It was the fall of European nobility, especially after the French Revolution, that caused Gobineau to become so pessimistic about the future of white civilization, since governments were falling into the hands of the middle and lower classes. He believed that the basis of this decline was the mixing of races and classes that was destroying the noble fabric of Europe. A vivid illustration of the psychopathology of racism is the fact that Gobineau married a "Creole" and sired mixed-race children. He drew on writers of his day who were racializing history and linguistic discoveries—for example, new knowledge that the Germanic languages, together with Greek, Latin, and Persian, were all derived from a common "mother tongue," Aryan. He argued that a single race corresponded with this linguistic family (an argument to be made many times again) and that civilization itself was born from the Aryan race of men. Human groups had been classified into physical types or races for more than a century, and Gobineau saw his work as bringing together the history, anthropology, archaeology, and linguistic studies that would confirm his theories about racial inequality.

The fundamental racist thesis of *Essai sur l'inégalité des Races Humaines* is outlined by Gobineau in his dedication:

> I was gradually penetrated by the conviction that the racial question overshadows all other problems of history, that it holds the key to them all, and that the inequality of races from whose fusion a people is formed is enough to explain the whole course of its destiny. I convinced myself that everything that is great, noble and fruitful . . . all in art, science, and civilization . . . belongs to one family alone, the different branches of which have reigned in all of the civilized countries of the universe.

These words are repeated almost verbatim in the opening of Hitler's *Mein Kampf* (Biddiss 1970, 25). Gobineau thus earned another credential in the rogues' gallery of racists.

Gobineau was neither a committed polygenist nor a committed monogenist, for he was not truly competent enough to engage in that major scientific debate. He did dismiss the original single Adamite pair of humans, for "what of his likeness, character and descendant families we cannot know, . . . but we must acknowledge that Adam is the ancestor of the white race." Confining his commentary to "the races of the second stage," after the great flood, which are naturally divided into three—the white, the black, and the yellow—Gobineau outlines his thesis of racial hierarchy. He notes, "I must take my choice from the vocabulary already in use." Choosing to overlook Blumenbach's twenty-eight varieties or Prichard's seven races, Gobineau helped to solidify the tripartite classification of race that became the standard in the twentieth century.

1. The white men are: Caucasian, Semitic, Japhetic.
2. The black men are: Hamites (generally following the biblical divi-

sion of the sons of Noah, Japhet, Shem, and Ham and the dispersal to three mountains, the Caucasus for the white, the Atlas for the black, and the Altai for the yellow).
3. The yellow are: Altaic, Mongol, Finnish, and Tartar. (Races of third and fourth orders are created through mixtures of the three basic races, such as Polynesians, who are mixtures of black and yellow.)

Adding class to race, the would-be aristocrat Gobineau saw the white race as the nobility, the yellow race as the bourgeoisie, and the black race as the commoners, the latter two being the vassals and the slaves, respectively, of the superior white race. Adding sexism to his racism, Gobineau saw the superior northern races as male, while the inferior southern races were female.

Listing ten civilizations, Gobineau notes that the Negro race is not the initiator of any civilization; only when it is mixed with some other race can it even be introduced to civilization. He does note seven non-European civilizations—the Egyptians, Assyrians, Indians, and Chinese; and three New World cases, the Alleghanians, Mexicans, and Aeruvians—however, all are derived from the Aryan race. The first were the Indians, who were derived from a branch of Aryans migrating from their primitive home in central Asia; the Egyptians came next, with civilization brought to the Nile by the Indians; the Assyrians were derived from the white descendants of Noah's sons; the New World civilizations resulted from Aryan colonization. The European civilizations include the Greeks, Romans, and the Germanic races, which are likewise derived from the Aryans, and which "transformed the Western mind" (Biddiss 1968, 122–23). The English were the best of the Aryan race, having by far the best constitution of the Europeans.

Of the three basic races Gobineau writes:

The negroid variety is the lowest and stands at the foot of the ladder. The animal character, that appears in the pelvis, is stamped on the Negro from birth, and foreshadows his destiny. His intellect will always move within a very narrow circle. If his mental facilities are dull or even non-existent, he often has an intensity of desire, and so of will, which may be called terrible. Many of his senses, especially taste and smell, are developed to an extent unknown to the other two races. . . . Finally, he is equally careless of his own life and that of others: he kills willingly, for the sake of killing; and this human machine . . . shows in the face of suffering, either a monstrous indifference or a cowardice that seeks a voluntary refuge in death.

The yellow race is the exact opposite of this type. . . . The yellow man has little physical energy, and is inclined to apathy. He tends to mediocrity in everything; he understands easily enough anything not too deep or sublime. He is practical . . . he invents little, but can appreciate and take over what is useful to him. The yellow races are clearly superior to the black. Every founder of a civilization would wish the backbone of his society, his middle class, to consist of such men. But no civilized society could be created by them.

Now we come to the white peoples. These are gifted with . . . an energetic intelligence. They have a feeling for utility . . . [and are] more courageous and ideal than the yellow races. They . . . have an extraordinary instinct for order, not only as a guarantee of peace and tranquility, but as an indispensable means of self-preservation. At the same time, they have a remarkable love of liberty, hostile to the formalism under which the Chinese are glad to vegetate, as well as to the strict despotism which is the only way of governing the Negro. The white races are distinguished by an extraordinary attachment to life; they know better how to use it and they are more sparing of life. When they are cruel, they are conscious of their cruelty; it is very doubtful whether such a consciousness exists in the Negro. The principal motive is honor . . . which has played an enormous part in the ideas of the race from the beginning. . . . On the other hand, the immense superiority of the white peoples in the whole field of the intellect is balanced by inferiority in the intensity of their sensations. (Gobineau, in Biddiss 1968, 135–37)

These passages readily can be deconstructed and critiqued by the average early twenty-first-century reader, and reading and discussing them would make a good class project. They are quoted here at some length because they refer to the commonplace understanding of race that is part of the Western legacy of racial stereotyping. The continuing persistence of these sentiments in today's world can be easily discerned; the intermediate "barbarian" position of the yellow race between the "civilized" whites and the "savage" blacks is still imprinted on the Western mind. Herrnstein and Murray's *The Bell Curve* (1994) gained widespread public attention because it reversed the usual position of white over yellow and black, with yellow over white and black inferiority still in its usual place.

### Aryan Supremacy

"There is no true European civilization, among the European peoples, where the Aryan branch is not predominant," writes Gobineau (Biddiss 1970, 144). The Aryans are descended from Japhet, the white son of Noah, who is superior to his brothers, the Semites and Hamites. Gobineau derived his confidence about race from the linguistic discovery that Sanskrit is the source of Latin, Greek, and other European languages; hence there is one great language family, one great race. This fallacy has been pointed out repeatedly in this book. Gobineau considered the Aryans to be the most noble, intelligent, and vital branch of the white stocks, but their very vigor and love of conquest makes them vulnerable to miscegenation, which was responsible for their downfall, according to Gobineau. His greatest preoccupation was to trace the decline of German Aryans from the Teutonic invasions, a historical parallel, he felt, to the decline of Greece and Rome from contamination with Semitic peoples, whom he regarded as carriers of black blood (Biddiss 1968, 123–24).

Beyond this, all of Gobineau's ten civilizations were derived from Aryan peoples. Today this is regarded as absurd diffusionism, an unsupportable contention that all civilized cultures come from a single source. Yet the doctrine of Aryan supremacy was an ideology that profoundly affected the twentieth century and is echoed still in contemporary neo-Nazi, white supremacist groups, such as White Aryan Nation.

It is a popular misconception that modern anti-Semitism was developed by Gobineau; this misconception is probably a result of the personal and intellectual links between him and what developed into the Nazi movement. However, the specific doctrine of anti-Semitism directed against European Jewry was developed more by his intellectual and political disciples, especially Houston Chamberlain (1855–1926) and German composer Richard Wagner. Wagner visited Gobineau and became so enamored of the latter's work that he founded the Gobineau Society in 1881 in Beyrouth, Germany, dedicated to spreading the creed of Teutonic or Nordic supremacy (Chase 1980, 91). Chamberlain's work *The Foundations of the Nineteenth Century* (1899) expresses an admiration of the Jews for their racial purity, but claims that they remain always "the aliens among all peoples." Aided by the princes and the nobles who needed their money, the Jews were, according to Chamberlain, the cruel exploiters and merciless destroyers of all nations (Sorokin 1928, 232). Chamberlain became a German citizen and the son-in-law of Richard Wagner. Chamberlain's writings and the political movement of Gobineauism had a direct bearing on Nazi ideology. Hitler went to Beyrouth, where he was received by the Wagner family and met the old and infirm Chamberlain. Chamberlain was impressed with Hitler as an "awakener of souls"; he said Hitler's visit "transformed the state of my soul" (Chase 1980, 91).

Gobineau regarded the Jews as but one branch of the Semitic family. Being hostile to miscegenation, he admires the relatively closed nature of Jewish society and its isolation from other Semites. To the degree that Jews had become tainted with black elements they had become debased, but the same could be said for European groups as well, so Gobineau makes no special case for Jewish anti-Semitism.

In fact he expresses admiration for the Jews' achievement in the environmentally hostile and arid Palestine. "And what did the Jews become, in this miserable corner of the earth? They became a people that succeeded in everything it undertook, a free, strong and intelligent people, and which before it lost, sword in hand, the name of an independent nation, had given as many learned men to the world as it had merchants" (Biddiss 1968, 78). He further observes that environment seemed to have little effect on the physical character of the Jews in various far-flung places of refuge after their dispersal.

The descendants of Gobineau's philosophy are both notorious and less well known. The links from Gobineau to Houston Stewart Chamberlain to Richard Wagner and Adolph Hitler have already been mentioned. Less well known are the Gobineau societies that were founded in Europe and America at the turn of the century. These led directly to the formation of eugenics societies, which influenced public policy in these countries regarding "weaker" and "stronger" races, sterilization laws, and immigration quotas. The idea of the progressive weakening of the white race, evident in Gobineau's pessimistic view of race history, has descendants in the views of overtly neo-Nazi and white militia organizations in Europe and the United States, which see their political goal as one of survival of the white race. Some authors have lamented the "birth dearth" (Wattenberg 1987), saying that not enough white babies are being born in the postindustrial nations of Europe and America, where birth rates have dropped to zero population growth or less. Others call for European unity against the colored hoards of Africa and Asia, whose birth rates exceed those of Europeans (Fouque 1958). Gobineau is indeed a major figure on the historical landscape of nineteenth- and twentieth-century Europe and America. Although Gobineau was never admitted to any learned society in France, the major political and social influence of his work can be felt today. Why, it must be asked, were antiracist scholars of these times ignored, marginalized, and finally obscured, while the perverse ideas of Gobineau held sway over the nineteenth and twentieth centuries? One of these powerful but forgotten figures is the Haitian scholar-activist Firmin.

## Joseph Anténor Firmin: Pioneering Anthropologist and Critical Race Theorist

Joseph Anténor Firmin, a pioneering but obscured Haitian anthropologist, wrote a response to Gobineau in 1885 entitled *De l'égalité des Races Humaines, Anthropologie Positive* (now translated as *The Equality of the Human Races: Positivist Anthropology*, 2000). This book, translated into English by Haitian scholar Asselin Charles and introduced by me as a historical work of anthropology in 2000, is far more than a simple rejoinder to Gobineau's racism. It is one of the earliest anthropology texts that uses the question of race to emphasize the importance of the new discipline's humanistic and scientific understanding of our species. Firmin not only confronts Gobineau, but he also challenges the racist physical

Figure 4.1.   Anténor Firmin, pioneer of anthropology.

anthropology of Paul Broca, founder and head of the Anthropology Society of Paris. Firmin and another Haitian colleague, Louis-Joseph Janvier, were members of the Anthropology Society in the 1880s, at a time when it was dominated by polygenist thought, and racial differences and inferiority were measured "scientifically" through craniometry and other physical measurements and purported characteristics of the various races. While Firmin's pioneering work is just coming to light, Broca's name has become synonymous with the pseudoscientific idea of phrenology, the determination of mental abilities and "criminal types" by feeling bumps on the head.

So far as I am able to determine, Firmin introduced into anthropology the scientific fact that melanin is responsible for skin pigment. This is not mentioned in two earlier works, neither specifically in Tylor's *Anthropology* (1881) nor in Martin Delany's *Principia of Ethnology: The Origin of Races and Color* (1879). Firmin emphasizes the influence of the environment on race, using the examples of pigmentation and hair form, which he suggests are linked to dryness and humidity in climate. Delany, an *Adamite monogenist*, writes that the original color of God's creation was rouge, which lightened or darkened according to its concentration. Delany claims that the same substance that causes white skin color causes black and yellow skin color (1879, chapter 6). Tylor describes the mucous layers of the skin, where small grains of black, brown, or yellow pigment are concentrated. He notes the medical term, "melanism," for normal areas of dark skin pigmentation in whites, such as the areola of the breast, and for a condition in whites in which dark patches resembling Negro skin appear on the body. However, Firmin appears to be the first to identify the source of human skin color as melanin within an anthropology text.

Firmin was a strong critic of polygenism, with more of his critique directed against Broca than against Gobineau. Firmin asks, Are there several human species or only one? He writes:

> Everything suggests that there is only one human species, if we understand the term as defined by most scientists. However, while admitting the unity of species, we absolutely reject the idea, Adamic or other, that all human beings descend from a single couple. This idea seems so contrary to reason and to the very history of our planet that it does not deserve discussion. (1885, 77)

Thus, although Firmin correctly states that monogenism is accurate science, he is careful to distinguish between the scientific unitarian theory and religious Adamic monogenism, the latter being an article of faith drawn from theology, not science. The unitarian theory is based on scientific deduction, drawing on the physical and moral qualities of the different human races, which are easily explained by the influence of environmental and other factors.

Broca writes on polygenism: "The difference in origin in no way implies the subordination of certain races . . . only the idea that each human race appeared in a specific region of the world and that it was . . . the crowning fauna of that particular region" (1869, 506). Firmin retorts:

> Assuming different origins of races, there is nothing to suggest that it has not sprung everywhere with the same organic constitution, confirming the existence of a single blueprint. Paleontologists have shown similar fossil species at various places on earth; from being originally similar during the course of evolution they became different under the influence of environment and habitat from one another, variations in forms, colors, physiognomy but all sharing the same basic blueprint, but under no less powerful a force of adaptation. These facts are consistent with the elegant laws of natural selection formulated by Darwin. Applied to humans, the inner constitution of the diverse races carries the proof of the unity of the species; there is not a single "zootaxic" difference among humans save skin color and hair form. *My hypothesis, albeit not a new one, seems very bold. As far as I know, it has never been presented in this guise before.*

Why? Firmin asks. "Because the polygenist scientists do not accept the unity of the human species, and the [religious] monogenists are not scientists" (1885, 81).

Broca thought that the physical configuration of the Negro was midway between that of the European and that of the ape (Firmin 1885, 57). For our purposes, Broca's conclusions thus can be viewed both as racist, in that the ranking of racial difference was central to his analysis, and as racialist, in that race as a biological phenomenon was a major factor in his writings. "He will neither be praised as a brilliant craniologist nor as a systematic ethnologist," Firmin correctly predicts of Broca's place in anthropological history. Yet today Broca's name is well known and Firmin's remains obscure.

For other scientists of the day the two extremes of humanity were represented by the European and Negro, and a sharp opposition between the Ethiopian's peripheral nervous system and that of the more developed European. Firmin cites A. de Quatrefages's (*L'Espèce humaine*) assertion that black people sweat less than white people (Firmin 1885, 60). Firmin can hardly contain his judgment of such racialist assertions. He writes that: "scientific progress will deal a death blow to all of their conclusions. I shall not bother to discuss the issue of the putative odor that is supposedly a particular characteristic of the Negro race. The idea is more comical than scientific" (1885, 62–63).

As for Negro mental inferiority, "It is quite evident today, then, that regardless of what has been said about their putatively innate lack of abilities, men of color are capable of all sorts of intellectual achievements. Outside the Republic of Haiti I could identify other striking examples, men such as Gerville Reache, Lacascade, Frederick Douglass, and so many other remarkable mulattoes in the U.S. and various colonies" (Firmin 1885, 77).

The scientific desperation of the polygenists led them to dismiss the Haitian case as "inconclusive" because it was the result of interbreeding between blacks and whites of Celtic and Iberian origins and not of (presumably superior) Germanic or Saxon origins. Firmin writes of the embarrassing displays he witnessed by ethnographers at every conference; they debated, for instance, whether the true Celts are dark haired or blond. The dark-haired Irish were often called "black Irish."

Of the Negro's so-called insensitivity (asserted as a racial characteristic by Gobineau) Firmin writes that were this accurate, it would have been based on the observation of blacks "stupefied by their infernal treatment and desensitized by numerous whippings" under slavery (Firmin 1885, 63). It is worth noting that the racialist physical anthropologists of the nineteenth century, in their adherence to the biological significance of race, failed to take into account centuries of the harsh conditions of slavery, which affected biological factors such as morbidity rates. Needless to say, for these early anthropologists cultural factors impacting on race classification and racism went unnoticed, in contrast to Firmin's sociological explanation for alleged Negro insensitivity.

The "problem" of race mixing is one of the central points of Gobineau's thesis as to why the formerly pure European races were now falling into decline and degradation. Firmin's position draws attention for the first time to the favorable mixing of races that has taken place in the New World. European racial classification, as we have seen, conceived of static and fixed races without taking into consideration the great amount of mixing that had taken place for centuries, creating the "Creole," "mestizo," and other "colored" populations of the New World colonies and possessions of Europe.

Countering the racist idea that the offspring of a racially mixed couple, a "mulatto" (from the word "mule"—the infertile offspring of a mare and donkey), is indeed infertile, Firmin notes the fecund hybridization in other species, such as that of a rabbit and hare (leponid), a mixed species that has remained fertile for seven generations. Further, Broca's contention that from north to south and from light skin to dark skin the races are naturally ordered from superior to inferior left out the important case of the New World, which would present the strongest argument against his theory because of the New World hybridity. This *métissage* Firmin believed to be a eugenic race mixing, that is, a biological phenomenon that is on the whole positive for diversifying the human species. At the time of Firmin's writing the racist eugenics movements were not organized, so it is possible to contrast Firmin's positive use of the term "eugenic" with its later use to describe the dire, "dysgenic" consequences of race mixing.

Firmin observes "that human beings have always interbred wherever they have come in contact with one another, so that the very notion of races is questionable. Indeed, if not for this fact of the essential unity of humanity, it would be difficult to explain the eugenic crossbreedings that have made the surface of the planet sparkle with more human colors than there are nuances in the rainbow" (1885, 64). (I particularly like this passage because it foreshadows the ideas of the Rainbow Coalition of civil rights leader Jesse Jackson in the 1970s, and was also adopted by postapartheid South African movements to construct a new multiracial "rainbow" country.)

"Métis," persons of mixed-race ancestry, suffer inferior health, longevity, and intelligence, according to Broca, thus showing that blacks and whites probably do not belong to the same species. Broca avoided the obvious question posed by Firmin: Are all of the children of the English, the French, or the German equal to their parents in terms of health, longevity, and intelligence? For Broca, "The union of a Negro and white woman is very often sterile, whereas the union between a White man and a Negress is always fecund," and has to do with the length of the "Ethiopian" penis, which is greater than the length of the Caucasian vagina. So the sex act between a Caucasian man and an Ethiopian woman is easy, while the act between an Ethiopian man and a Caucasian woman is difficult, painful, and most often infertile! (Firmin 1885, 66, quoting Broca, *Memoires d'Anthropologie*). Despite its nonsensical premises, this racist view of Negro and white sexuality persisted and lingers to this day, with the myths of black sexual prowess and weak libido in whites.

"Are all of the New World mulattos infertile?" asks Firmin. The immense number of "métis" found wherever blacks and whites have been in permanent contact with one another is obvious, and the fecundity of mulattoes is a well-known fact. The Dominican population of Hispaniola offers initial proof that among both first-generation mulattoes and subsequent generations the unions of mixed-race persons are as fecund as those between pure-race individuals.

"Of Haiti, the old French section of Hispaniola," Firmin writes,

I can speak with even greater confidence, since it is my motherland, my native country. There I have made the same observation, and the evidence is irrefutable. Since independence the Whites have left making unions between Whites and Blacks rare. Despite this fact the number of mulattoes in Haiti has more than doubled. The cause resides in sociological factors not biological ones. (Firmin 1885, 69)

As for the social condition of the mixed-race métis, their fate was a life of shame and misery as the products of irresistible libidinous moments when the master was drawn to the slave. Firmin sympathetically describes the painful position of the mulattoes, who were "treated with more contempt than the Black and they were subjected to the whip, the knife, the gallows if they protested or claimed their rights to their fathers" (Firmin 1885, 73). As a black Haitian, Firmin might have been less sympathetic to mulattoes, for the racial divide in Haitian economic, political, and social life was then and remains today a powerful force. However, Firmin attempted to create an objective science; when he praises black accomplishment, especially in the heroic Haitian Revolution—which produced the world's first black republic in 1804—he excuses himself for the appearance of black chauvinism. When E. B. Tylor extolls the accomplishments of the white race he does so more matter of factly, without apology; they are a people "throughout history growing more dominant intellectually, morally, and politically on the earth" (1881, 105–6).

Naturally Firmin disagreed strongly with Gobineau's claim that the Negro race did not give rise to any civilization. Firmin cites Egypt and Nile Valley civilizations that are Negro and African. He further cites the

"Ethiopians," whom the Greeks called the "people of the burnt faces," which we now understand to have been their reference to the Nubian kingdoms of Kush and Meroë. These kingdoms rivaled and in some cases ruled Egypt from the fifth century BCE to the end of Pharaonic rule and continued as Christian kingdoms until the coming of Islam.

In summary, the works of Gobineau and Firmin are divergent on every point regarding the unity of equality of all members of the human species. The two contrasting works arguing for the inequality/equality of races were written by the respective authors when they were both in their prime, between thirty-five and forty years of age, one full of pessimism about the human race, the other full of optimism, with a secure vision of the ultimate truth of human equality. The radical differences between the two might suggest that they belonged to different eras, but the truth is that in every era racist and liberal or antiracist writers have existed side by side, although history has not treated their writings equitably.

Few today are interested in Negro history because they feel the matter already settled: the Negro has no history. . . . I remember my own rather sudden awakening from the paralysis of this judgment taught me in high school and in two of the world's great universities. Franz Boas came to Atlanta University where I was teaching history in 1906, and said to a graduating class: you need not be ashamed of your African past; and then he recounted the history of Black kingdoms south of the Sahara for a thousand years. I was too astonished to speak. (W. E. B. DuBois 1939; referring to Boas 1906).

## THE SOCIAL DARWINIST AND EUGENICS
## MOVEMENTS AND THEIR CRITICS

### Social Darwinists Sir Francis Galton and Lothrop Stoddard and Their Critic Franz Boas, 1900–1940

Many students are trained to accept a simple notion of Darwinian evolution that species evolve from simple to complex, that natural selection and the "survival of the fittest" weed out inferior genes and produce optimum physical results in all life forms. The laws of evolution can occasionally take a wrong turn, and the result can be a maladapted saber-toothed tiger, but nature corrects itself through extinction, and life continues to reproduce itself. Darwin was cautious about applying his ideas to human society, and it was Herbert Spencer, not Darwin, who coined the phrase "survival of the fittest," which has come to summarize evolution.

However, many racially motivated authors of the nineteenth and twentieth centuries took the ideas of Darwin—heredity, struggle for life, variability, natural selection, and survival of the fittest—and typed societies as "fit" or "unfit," with some capable of rising to the highest evolutionary levels of civilization, others left hopelessly behind in lower stages of barbarism and savagery. These authors are referred to as "social Darwinists," and their ideas about the higher and lower stages and levels of humanity were anything but progressive, but they too form a part of our intellectual heritage in anthropology and the social sciences. Human beings are fundamentally unequal as a matter of heredity, and men of genius are found among those societies that have created civilization. Spencer claimed that "savage" and "semicivilized" people represented the lower stages of biological evolution, making a basic error by confusing biology and culture. The near genocide of Native American peoples was explained as their lack of fitness for civilization from a social Darwinist perspective. The European colonization of African peoples was justified as a means of making them more fit for civilization.

Social Darwinism viewed societal development as a law of nature, just like the biological laws of evolution. Societies or individuals could try to go against these laws and become civilized, but they were doomed to failure and a reversion to an uncivilized state; thus, only very limited social progress was possible. A classic social Darwinist statement comes from the American William H. Brown's analysis of his visit to South Africa at the close of the nineteenth century: "Throughout history, human progress has resulted largely from the forcible encroachment of nations of superior characteristics and customs upon races of lower development. Without radical measures there is little hope for the rapid improvement of those tribes which are thoroughly satisfied with their depraved condition" (Brown 1899).

A typical social Darwinist justification for the American crime of slavery comes from Brown's comparison of African and American Negroes:

> That forced servitude, even in the abhorrent form of chattel slavery, has exerted a potent influence in the uplifting of primitive man, is exemplified by its results upon the negro in America. Through an apprenticeship of bondage, the negro has been removed from a state of barbarism and superstition and placed among the most progressive of all races. (Brown 1899, 390–91)

### Eugenics (Selective Breeding of Humans) and the Survival of the Fittest

Sir Francis Galton, a social Darwinist and advocate of eugenics, wrote the racist work *Hereditary Genius* in 1869. This book remained a standard through the end of the nineteenth century, and Galton was knighted for ideas stated in this and other works. In *Hereditary Genius* he claims that the races are fundamentally unequal and that the Negro race has failed to produce a single man of genius in its entire history (1869, 325–37). More than any of his contemporaries Galton made a science of racism. His "objective" study of men of genius—with mental capacity graded from A to G, A being the lowest, G the highest, and X the truly exceptional—shows that genius is an inherited trait and clusters in families, populations, and nations. In ancient Greece, he calculates, there was one man of the highest genius per 4,822, while in England the genius rate is much higher, especially among its nobility. This should bring a smile to any follower of the scandals of the British monarchy! Environment cannot create a genius out of a mediocre man; however, a genius can overcome a disadvantaged environment. Galton was the first to study twins, attempting to show the greater effect of heredity over environment. This was the debut of the heredity-versus-environment debate with regard to individual and group intelligence that rages on today. The latest act played out with the publication of *The Bell Curve* in 1994, which incidentally the authors open with a deep bow in the direction of Sir Francis Galton. Making a "science" of human intelligence, Galton created the first tests of innate ability and the first bell curve, with an average bulge in the middle and equal and opposite extremes at the high and low ends of intellect. Galton had his critics then, as the authors of *The Bell Curve* have theirs today, but what continues is the weight given then and now to the hereditarian hypothesis that race, social class, and intelligence are genetic traits.

Galton's work gave a great impetus to the eugenics movement, which had the goal of social restructuring through selective breeding, favoring the fertility of the alleged best of the human species over the biologically and mentally inferior. Legislation making possible the sterilization of selected populations was the next step.

It often surprises students to learn that the first case of eugenics legislation was not in Nazi Germany, but in the United States. The chief proponent of the American eugenics movement was Charles B. Davenport, who established a eugenics section of the American Breeders' Association (ABA) "to investigate and report on heredity in the human race" and to "emphasize the value of superior blood and the menace to society of inferior blood" (Chase 1980, 114). Davenport traveled to England in 1897 to meet Galton and became an early convert to eugenics. He wrote to Galton in 1910, saying that a Records Office in Eugenics had been established and hailing Galton as the "founder of the Science of Eugenics"—he went on to say that they hoped the office would include both positive eugenics and negative eugenics, the "weeding out" of bad strains of inferior human traits. Research committees were set up within the ABA eugenics section dealing with the heredity of: feeble-mindedness, insanity, epilepsy, criminality, deaf mutism, eye defects, sterilization, genealogy or inheritance of mental traits, and immigration.

Supporters of American eugenics included overt racists and elitists, as well as others who saw in eugenics a scientific way to improve life for all. Liberals such as Franz Boas were initially attracted to its "potential," but the policies and programs of the eugenics movement soon revealed its true nature and intent.

"Bad blood" consisted of supposed hereditary traits such as pauperism, the major genetic defect of the poor; insanity; low IQ test scores; homelessness; pellagra and other diseases of the chronically poor. Selective mating with superior Nordic people would have the positive effect of race betterment, while the prevention of the breeding of inferiors would prevent racial deterioration. All of this would benefit society, which would not have to waste its tax dollars on health, education, and employment benefits for those races and social classes that are doomed by their inferior genes to be uneducable, unhealthy, unemployable, and immoral (Chase 1980, 116–17).

The American eugenics movement had two goals: 1) to restrict the immigration of non-Nordics, and 2) to have every state enact laws for the compulsory sterilization of people of "bad heredity." Efforts between 1897 and 1907 to pass legislation in the states of Michigan and Pennsylvania failed due to ethical, religious, and scientific questions that politicians had about the use of forced sterilization. But Indiana broke the deadlock with its approval of an act to "prevent procreation of confirmed criminals, idiots, imbeciles, and rapists" held in state institutions and certified as beyond rehabilitation. Washington, California, and Connecticut passed nearly identical bills in 1909, while the governors of the states of Vermont, Nebraska, and Idaho vetoed comparable bills on the grounds of being unwarranted and inexcusable discrimination (Chase 1980, 126).

Undaunted, Harry Hamilton Laughlin, head of the Eugenics Record Office, prepared in simple form and language a Model Eugenical Sterilization Law, which was widely distributed to the press, as well as government, education, and religious leaders. This model legislation was to affect

all persons in the state who, because of degenerate or defective hereditary qualities are potential parents of socially inadequate offspring. . . . An Act to prevent the procreation of persons socially inadequate from defective inheritance by authorizing and providing for eugenical sterilization certain potential parents carrying degenerate hereditary qualities. The "socially inadequate" classes, regardless of etiology or prognosis include the following: 1) Feeble-minded 2) Insane 3) Criminalistic (including the delinquent and wayward) 4) Epileptic 5) Inebriate 6) Diseased (including the tuberculous, other legally segregable diseases) 7) Blind 8) Deaf 9) Deformed 10) Dependent (orphans, homeless, tramps, and paupers). (quoted in Chase 1980, 134)

As cruel and inhumane as this model legislation sounds today, it is even more shocking to learn that thirty of the forty-eight states eventually passed some version of it by the time of the Great Depression. The state of Vermont, whose governor had vetoed an earlier version of eugenics legislation, capitulated and is still suffering from the stigma of its decision to enact a eugenics sterilization law in 1931. The legislation, much like the model bill, was preceded by a twelve-year Vermont Eugenics Survey in which an independent team of social scientists studied "good" and "bad" families in the state with an eye to eliminating the state's "degenerate" bloodlines and replenishing "old pioneer stock." The data, unearthed by researchers in the 1980s and not systematically studied until the 1990s, consisted of forty crates of reports stored in a laundry room in a state mental hospital. The 1931 law resulted in the sterilization of several hundred poor rural Vermonters, Abenaki Indians, and others deemed unfit to procreate. The documents do not indicate how the legislation was enacted or whether the sterilizations were presented as an option or an order. One scientist, Henry Perkins of the University of Vermont, came up with a theory of "pedigrees of degeneracy" that singled out certain families as "dysgenic," families that current research indicates are still referred to as "the troublemakers" in Vermont's public high schools (Gallagher 1999). The eugenics laws were not rolled back until the 1960s and 1970s. This is research from just one state, and a relatively rural, underpopulated state; records from other states may tell more dramatic and shocking stories. It might be that the documentation of the effects of eugenics legislation has been stored in other "laundry room"–like locales to obscure a shameful period in American history that bears far too many similarities to later events in Nazi Germany.

The origin of these laws antedated by twenty years the 1927 German voluntary sterilization law, which was followed six years later by the Nazi compulsory sterilization laws of 1933. Laughlin's Model Eugenical Sterilization Law was adopted wholesale by the Germans and applied by the Nazi eugenics courts to "social inadequates," including the genetically mentally deficient, mentally ill, epileptic, blind, and deaf, as well as chronic alcoholics and people with any grave, inherited physical defect. Soon, being Jewish, or Gypsy, or homosexual, or Slavic came to be viewed as an "inherited physical defect," and the Americans who had innovated the eugenics legislation would find themselves confronting a monster that was partly of their own making. Under the Nazis an average of 165,000 German men and women per year were sterilized against their will, 450 per day. Nor was Germany alone in this quest for government-sponsored genetic purity. The Swedish government involuntarily sterilized as many sixty thousand of its citizens with undesirable traits such as psychopathy, a vagabond life, a low IQ, or "unmistakable Gypsy features." The welfare state apparently embraced eugenics as a cost-saving measure for its expensive social programs.

By 1968, sixty-five thousand Americans had been sterilized in thirty states against their will as a result of the eugenics laws, over 52 percent for being labeled "mentally retarded." In most states a diagnosis of mental retardation was made on the basis of IQ tests, the effects of which will be addressed in chapter 5.

Despite the political and military defeat of the eugenics-based policies of the Nazis, the idea of eugenics did not die out. It resurfaced in the wake of the gains made by the civil rights movement, especially in the field of compensatory education. A 1969 article by eugenicist Arthur Jensen, published in the *Harvard Educational Review*, "How Much Can We Boost IQ and Scholastic Achievement?" challenged the utility of the government spending money on Operation Headstart. At the article's base was Jensen's eugenics argument that "current welfare policies, unaided by eugenic foresight, could lead to genetic enslavement of a substantial segment of our population" (quoted in Chase 1980, 470).

The history of U.S. antimiscegenation laws shows that the majority of southern and border, former nonslave states, as well as Oklahoma, had statutory restrictions on racial intermarriage until the late 1960s, and in other cases until the dawn of the new millennium. Alabama dropped its statute only in 2000 due to shame and disgrace, as happened with lynching. The fear of interracial couples still pervades southern and American racial history.

The U.S. Supreme Court did not declare miscegenation laws unconstitutional until 1967 (*Loving v. Brace*), in the wake of the mass civil rights movement. What may not be appreciated is the number of southern states whose miscegenation laws were placed on the books in the 1950s—not a century before, at the end of slavery, but at a time when fears of a desegregated society were spreading throughout the white communities of the south. In 1953 North Carolina passed legislation stating: "All marriages between a white person and a person of negro descent to the third generation inclusive, are forever prohibited, and shall be void" (Domínguez 1994, 269, quoting NC Gen. Stat. 14–181).

North Carolina's statute was not repealed until 1973; in Maryland a similar statute was repealed in 1967; and Texas Article 4607, adopted in 1951, was repealed in 1969.

Alabama, Arkansas, Georgia, and Virginia prohibited marriages between white persons and persons with any discernible trace of Negro blood (the one-drop rule). Two of the border states, Kentucky and West Virginia, prohibited until 1968 intermarriage between whites and mulattoes or persons of the Negro race, but they failed to define the rules of descent and prohibition. Oklahoma followed southern patterns by prohibiting miscegenation in 1954 and repealing that prohibition in 1969. The state of Virginia included Indians as well as "colored" persons in its anti-miscegenation law, retaining it until 1968.

The Tennessee statute (46–402, passed in 1955) repealed only the following language in 1978: "The intermarriage of white persons with negroes, mulattoes, or persons of mixed blood descended from a negro to the third generation inclusive" (quoted in Domínguez 1994, 269). Florida, Mississippi, Missouri, and South Carolina prohibited marriages between white persons and persons of one-eighth Negro blood (so-called octoroons) or more. The 1957 Florida statute and the 1953 Missouri statutes were repealed in 1969. The words "Negro," "colored," "colored persons," "mulatto," and "persons of color" were applied for people having one-eighth or more Negro blood—that is, one or more great-grandparents of "Negro" blood. The Alabama and Mississippi statutes were not repealed until after the new millennium.

This fear of interracial dating and marriage is dramatized in the high school in Butler, Georgia, which held segregated proms—one for blacks and one for whites—for thirty-one years after the school was integrated, from 1971 to 2002. Public schools that ignored federal orders to desegregate long after *Brown v. the Board of Education* in 1954 were finally forced to integrate, but held onto rigid customs preventing socializing between blacks and whites. In Butler, Georgia, the walls of segregation were finally torn down by the students themselves, 75 percent of whom supported a student proposal to hold a single prom (*Providence Journal* 2002).

### Franz Boas and the Mainstreaming of Antiracist Anthropology

Franz Boas is widely respected as the father of American anthropology and as a scholar who publicly pronounced his staunch antiracist views. He founded the first major anthropology department, at Columbia University, in 1905 and headed it until his death in 1942. This department transformed the field from one with a relatively narrow geographical and physical anthropological base in the nineteenth century into a discipline focusing on the integrated, holistic study of humanity using its cultural, physical, archaeological, and linguistic features. Boas's egalitarian view came to dominate American anthropology and eventually eclipsed the old racist physical anthropology. Throughout the first half of the twentieth century he trained many of the most important names in the field, from Margaret Mead and Ruth Benedict to the major pioneer in the field of African cultural survivals in the Americas, Melville Herskovits, as well as the great novelist Zora Neale Hurston and the author of the classic work on the fallacy of racial myths, Ashley Montagu. Boas was a supporter and friend of the titan of black studies in the United States, W. E. B. DuBois, who credits Boas with his awakening to the great cultural traditions of precolonial Africa. Simply put, Boas's influence was immense on the mainstreaming of anthropology in university and intellectual life.

His ethnographic work focused on the native peoples of the American northwest coast, and he produced volumes of detailed study of their languages, myths, and material culture. As a younger scholar he carried out a great number of physical anthropological studies of human variation, and he was an enthusiastic measurer of diverse crania. However, he was unlike his physical anthropological contemporaries in that his study of the crania and changes in bodily form of immigrant populations in the United States led him to opposite conclusions. Boas found that physical characteristics of humans are malleable, not fixed, and that they are subject to environmental factors resulting in change even from one generation to the next. His studies in Worcester, Massachusetts (when he was professor of anthropology at Clark University), of first-generation Italian and Jewish groups demonstrated to him that their physical growth and condition had changed and improved dramatically over the period of a single generation in America (cf. Boas 1911). This contradicted the view of racialist scholars that "fixity of type" in race bore little susceptibility to environmental forces.

Boas's greatest contribution to the study of race was his emphasis on the role of heredity and environmental factors on the plasticity of race and his critique of eugenics. Being of the first post-Mendelian generation of anthropologists he was able to apply the newly understood laws of inheritance. He understood the important difference between densely populated regions with multiple ancestors, such as in Europe, and regions with relatively sparse populations with fewer ancestors, such as the homelands of American Indians, whose genetic makeup would be magnified in subsequent generations rather than lessened or diluted through the effects of genetic mixing. This "founder's effect" in genetically isolated breeding populations is recognized today as a significant force in human evolution and the development of microevolutionary differences we have called race.

Through studies of American immigrant and resident populations in varying environmental circumstances over several decades Boas discovered that children of immigrants were taller and weighed more on average than their parents. He further showed that environmental factors such as disease and a lack of health care in early childhood, as well as poor nutrition, had retarding effects on growth, while fresh air, sunshine, and physical exercise all had a positive effect on growth and development. His study comparing Negro children in New York public schools and in orphanages demonstrated the effect of their respective environments on their differing average size and body weight. Boas proved that environmental influence has a significant effect on physical form, at the time most strongly assumed to be associated with race. Today the link between good nutrition and overall health is scientific common sense and is as associated with differences in class as race, as we recognize the risks to physical and mental growth and development that a poor standard of living conveys. But in Boas's time the role of the environment was a new finding, and groups could be blamed for their physical weaknesses, very much in a social Darwinist worldview of blaming the victim.

Franz Boas's response to eugenics advocates took place at the height of their influence in the United States and before the "final solution" was conceived in his native Germany. Boas's Jewish ancestry undoubtedly sensitized him to prejudice and discrimination toward others. Boas wrote a chapter on eugenics in his book *Anthropology and Modern Life*, written for a popular audience and published in 1928. While Boas concedes the potential that a eugenic approach might have toward the alleviation of human suffering in theory, he is profoundly skeptical of the ability of eugenics laws to raise the overall physical and mental well-being of the population. As an advocate of the important role of the environment, Boas holds that "no amount of eugenic selection will overcome the social conditions that have raised a poverty and disease-stricken proletariat which will be reborn from even the best stock so long as the social conditions persist that push human beings into helpless and hopeless misery" (1928, 118). In this vein Boas is particularly critical of the eugenic claim that criminality or other obvious social pathologies could be hereditary. Eugenics, therefore, should not be allowed to deceive us that a race of supermen can be created. "Eugenics is not a panacea that will cure human ills; it is rather a dangerous sword that may turn its edge against those who rely on its strength" (Boas 1928, 121).

Boas's most popular works written for a general audience relate to central anthropological questions that touch directly on themes of racial-cultural equality. His volume of previously published articles, *Race, Language and Culture* (1948), is a definitive statement on the necessary separation of these three often confused aspects of human identity. And his *The Mind of Primitive Man* (1911; 1938) and *Race and Democratic Society* (1945) were republished or written when Nazism was at its peak in his native Germany, and are his classic polemical works on the subject of race and racism. He feared the political implications of the rise of racial identity and solidarity, which displace or enhance feelings of national or religious identity. The clear but unstated reference was to the rise of Nazism in Germany; his ideas regarding race may have been the reason his books were banned and then burned in Nazi Germany. Boas's Jewish ancestry, no doubt, was also a contributing factor.

Boas certainly advanced the study of race beyond its racialist and racist origins in physical anthropology, but he did not "go the full distance" in terms of basically challenging the scientific validity of race. A race he defined as a biological unit, a population derived from common ancestry that by virtue of its descent is endowed with definite biological characteristics (1938, 37). The idea of race as common biological ancestry, in Boas's view, needs to be separated from the idea of racial superiority and inferiority, which he found to be utterly subjective and emotional. However, Boas took the measurement of racial difference seriously, such as variability of stature by race and at different developmental stages; cephalic index, the length-breadth ratio of skulls; and the observable phenotypic differences in skin pigmentation, hair form, and face and eye shape. Boas was careful to point out that such physical measurements and classifications had descriptive value but no further biological significance. Countering racist writers such as Lothrop Stoddard and Roland B. Dixon, Boas would not accept the idea of long headed (dolichocephalic), blond, narrow-nosed European groups as in any sense a pure racial stock. However skeptical he was about existing racial classifications, Boas did not discard them altogether, and he followed what had become the accepted science of the three great races, Mongoloid, Caucasoid, and Negroid.

Boas was strongly affiliated with many different public condemnations of racism in its many forms; he associated with black intellectuals, objected to the plight of the Negro in America, and encouraged the anthropological study of Negroes in the Americas; he also condemned Nazism in his native Germany. It is based on these public postures that he has earned a high place in antiracist circles. But as Vernon J. Williams (1996) has pointed out, Boas was not without his scientific reservations about the absolute equality of Negroes with whites. While he found no proof of Negro inferiority when comparing the bulk of the Negro population with the bulk of the white population, he equivocates that perhaps "the race [Negro] would not produce quite so many men of highest genius as other races" (1938, 268). He saw the importance of brain weight as indicative of mental faculty and saw the evidence as heavily favoring whites. "There are sufficient data available to establish beyond a doubt the fact that the brain-weight of the Whites is larger than that of most other races, particularly larger than that of the Negroes" (1938, 103). Here Boas seems to accept the measurements and studies of known racialist scholars, such as Topinard's cranial measurements and Galton's study of upper-class English schoolboys, whose heads were measured as larger than those of average students (1938, 104). These studies, Boas cautioned, should not be overestimated, and he cautioned against the hasty interpretation that relative brain size always indicates genius, noting that not all the brains of eminent men are unusually large. But in the end he failed to abandon the general correlation between brain size and "increased faculty." He might have been more skeptical, since Galton's nineteenth-century social Darwinism and advocacy of eugenics policies were well known in the twentieth century. He observed of Australian Aboriginal peoples that they exhibit "a number of rather primitive features that set them off sharply from other races"; his hypothesis that they may have differentiated at an early period and been crowded back by more successful races into remote corners of the world has a social Darwinist ring to it.

Notwithstanding these reservations about full Negro equality, Boas stuck by his environmentalist arguments, noting that there is no proof that race is responsible for the conditions observed by ethnologists in the poorest Negro communities. Boas's sensitivity to the historical context of the American Negro's inferior social status is evident in the following quotation:

> The traits of the American Negro are adequately explained on the basis of his history and social status. The tearing-away from the African soil and the complete loss of the old standards of life, which were replaced by the dependency of slavery and by all it entailed, followed by a period of disorganization and by severe economic struggle against heavy odds, are sufficient to explain the inferiority of the status of the race, without falling back upon the theory of hereditary inferiority. (1938, 270)

Boas further stimulated interest among both black and white Americans in the study of African culture. This is notable, since the United States did not have the same direct colonial interest in the African continent as Europe, and this helped to diversify the American ethnological preoccupation with the American Indian. Boas knew about ancient African kingdoms and describes indigenous African cultures as those of a "healthy primitive people with a considerable degree of personal initiative, with a talent for organization, with imaginative power, with technical skill and craft" (1938, 270). Each of these descriptive phrases counters a racist stereotype that was extant at the time of Boas's writing.

He also attempted to bring attention to the study of "mulattoes" in the New World—mixtures of African peoples with Latino and white populations. He questioned, as Firmin had done fifty years before, the hereditary weakness or inferiority of the hybrid mulatto, and he castigated the government for its failure to take notice of or give scientific support for the study of the question, which was of paramount importance to the welfare of the nation.

Boas concludes his most important book on race with remarks that in some ways presage Martin Luther King's "I Have a Dream" speech—"Freedom of judgment can be attained only when we learn to estimate an individual according to his own ability and character" (1938, 272).

## Lothrop Stoddard: Eugenicist, Immigration Opponent, Nazi Sympathizer

Several racist writers of the first decades of the twentieth century might have been selected for a comparison with Boas, among them Madison Grant, whose *The Passing of the Great Race* echoes Gobineau's pessimism about the decline of the great white race, or Aleš Hrdlička, a contemporary of Boas who taught racialized physical anthropology to generations of students. Hrdlicka's influence continued well into the civil rights period, and his moral message questioned fundamentally the inequality of races.

But I selected Lothrop Stoddard because his racist ideas were especially directed toward racial policy, he provides a good contrast to Boas's antiracist public postures, and he has relevance to contemporary antiimmigrant sentiment. Stoddard published two highly influential racist works that led to the restrictions on immigration in the 1920s, *The Rising Tide of Color* (1920) and *The Revolt against Civilization: The Menace of the Underman* (1922). He was hailed as a prophet and savior of Western and American civilization by no less than president Warren G. Harding and the new convert to eugenics and founder of the modern birth control movement, Margaret Sanger (Chase 1980, 292). Stoddard testified often as an expert witness before the U.S. Congress, warning against opening America's door to inferior stocks of Jews, eastern Europeans, and other non-Nordic types. Like many other racist writers of his time, Stoddard was of the "best" American stock, Harvard educated with a law diploma and a doctorate in history.

*The Races of Europe* (1924, 96) followed a French racialist classification of European types. It posited three different European stocks, each quite distinct, but all superior to the "yellow Mongolian" and the African Negro races. The Nordics were said to be descended from Aryans, whose association with empire and conquest make them the superior Europeans; while the Alpine peasants of Poland, Russia, south Germany, and France have been bred more as a subject people; and the darker, emotional Mediterranean stock is undisciplined by nature and retreats before the attacks of both Nordics and Alpines. According to Stoddard, it was the great good fortune of the United States that it had attracted large numbers of the Nordic stock, and it was this superior European that Stoddard wanted to encourage and protect by way of immigration quotas. It is worth noting that racism as an ideology can extend to different groups of Europeans, as can be seen here: Aryan Nordic northern Europeans stand in a superior position in general to the peoples of eastern and southern Europe. Now, stop and think about the once popular Polish jokes that emphasized the stupidity of Poles, while the jokes about Italians focused on their lack of bravery in battle. So many of the stereotypes we perpetuate are rooted in racist works or ideas like these of Stoddard. Racial mixture, especially the "mongrelization" of Nordic peoples with inferior Alpine stock—Germany being a case in point—has lead to their decline, according to Stoddard. It is to America that Stoddard looks for the salvation of the Nordic race!

The United States was founded by men of Nordic stock, Stoddard claimed, and its institutions and ideals are the fruit of the Nordic spirit—if the United States should cease to be a Nordic land our America would pass away. America has been misguided by the belief that the environment rather than heredity is the chief factor in human affairs. This has lulled the American people into a false confidence and optimism that is not justified by the "realistic" science of race. The old American stock that built the country was Nordic stock, and its dilution with the waves of immigration from inferior southern and eastern Europe European stock places the nation in great peril. Stoddard's hereditary hypothesis, published in 1924, proved more successful in terms of public policy than Boas's environmentalism in that the restrictions on immigration from these regions sought by works like Stoddard's were instituted. Quotas restricting immigration from southern and eastern Europe and favoring northern European immigration became law in the early 1920s. It is worth noting that IQ testing of the non-Nordic immigrants "proved" their inferiority, with many eastern and southern Europeans, including Russian Jews, scoring at the "moronic" or "feebleminded" levels, while Nordic intelligence tested at the above-average or higher levels. Small wonder, since the intelligence tests were administered in English at Ellis Island to new immigrants with little or no knowledge of English language or American customs.

Stoddard rejected the idea that America is a dynamic, multiracial, and multicultural nation ever changing—America was made by the great men from England and northern Europe who founded it, and not by all those people who "had been dumped down together at Ellis Island a few short years ago" (1922, 243). One can readily identify these chauvinistic sentiments with anti-immigrant sentiment today, and it is naive to believe that immigration quotas are not still affected by race, among other factors. Compare the recent experience of Haitian economic and political immigrants with that of immigrants to the United States from the former Soviet Union.

Stoddard's plea for America to develop a realistic racial consciousness was nothing short of a call to arms to keep the nation white. That the "real America" is white is still a prominent idea; its reconstruction into a genuine multiracial/multicultural society is still in progress, aided by rapidly changing demographics, especially a rising Hispanic population. It is useful for some white Americans who are descendants from Stoddard's "inferior" European stocks to read what was written about them in the past, so that they may empathize (using historical insight) with what is written or said about today's new immigrant populations.

Franz Boas struggled to show the plasticity of race, that physical form is profoundly affected by environmental factors, and that an open door to world emigration expresses the highest goals of American civilization. Lothrop Stoddard feared that the old America was being swept away by immigrant hoards from inferior racial stocks and believed that keeping America white and Nordic was crucial for its survival. Stoddard ends his racist polemic with a not so thinly veiled eugenics program that he believes each country should encourage through legislation and policy, as a way of "improving its racial stocks."

A Nazi sympathizer, Stoddard described his "audience" with Adolf Hitler and his instructive visit to a Nazi eugenics court in 1940. Between 1933 and 1939 the Nazis had officially sterilized 375,000 individuals; however, postwar estimates number closer to two million. Stoddard, our Harvard-educated social engineer, had paraded before him "obvious" candidates for sterilization, including an "ape-like" man with a history of homosexuality married to a Jewess, with whom he had already had three inferior children, a feebleminded seventeen-year-old girl, a manic-depressive, and an eighteen-year-old deaf-mute. These cases were "carefully and patiently" considered by the German eugenics court and were postponed until further clinical and psychological studies could be carried out, a judgment far too lenient in Stoddard's opinion. The experience left the Boston Brahmin convinced that the policy of German sterilization was "weeding out the worst strains in German stock in a scientific and humanitarian way" (Stoddard 1920, 196).

## Contrasting Postwar Anthropologists: Antiracist Ashley Montagu (1905–1999), and Racialist and Racist Carlton Coon (1942–1962)

Though the authors were anthropological contemporaries in the mid-twentieth century, Ashley Montagu's *Man's Most Dangerous Myth: The Fallacy of Race* (1942) and Carlton Coon's *The Origin of Races* (1962) could not be more different. From a strictly chronological point of view one might guess that the later book would have the more enlightened view of race, but that is not the case. Coon's book, espousing a neopolygenist view of the separate and unequal origins of races and published at the peak of the civil rights movement, was used by segregationists to add scientific weight to their opposition to the integration of America's public schools. If the races originated separately and at earlier and later time periods, then it could be argued that the races are in fact unequal from an evolutionary and biological standpoint.

Twenty years earlier, at the height of the Nazi power in Europe, Ashley Montagu had warned about the social and political dangers of racial myths, but his message was relevant to more than one particular time and place. It is a telling point that his work has reached its sixth edition and has lost none of its relevance or power.

Coon's *The Origin of Races* was still generally a current book when I came into anthropology as an undergraduate in the 1960s, and what astonishes me today is that I can't recall a single critical remark made about the book or Coon's ideas. Moreover, when the popular Time-Life imprint published a number of books with anthropological themes the section on "Races of Mankind" from the book on human evolution used Coon's five-part racial classification without comment, presumably presented as the best science of the day. There were pictures meant to be typical of Coon's races: Caucasoid, Mongoloid, Congoid, Capoid, and Australoid. On the surface they may have appeared to be harmless new ways to talk about the old subject of race, but a closer examination of Coon's thesis in *The Origin of Races* might have provoked a stronger reaction.

*The Origin of Races* advertised itself as the "first detailed history of the evolution of the five races of man—a pioneer work, a milestone of scientific thought." Carlton Coon's credentials were impeccable: professor of anthropology at the University of Pennsylvania and curator of ethnology at the university museum, president of the American Association of Physical Anthropologists, recipient of a Harvard doctorate, and a local television personality in Philadelphia for the award-winning program "What in the World?" I recall being a fan of this program as a child growing up in Philadelphia in the 1950s. During World War II Coon had worked for Army intelligence in North Africa and was considered an authority on Arabs in addition to an expert on race matters.

Coon dedicates *The Origin of Races* to a somewhat obscure physical anthropologist, Franz Weidenreich, who had studied the fossil human Sinanthropus and concluded that "he" was indeed an example of *Homo erectus* and that racially he was Mongoloid. Again, on the basis of a single skull a general theory was generated that races originated separately and that race variation is older than species evolution—that is, a Mongoloid *Homo erectus* preceded the later appearance of *Homo sapiens*. Coon asserts that of the five races the Australoid is the most archaic and therefore the most primitive. Throughout Coon fuses cultural and biological evolution, a grave error in anthropology by this time. Though an acknowledged expert on race, Coon fails to cite a single work of America's most famous antiracist anthropologist, Franz Boas. As proof of the biocultural backwardness of Australoids Coon asks, "How could the Australian aborigines in the 19th century be living in the same condition as Europe 100,000 years ago if they hadn't evolved separately? And how could there be thousands of different languages if humans have a common ancestry?" These simplistic questions, after a century of anthropological studies of ethnology, show either Coon's poor understanding of human cultural history and evolution or his use of ethnology for a racialist agenda.

For Coon, Africa was still the "darkest continent" in terms of racial evolution. He was writing after the Leakey family's discovery of Zinjanthropus, when Darwin's idea that humans originated in Africa was actively being confirmed with hard scientific evidence. Coon wrote that three of the five races crossed the line to *Homo sapiens* (modern humans) outside of Africa. Today paleoanthropologists have evidence that all three human subspecies emerged and matured in Africa, and some accept that the original dispersal of *Homo sapiens* came from Africa around two hundred thousand years ago. Yet Coon concluded only a few decades ago, "If Africa was the cradle of mankind, it was only an undifferentiated kindergarten. Europe and Asia were *our* principal schools" (1962, 656; emphasis mine). Coon follows all of the racialist writers and nineteenth-century craniologists who drew a line between "white" and "black" Africa, with the "Negro line" just south of the Sahara (just where it is today), and not surprisingly Coon views the Congoid Pygmies and the Capoid Bushmen as the most primitive peoples of the continent.

According to Coon, the more recently emerged races, and therefore generally the more advanced from an evolutionary perspective, are the Mongoloid and Caucasoid races. Their relative advancement Coon determines, not by the then discredited craniology and measures of prognathism, but with "new" diagnostic anthropometric criteria including "facial flatness" and size of dentition. Mongoloids and Capoids have a more accentuated appearance of facial flatness, reminiscent of the apes and Australopithecines, while at the opposite extreme are the Caucasoids, whose beaklike faces are reminiscent of lower primates (Coon 1962, 364). Given that reduction in tooth and mandible size are general trends of human macroevolution and moves toward modern *Homo sapiens*, Coon hypothesizes that difference in the size of teeth is a significant racial

marker. His five races are divided by tooth size into microdont, mesodont, and megadont types, with—Guess what?—Australoids and Con-
goids having the largest, megadont, teeth; while Bushmen (Capoids) and
Mongoloids are mesodont; and only Caucasoids possess the highly
evolved small microdont teeth (Coon 1962, 354). Coon sees brain size as
the dividing line between *Homo erectus* and *Homo sapiens*, but the all-
important racial differences are most evident in tooth morphology and
degrees of facial flatness.

These ideas were written in 1962 and not 1862, revealing the persistence
of racial myths. Coon's work restated virtually every racial myth and kept
intact the basic Caucasoid-Mongoloid-Negroid/Australian hierarchy
with his scientific evidence. Coon continues the age-old warning about
race mixture when he asserts that "racial intermixture can upset the
genetic as well as the social equilibrium of a group" (1962, 661). As for
Caucasoid origins, he is not certain, but he places the mature Caucasoids
in southwest Asia and the Near East as the creators of the Neolithic food-
producing revolution and thus the founders of modern civilization. To
achieve this he includes among the Caucasoids all the "civilized" peoples
of the region, not only Europeans, but Middle Eastern whites from
Morocco to West Pakistan and most of Aryan India. Although Coon's 724-
page *The Origin of Races* has the heft and appearance of an important work
of science, it is warmed-over polygenism—perhaps its last hurrah.

Unlike Coon's effort to refine scientific racism, Ashley Montagu's 1942
*Man's Most Dangerous Myth* is an all-out assault on racism. His subtitle,
*The Fallacy of Race*, makes this work among the first in anthropology to
place the word "fallacy" in a book title and thus attempt to undo the
damage that had been done in the name of the science of race. The lack
of any biological value to the race concept, combined with the profound
racialist and racist bias applied to the study of race, makes a sufficient
case for Montagu to advocate an end to the use of "race" in scientific discourse, and its replacement with the term "ethnic group." In making his
argument against the race concept Montagu pronounces an end to the old
physical anthropology that focused on craniometry, cephalic index, and
facial angle as measurements of significant racial difference and its
replacement with the new biological anthropology, capable of studying
human variation without the use of race. Montagu asked anthropologists
in 1942 to acknowledge that they had played no small part in the creation
of the myth of race, which had assumed dangerous proportions. Moreover, he lamented the fact that very few antiracist voices were raised in
anthropology prior to Boas's and his own.

American anthropology responded positively to Montagu's advice,
especially after the horror of what Nazi racist ideology and practice had
wrought during the Second World War. Studies of "race" focused more

on exploding racial myths and an examination of the biological adaptation of human populations, often described as "clines" or "breeding populations." One of the "new" physical anthropologists, Frank Livingstone, declared in 1964, "There are no races, there are only clines" (quoted in Montagu 1942, 17).

What is notable is how unsuccessful anthropologists and biologists have been in eliminating the race concept, now more than fifty years after Montagu's call and the generally positive response from anthropologists. Likewise, "race" has not disappeared from the discourse of science, leading some anthropologists to comment on the dogged persistence of the race concept (Harrison 1995). That persistence may be a result of anthropology's and society's ambivalence about race and the consistent denial of the linkage of race with racism. Early physical anthropology actually contributed to a great deal of racial mythology; the field then retreated from the race concept without honestly confronting its own history and its part in the construction of race as wedded to racial hierarchies.

Loring Brace writes, in his foreword to the sixth edition of Montagu's antiracist classic, that *Man's Most Dangerous Myth* was so far ahead of its time in undermining the biological issue tied to race that both anthropology and society are just now beginning to catch up (Montagu 1942, 15). He also describes Ashley Montagu as a St. George who has come to help us slay the dragon of racism, first in the darkest hours of World War II and now again in our latest hour of need. It is indeed a sobering observation that so little has changed, and that Ashley Montagu has been a contemporary of both the neo-polygenist Carlton Coon in the 1960s and the authors of *The Bell Curve*, Herrnstein and Murray, in the 1990s.

## Antiracist Activism

Throughout the history of racial hierarchies and exclusion there have been forward-thinking, courageous activists who have stood firmly against racist laws and practices and who have placed their lives and fortunes in jeopardy in support of racial equality. In the last decades of his life Herbert Aptheker, well-known chronicler of American slave revolts and curator of the papers of W. E. B. DuBois, devoted time to the history of antiracism in the United States (1993). This is a rich and dense history, not a thin one. Aptheker's survey of American antiracism reveals several general patterns of white engagement: 1) antiracism is more common among lower classes; 2) antiracism is more common among white people who have had significant experiences with people of African origin; 3) antiracism appears to be more common among women than men (Aptheker 1993, xiv). Religiously based antiracist organizations—from the Quakers and Unitarians to liberal Baptists—are inspired by their theology to understand human equality and to practice it in various ways. Symbolic and real acts of antiracism characterize the life of Thaddeus Stevens, one of Pennsylvania's representatives in the House in Washington, who argued vigorously for the equal rights of newly emancipated slaves in 1865. "This is not a white man's government," he thundered; "that idea is political blasphemy." For twenty years, until his death in 1868, Stevens lived with a black woman, Lydia Hamilton Smith, always addressed as "Mrs. Smith," and as he was nearing death he made certain that his remains would not be buried in a segregated cemetery. He had these words carved on his tombstone:

> I repose in this quiet and secluded spot,
> Not from any natural preference for solitude
> But, finding other Cemeteries limited as to Race by Charter Rules,
> I have chosen this that I might illustrate in my death
> The principles which I advocated
> Through a long life.
> EQUALITY OF MAN BEFORE HIS CREATOR.
> (quoted in Aptheker 1993, 195)

The social and legal bans on interracial marriage (not sexual liaisons) were defied time and again from the times of nineteenth century abolitionism to the second Reconstruction that was the civil rights movement of the 1950s and 1960s. During abolitionist times and the Civil War white activists such as Wendell Phillips, Harriet Beecher Stowe, and Horace Greely flouted interracial intimacy conventions and advocated race mixing as "God's own method of crushing out the hatred of race and civilizing and elevating the world." Greely, founder of the *New York Tribune*, promoted his Ten Point Program favoring miscegenation, writing that "the solution of the Negro problem will not be reached in this country until the public opinion sanctions a union of the two races. As the Negro is here and should not be driven out, there should be no impediment to the absorption of one race into another." Scandalizing slave owners, he continued, "Legitimate unions between whites and blacks could not possibly have any worse effect than the illegitimate unions that have been going on for more than a century in the South."

Indeed, mixed-race children had become so common by 1850 that the government began to count "mulattoes" as a separate category in the national census. Fearing whiteness might be dissolved by such abolitionist advocacy and a southern demography where black slaves vastly outnumbered whites, southern states began to pass their anti-miscegenation laws preserving "racial purity."

The modern civil rights movement had many white heroines and heroes, as well as martyrs. The white and black Freedom Riders of the summer of 1963 boarded buses in Washington, DC, and rode into the Jim Crow South in an effort to integrate segregated bus stations. Along the way these young black and white students—among them John Williams, now U.S. representative from the District of Columbia—were harassed, beaten, and arrested for their principled stand. Despite the dangers and death threats they continued from Atlanta to Montgomery and Birmingham, setting an example for student activism that continued with the anti–Vietnam War student protests of the later 1960s and 1970s.

## REFERENCES

Aptheker, Herbert. 1993. *Anti-Racism in U.S. History: The First Two Hundred Years*. Westport, CT: Praeger.

Biddiss, Michael D. 1968. *Father of Racist Ideology: The Social and Political Thought of Count Gobineau*. New York: Weybright and Talley.

——. 1970. *Gobineau: Selected Political Writings*. London: Jonathan Cape.

Boas, Franz. 1906. "The Negro's Past." Commencement address at Atlanta University, May 31. Atlanta University Leaflet, no. 19. Repr. in *Race and Democratic Society*. New York: J. J. Augustin, 1945, 60–69.

——. 1911. *Changes in Bodily Form of Descendants of Immigrants* (final report). Washington, DC: Government Printing Office.

——. 1928. *Anthropology and Modern Life*. New York: Norton.

——. 1938. *The Mind of Primitive Man*. Rev. ed. New York: Macmillan.

——. 1945. *Race and Democratic Society*. New York: J. J. Augustin.

——. 1948. *Race, Language and Culture*. New York: Macmillan.

Boas, Franz, with Helene Boas. 1912. "The Head Forms of Italians as Influenced by Heredity and Environment." *American Anthropologist*, n.s., 15:338–39.

Broca, Paul. 1869. *Memoires d'Anthropologie*. Proceedings of the Paris Anthropological Society, vol. 3:506.

Brown, William Harvey. 1899. *On the South African Frontier: The Adventures and Observations of an American in Mashonaland and Matebeleland*. New York: Charles Scribner's Sons.

Chamberlain, H. S. 1899. *The Foundations of the Nineteenth Century*. Repr., New York: Lane, 1910.

Chase, Allan. 1980. *The Legacy of Malthus: The Social Costs of the New Scientific Racism*. New York: Knopf.

Coon, Carlton S. 1962. *The Origin of Races*. New York: Knopf.

Delany, Martin R. 1879. *Principia of Ethnology: The Origin of Races and Color*. Philadelphia: Harper and Brothers.

Domínguez, Virginia. 1994. *White by Definition: Social Classification in Creole Louisiana*. New Brunswick, NJ: Rutgers University Press.

DuBois, W. E. B. 1939. *Black Folk, Then and Now*. New York: H. Holt.

Firmin, Joseph Anténor. 1885. *The Equality of the Human Races: Positivist Anthropology*. Translated by Asselin Charles, introduced by Carolyn Fluehr-Lobban. Repr., New York: Garland, 2000.

Fouque, Charles. 1958. *Defense et Illustration de la Race Blanche: A la Memoir du Comte Gobineau*. Lyon.

Gallagher, Nancy L. 1999. *Breeding Better Vermonters: The Eugenics Project in the Green Mountain State*. Hanover, NH: University Press of New England.

Galton, Sir Francis. 1869. *Hereditary Genius*. London: Macmillan.

Gobineau, Arthur. 1853–1855. 1967. *Essai sur l'inégalité des Races Humaines*. 4 vols. Paris: Belfond.

———. 1856. *The Moral and Intellectual Diversity of Races*. Translated by A. Collins. Philadelphia: J. B. Lippincott.

Grant, Madison. 1916. *The Passing of the Great Race*. New York: Charles Scribner's Sons.

Harrison, Faye V. 1995. "The Persistent Power of 'Race' in the Cultural and Political Economy of Racism." *Annual Reviews of Anthropology* 24:47–74.

Herrnstein, Richard J., and Charles Murray. 1994. *The Bell Curve: Intelligence and Class Structure in American Life*. New York: Free Press.

Montagu, Ashley. 1942. *Man's Most Dangerous Myth: The Fallacy of Race*. 6th ed. Repr., Walnut Creek, CA: AltaMira, 1997.

*Providence Journal*. 2002. "For Georgia High School Students, Integrated Prom Will Be a First." April 21.

Ripley, Wiliam Z. 1899. *The Races of Europe*. In Chase 1980.

Sorokin, Pitirim. 1928. *Contemporary Sociological Theories*. New York: Harper and Brothers.

Stoddard, Lothrop. 1920. *The Rising Tide of Color into the Darkness: Nazi Germany Today*. New York: Duell, Sloan, and Pearce.

———. 1922. *The Revolt against Civilization: The Menace of the Under-man*. New York: Charles Scribner's Sons.

"Vermont Eugenics Project Unearthed." 1999. *Providence Sunday Journal*, August 8, A3.

Tylor, E. B. 1881. *Anthropology: An Introduction to the Study of Man and Civilization*. Repr., New York: D. Appleton, 1902.

Wattenberg, Ben. 1987. *The Birth Dearth*. New York: Pharos Books.

Williams, Vernon D. 1996. *Rethinking Race, Franz Boas and His Contemporaries*. Lexington: University of Kentucky Press.

# 5

# Race, Intelligence, and Mental Testing

## SO-CALLED RACE AND SO-CALLED INTELLIGENCE

N o dividing line between supposedly superior and inferior races has been more insidiously defined, or more cruelly refined, than the alleged linkage between race and intelligence. The relentless pursuit of the proof of inferiority of non-European peoples by European and American scholars represents a shameful chapter in the history of science, including anthropology. The arrogant assertion of European racial superiority, using nothing more than a self-proclaimed achievement of higher civilization, combined with a denial of any comparable accomplishment among non-Europeans, produced the single most powerful rationale for European expansion from 1492 onward. The subsequent centuries remained immune from criticism for the racist practices associated with the holocausts suffered by indigenous peoples in the New World, four centuries of capture and enslavement of Africans, and the colonization of the majority of the world's geography and peoples by European powers. The innate intellectual and cultural inferiority of "peoples of color" was so unassailable in the minds of Europeans that the more liberal among them spoke in terms of the "childlike" simplicity of the "backward races," while the less guilt ridden justified every atrocity in terms of events having little or no consequence in the grand scheme of civilization. It is rare that so much history can be explained by simple truths; however, Europeans' declaration of their own superior intelligence and civilization, proven with their own methods of science and historical analysis, provided the essential but false ideological justification for their unchallenged power and influence since 1492.

Much of European and American sociology and anthropology was built on the questions of race, intelligence, and the innate or acquired capacity for civilization. Many of the founders of French, British, and American anthropology were committed to the "scientific" study of racial difference, intelligence, and hierarchies of people. The creators of physical anthropology thought they were conducting science when they moved beyond mere phenotypic description of race to the measurement of skulls, facial features, long bones, and other physical features to analyze race. Many were enamored with the Darwinian revolutionary view of mankind and were quick to apply crude evolutionary schemes to race, particularly the relative nearness to or distance from apes and apelike characteristics. Such was the cause for the fascination with the measurement of difference, anthropometry, craniometry (the measure of physical features and the cranium), and a special measure of the facial angle—showing relative prognathism, or forward protrusion of the jaw, indicating a presumed closeness to ape physiognomy. The following is a review of this peculiar history.

## ANTHROPOMETRY, CRANIOMETRY AMOUNTING TO "SKELETOMANIA"

### Craniometry: Cranial Capacity, Facial Angle, Dolichocephaly, Brachycephaly

The cephalic index was invented by Paul Broca, a nineteenth-century French physical anthropologist who was a polygenist committed not only to the idea of separate origins of races but to a hierarchical view of human races. Firmin's response to European racializing of race in his 1885 work *De l'égalité des Races Humaines: Anthropologie Positive* (*The Equality of the Human Races: Positivist Anthropology*, 2000) is largely directed against the science of race constructed by Broca's craniometry, including the all-important cephalic index. The index was measured by calculating the breadth of the head above the ears expressed as a percentage of cranial length from the forehead to the base of the skull. Broca invented many of the instruments of the "science" of *craniometry*, including the craniograph, the goniometer (to measure facial angle), and the occipital goniometer (to measure angle of the back of the skull). Broca painstakingly took 180,000 measurements of the approximately 500 skulls in the Anthropology Society of Paris Museum in order to scientize his theories about race.

For Broca, a head with a *cephalic index* above eighty (assuming a length of one hundred) was classified as a *brachycephalic* head; when the number fell below seventy-five, a head was classified as *dolichocephalic*. Indexes falling between seventy-five and eighty were classed as mesocephalic. Some scientists became skeptical of craniometry when it was discovered that the shape of the skulls of Negroes and Scandinavians were similar enough to be classed together as dolichocephalic; it was apparent that something was wrong! (Haller 1971, 16). The basic formula for cephalic index held that northern European peoples were dolichocephalic, and that was the superior type; inferior types were characterized as brachyce-phalic, including Mongoloids from East Asia and Mongoloid-contacted groups such as eastern Europeans. Poles, Hungarians, Ukrainians, and other eastern Europeans were also scientifically categorized as "inferior brachycephalic" types by Nazi physical anthropologists using these same craniometric measurements seven decades later.

## Cranial Capacity and the Ranking of Race

The "science" of race progressively moved from the gross measurement of the skull and its exterior surface to the interior measurement of the brain, its gross weight, and cranial capacity. It was only logical that the next step should be to measure the difference in the capacity for intelligent thought among the various races; and the development of the intelligence test followed on these gross measurements of the brain.

Measurement of the brain cavity was the focus of anthropological studies by Samuel Morton in the United States, as well as Paul Broca, Paul Topinard, and J. J. Virey in France. Their technique was to pour anything from mustard seed to buckshot to water into human crania to measure their capacities in cubic centimeters. The assumption was that the size of the brain case was linked to the development of intellectual faculties, and that European brains were the largest, especially when compared with smaller, inferior African brains. A parallel relationship in the evolutionary stages of man—from savage, to barbarian, to civilized—was also theorized, with the conclusion that cranial capacity corresponded with the degree of civilization achieved. Thus, the European, with a cranial capacity of 100 cubic centimeters (cc), was at the top of the list, the apex of civilization; Mongols averaged 94 cc and American Indians 91 cc, approximating a midlevel barbarian stage; Negroes averaged 88 cc, South African Hottentots 86 cc, and Australian Aborigines 88 cc, occupying the lowest stage of savagery (Haller 1971, 18–19). Paul Topinard's nineteenth-century work comparing white and African brains has been cited by racist writers as recently as 1995 (Rushton); however, the American physical anthropologist C. Loring Brace examined the skulls that Topinard used in his study at the Musée de l'Homme in Paris and discovered that the Congolese and West African skulls from which his measurements were taken represented people 15 to 20 percent smaller in body size than the average European (Brace 1999). This story shows an important truth about the history of racism and science—if the facts do not support theories of racial inequality, just alter the study or change the facts. But it is important always to support your theory with facts and numerical data; that is what makes it appear scientific.

Samuel Morton's racist measurement of skulls and brains across a range of humanity (*Crania Americana*, 1839, and *Crania Aegyptica*, 1844). His 1849 "Observations on the Size of the Brain in Various Races and Families of Man" places northern European Teutonic brains in cubic inches at 92, with Chinese 82, and Hottentot and Australian tied for last place at 75 each (1849, 83). Morton went to great pains to demonstrate that Egyptian crania from classic Pharaonic times were Caucasian and not Negro, and that the allegedly more advanced, darker-skinned Hamites were the result of a positive admixture of lower African Negroes with more superior Asiatic elements.

So influential was craniometry and the myth of brain size as being linked to intelligence and civilization level that John Wesley, pioneering naturalist and founder of the geographical society that developed into the American Anthropological Association, and his fellow explorer and friendly rival William McGee both requested that after death their brains be removed, weighed, and compared by the Smithsonian Institution; the brains remain in the museum's "wet collection" (stored in formalin) today. More disturbing was the presence of the brain of the famous last Yaqui Indian, "Ishi," who was discovered and studied by anthropologist Alfred Kroeber at the University of California until Ishi died in 1916. Against Yaqui religious beliefs (well known to the anthropologists) Ishi was autopsied and his brain removed and given to physical anthropologist Aleš Hrdlička, a curator at the Smithsonian. After the Native American Graves Protection and Repatriation Act (NAGPRA) legalization of the return of American Indian remains from museums after 1990, two California tribes requested that Ishi's brain be returned for burial; it was finally repatriated in 1999, eighty-three years after its delivery to the museum (*Providence Journal* 1999).

One might think that the simplistic racialist generalization equating brain size with intelligence would have been left behind with the racist history of nineteenth-century Euro-American science. But in 1995 Canadian psychologist J. Philippe Rushton published *Race, Evolution, and Behavior*, in which he argues that Magnetic Resonance Imaging (MRI) comparisons of three different "races"—blacks, whites, and "Orientals"—shows that "Orientals" have the largest brains, averaging 1,364 cc, while whites come in a close second at 1,347 cc, and the average brain size of blacks—both Africans and African Americans—is 1,267 cc. That difference adds up to millions of brain cells—"Orientals" having 102 million more brain cells than whites, and whites having 480 million more brain cells than blacks—that allegedly account for historical and contemporary differences in racial performance. The only difference between Rushton's and Morton's craniometry is the rank order of "Orientals" over whites (Lieberman 2001). Blacks in 1995 remain where they were placed in 1839, at the bottom of the racial ladder. Rushton's assertions match well with the conclusions of another racialist and racist work that appeared a year earlier, *The Bell Curve* (Herrnstein and Murray 1994), in which the argument for "ethnic" ranking by intelligence has Asians in first place, with whites a close second, and blacks, as always, in last place.

### Facial Angle

Perhaps the most graphic portrayal of inferior types was provided with the invention of the facial angle, first suggested by Petrus Camper in the eighteenth century. A "horizontal line drawn through the lower part of the nose and the orifice of the ear" provided comparative data for the two extremes—an angle of less than 70 degrees described the orang or ape, while an angle of 100 degrees marked the perfect type, derived from ancient Greek sculpture; the "apelike" Negro fell toward the lower end of the scale (Haller 1971, 9). The revival by Camper of Blumenbach's argument for the ideal beauty of the Caucasian skull was welcomed in the nineteenth century; Camper added to it the idea that intelligence could be measured by the angle of prognathism.

Lambert A. J. Quetelet (1842) advanced theories about the facial angle and intelligence that became the basis of American Civil War anthropometric investigations. These showed a direct relationship between physical type, the standard of beauty as measured by the facial angle, and the proportion of intelligence, a measurement that favored the Caucasian. By 1860 the facial angle had become the most frequently used measure to explain the gradation of species from lower to higher, and the description of human types from inferior to superior. From the "apelike" Hottentot to the midrange "Chinaman" and Indian, to the near perfect Caucasian, the facial angle provided for Europeans and Americans yet another scientific proof of their superior intelligence and beauty.

The measure of the relative prognathism—protrusion or jutting forward of the jaw—especially of Negroes, pointed to a not-so-subtle closeness of Africans to apes. Prognathism as a measure of the degree of "primitiveness" was accepted anthropological science well into the mid-twentieth century. Because greater prognathism is found in all mammals except man, it followed that decreasing prognathism was a positive, progressive evolutionary trait. Negroes were viewed as invariable progna-

Figure 5.1.    Facial angle, measuring relative prognathism. From Robert
Wilson Shufeldt, *America's Greatest Problem: The Negro* (Philadelphia: F. A.
Davis Company, 1915).

thous; Mongoloids moderately so; and Caucasians only slightly so
(Kroeber 1948, 82).

## Anthropometry—"Skeletomania"

The term "skeletomania" was coined in 1878 by one of the first woman
anthropologists, if not the first—Clemence Royer of Paris, who is best
known for translating Darwin's *Origin of Species* into French. Skeletomania is an excellent way of describing the fanatic, inordinately intense
effort to measure human difference and have such measurements produce the desired result, that Europeans, especially allegedly pure ones
from noble, uncontaminated lineages, were physically superior to non-
Europeans. After measurement of the all-important crania, in which intelligence and civilization capacity rested, measurement of the long bones
(the ratio of arm and leg length) and the pelvis figured significantly in
developing hypotheses about lower and higher forms of humans and
their purported similarity to or distance from apes.

Comparisons of physical stature, of muscular strength, of sexual characteristics, and of longevity captured the imagination of nineteenth- and
twentieth-century racialist physical anthropologists. Dozens of other
measurements—the distance from the elbow to the fingertip, or between

the eyes, or between the nipples; the amount of perspiration; the thickness of the foot and heel; the length of the penis and size of female vulvae—all of these were added to make a "science" of anthropometry, each in its own way to measure racial difference of observable physical traits. Any physical trait could be racialized, and many were more imagined than real, such as the peculiar "odors" of different races or the types of oils secreted by the skin and glands of various races.

In the United States the Civil War period saw the greatest interest in the practical application of anthropometry. The question of the fitness of the Negro to serve in the Union Army after 1862 was a catalyst, as was the overall fitness of the federal army after a number of stunning Confederate victories. Eventually over 180,000 Negroes were inducted into the Union army, while some 15,900 examinations and anthropometric measures of troops were taken (Haller 1971, 26).

The racial categories by which the soldiers' measurements were tallied by the U.S. Sanitary Commission are of interest, as they show how the U.S. government classified races during the Civil War period. They included the following:

1) Whites
2) Full blacks
3) Mixed races
4) Indians

The report of the commission showed supposedly perceptible differences between Negroes from free states and those from slave states, and that mixed-race mulattoes were physiologically inferior to their original stocks. This scientific assertion made a point about the futility of trying to uplift the status of the Negro through racial mixture with whites. A comparison of the brain weights of 405 autopsied Negro and white soldiers of the Eleventh Massachusetts Volunteers showed significant differences by "Grade of [skin] Color" from full white to full black, with grades of 3/4, 1/2, 1/4, 1/8, 1/16 indicating the amount of white blood in a person. Brain size and weight generally decreased on this sliding color scale from white to black (Hunt 1869).

Having won its place in American science after the war, anthropometry continued as a respectable science within university and medical establishments, as it also formed the basis for the practice and teaching of physical anthropology for the first half of the twentieth century. Simplistic racialist anthropometry was challenged before World War II by progressive scholars such as Franz Boas (*Race, Language and Culture,* 1920) and Pitirim Sorokin (*Contemporary Sociological Theories,* 1928). Sorokin referred, for example, to the "myth of the superior dolichocephalic

Figure 5.2.   Civil War African American soldier.

hypothesis" (273). But even Boas, who was known for racial liberalism, did not abandon totally the purported link between the brain case and intelligence. It was only after the horrific revelations of the uses to which physical anthropology had been put during the racist eugenics program of the Nazis that anthropometry was finally abandoned as having anything to do with objective scientific inquiry.

## SKIN COLOR AND INTELLIGENCE

Following the myth of "long-headed" or dolichocephalic superiority was a relationship between light or dark skin color and intellectual ability. Light skin color and blondness, like dolichocephaly, were supposed to be correlated with energy, talent, and superior mental qualities (Sorokin 1928, 273). It was actually contended in the early twentieth century that the upper classes of the Aryan or Nordic race of Western Europe were more blond than the lower classes or common peoples (Lapouge 1909; Onslow 1920–1921). This statement of fair-blond superiority stimulated research to counter the racialist hypothesis whereby wealthy and poor children with relative blondness and fair skin color were measured.

Likewise, British "men of genius" (Sir Francis Galton's term) were found to be mainly of "medium" skin color, not very light skinned and not very dark, along a European scale of pigmentation. On a rather amusing note, the British royal family were rated as *not* at the top of the list (i.e., the "fairest of them all") but also of "medium" skin tone. Reading this made me think of American comedian Joan Rivers's comment after having met British Queen Elizabeth, describing her as the "whitest woman I ever met."

Fast-forward to the 1970s: renewed arguments about race and intelligence swirled around school integration in the United States and "controversial" programs such as Project Headstart and its ability to affect children who are "born dumb." Audrey Shuey in his 1966 *The Testing of Negro Intelligence* suggests studying "Negroes with different shadings of skin color" to see what differences in intelligence exist. He laments that more refined studies correlating intelligence and skin color have not been undertaken and that light-skinned Negroes have been lumped with darker-skinned Negroes.

During the same period an effort to link the blood factor Duffy-Fy, found only in whites, with the increased intelligence of lighter-skinned Negroes who might also have Duffy-Fy because of white ancestors played the same card of associating lighter skin color with higher intelligence.

## RACE AND THE MEASUREMENT
## OF INTELLIGENCE

Pioneer in the Racialization of Intelligence:
Sir Francis Galton (1822–1911), Originator of the
Bell Curve

The publication of Francis Galton's *Hereditary Genius* in 1869 represented a milestone in the history of racialist scholarship.[1] Like Gobineau's *Essai sur l'inégalité des Races Humaines* (1853–1855), *Hereditary Genius* is a classic of both racialist (using race as a major framework of analysis) and racist (asserting that there are higher and lower races) writing, for it not only sets forth a theory of racial difference, but introduces to science the idea of a bell curve around which group, hereditary human intelligence can be measured and interpreted. For Galton, human intelligence varies from the highest genius to the least intelligent beings along a typical bell curve of frequency distribution. Following Darwin's ideas about the biological evolution of species, Galton adds the social to the biological and sets forth a hierarchy of ranked races and classes. Individual differences are the result of two principle factors, environment and heredity, but of these two heredity is by far the more important. Galton adds to this his fear that the lower races and poorer classes were out-breeding the upper classes and higher races. Fearing a dysgenic trend of future genetic inferiority, he advocates eugenic programs that would limit the number of "defective," "inferior" races and classes. Thus Galton's ideas and name are linked to the origins of the eugenics societies (some of which called themselves "Galton societies"), and he is closely identified with what came to be called "social Darwinism," or the application of the idea of the survival of the fittest to races and nations.

What is remarkable in the current period is that Galton's work, which may be judged to be both racialist and racist, is still cited without criticism as laying the foundation for the testing movement and for developing statistical methods for the analysis of data on individual differences (Anastasi 1988, 7–8). As foolish as many of his ideas sound today, it would be a mistake to dismiss the legacy of Galton, for his name is still respected in scientific circles beyond psychology and educational testing. His pioneering role in the measurement of race and intelligence was recognized most recently in Herrnstein and Murray's *The Bell Curve* (1994), which salutes Galton's work by using his central idea as its title. Galton grades men on a scale of genius from A to G, with G (genius) being the highest grade. The greatest majority of humans are found in the "mediocre classes," the bulge in the bell curve, with only a small number of people of great ability and an equally small number of mental defectives. Thus the rarity of genius and the vast abundance of mediocrity are no accident, but due to natural, hereditary forces. It just so happens that "genius" is

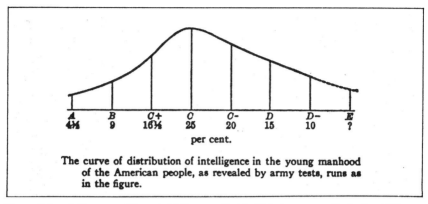

The curve of distribution of intelligence in the young manhood
of the American people, as revealed by army tests, runs as
in the figure.

Figure 5.3.   Bell curve of Francis Galton applied to U.S. Army recruits in the 1920s.

not found randomly among all humans, but is concentrated in the upper classes of northern Europeans. According to Galton, classical Greece and contemporary England possess the highest percentage of per capita geniuses of the first class, while the Negro race has failed to produce any man of genius in its whole history (1869, 325–37).

That it puts forward such nonsense as science should banish a book like *Hereditary Genius* to the wastebasket of history; however, this book was reprinted many times and was an inspiration to proponents of eugenics and social Darwinism well into the twentieth century. For Galton, genius clusters in families, and no matter how rich the social and cultural environments, they can never be sufficient to create a genius out of a mediocre man. If this is reminiscent of the question asked by Arthur Jensen in 1969—"How much can we boost IQ and scholastic achievement?"—in reference to poor and minority children in the Headstart program, it is because Galton's hereditary genius lies at the base of much of the literature that makes a false correlation between race, class, and intelligence.

## Intelligence Testing: IQ and Race

The first test of intelligence, the Binet and Simon Scale, was created in 1905 by Alfred Binet, who was given support by the French Ministry for Public Instruction to improve the condition of retarded children. The test was revised in France before it was adapted, in 1916, by L. M. Terman of Stanford University for use in the United States. It became known as the Stanford-Binet test, and for the first time the intelligence quotient (IQ) was used (Anastasi 1988, 10–11).

Intelligence testing has rested on two basic premises:

1) That intelligence can be measured objectively by tests yielding an intelligence quotient (IQ)
2) That IQ is largely inherited (from Galton forward it was asserted to be 80 percent hereditary, or more recently 60 percent, but always more important than environmental factors)

Since the beginning of intelligence testing, calculating and ranking differences by race has been a key feature of this enterprise. It remains so to this day, along with other measures of academic potential, such as the measure of Scholastic Aptitude Tests.

Galton invented the prototype of the intelligence test with his reaction time tests, which measured the rapidity of sensory responses of the eyes, ears, and brains of people to colors, sounds, and smells. When Galton's reaction time test was applied by R. Meade Bache to three groups by race—Caucasians, American Indians, and Negroes—the researcher found that Caucasians had the slowest reaction times and American Indians the fastest, with Negroes between the two. What did racialized science make of these findings? Of course, it concluded that rapid reaction time is inversely related to intelligence, so the slower Caucasians were actually smarter. Had the results been reversed—with Caucasians having the fastest response time—then the theory would have argued for a positive connection between intellectual development and reaction time.

The mental tests that succeeded Galton's reaction time tests were originally called the Stanford-Binet tests in the United States. The application of the French psychologist Alfred Binet's nonracialist interest in ability testing was a considerable alteration of his views. A rigorous scientist, Binet was unable to define or accurately measure what he called "general intelligence." By studying the abilities of individuals, including his two very different daughters, he differentiated two distinct learning styles, "objective" and "subjective." He developed tests to experiment with kinds of intelligence. His complex view of intelligence was more in tune with modern psychology; however, he died somewhat prematurely in 1911, before his view had prevailed. His tests were grossly oversimplified and made into the first standardized intelligence tests, which were then graded according to an intelligence quotient (IQ). "Mental age" was divided by a person's chronological age and multiplied by one hundred, with the net result being the intelligence quotient.

$$\frac{\text{mental age}}{\text{chronological age}} \times 100 = \text{Intelligence Quotient}$$

Before anyone knew what intelligence was—if it was a single measurable trait, or a complex combination of factors, as we now believe—a very scientific-looking formula came to be accepted as showing the innate intellectual capacity of an individual (Chase 1980, 232). This quickly translated into a deeply held cultural belief that intelligence is reducible to a single number above or below one hundred, signifying "above-average" or "below-average" intelligence. Countless individuals and parents have anguished about IQ test results and what their own or their children's inherited intellectual capabilities might be. Averages of group intelligence have been even more pernicious, as Negroes, immigrant populations, and today's non-English-speaking resident aliens are consistently evaluated as being "below-average" in intelligence.

Never permitted a neutral scientific arena, the Binet intelligence test were first adapted by the eugenicist-psychologist Henry Herbert Goddard for the screening of immigrants at Ellis Island. Using the Binet tests Goddard was able to "prove" that certain undesirable non-Anglo-Saxons—especially Jews, Hungarians, Poles, Russians, and Italians—were "mentally defective." These immigrants were usually third-class steerage passengers, and as a group they were found to have low, even moronic levels of intelligence. Goddard found that 83 percent of Jews were "feebleminded," a "hereditary" defect that they shared with 80 percent of Hungarians, 87 percent of Russians, and 79 percent of Italians. In a 1917 article, "Mental Tests and the Immigrant," Dr. Goddard writes:

> Assuming that they are morons, we have two practical questions: first, is it hereditary defect or; second, apparent defect due to deprivation? If the latter, as seems likely, little fear may be felt for the children. Even if the former, we may still question whether we cannot use moron laborers if we are wise enough to train them properly. (1917)

The tests of immigrants "proved" what eugenists had warned, that immigrants from southern and eastern Europe were inferior and that, along with dangerous mixing with black people, each had a potential dysgenic effect on the American populace. The mean intelligence test scores for immigrant army recruits showed a clear hierarchy of European peoples. The percentages of inferior test scores reported by Lothrop Stoddard (1922) are as follows:

1) England: 8.7 percent
2) Holland: 9.2 percent
3) Denmark: 13.3 percent
4) Scotland: 13.6 percent
5) Germany: 15.0 percent
6) Sweden: 19.4 percent
7) Canada: 19.5 percent
8) Belgium—24.3 percent

9) Norway: 25.6 percent
10) Austria: 37.5 percent
11) Ireland: 39.4 percent
12) Turkey: 42.0 percent
13) Greece: 43.6 percent
14) Russia: 60.4 percent
15) Italy: 63.4 percent

(summarized in Chase 1980, 260)

Today one needs only to reflect on these results to see how slowly stereotypes about ethnicity and mental ability pass away. Stoddard's graph of ability among whites, "colored," and officers in the army graded A through E had the vast majority (84 percent) of officers in the A and B range, while the vast majority of "colored" draftees (74 percent) were in the D and E range. Whites (i.e., ethnic immigrants) clustered in the C and D range, with 72 percent of draftees in this range. These tables and ranges, writes Stoddard, speak for themselves (1922, quoted in Chase 1980, 260).

What to do with the children of the immigrants who passed the screening and made it into the American "Promised Land?" It fell to Lewis Terman of Stanford University to revise the Binet test for group intelligence testing of school children. His revision of the Binet test in 1916 became known as the revised Stanford-Binet IQ test and added to the earlier test more cultural information that children acquired as members of families. Test results for the revised Stanford-Binet showed that native-born white children had an average IQ of 106.5, while, for example, the average IQ of children of Italian immigrants was 85, and the average native-born Negro child's IQ was 83.

It was the Stanford-Binet IQ test that I was administered in the 1950s, and it is still the Stanford-Binet test that is the basic test of intelligence for children today. Establishing a base class line for scoring on intelligence tests, Terman found that the children of higher-status professional classes had higher average intelligence and mental age than the children of the laboring classes. Terman was quick to point out that the higher scores of higher-class children were not due to an apparent greater importance of culture and home life. Terman claimed that their high scores were actually more attributable to heredity, and that class status depends more on nature and inherent ability than on environmental influence. This judgment of the effect of class and heredity on intelligence persists to this day among some as an uncritically accepted assumption.

It was an easy step to move from intelligence differences based on class, European ethnicity, and heredity to those based on racial difference. When Terman's associates tested Negro, Mexican, and Spanish-Indian children in California, the IQ tests revealed:

> Their dullness seems to be racial, or at least inherent in the family stocks from which they come. . . . The whole question of racial differences in mental traits will have to be taken up anew and by experimental methods. The writer [Terman] predicts that when this is done, there will be discovered enormously significant racial differences in general intelligence. . . . Children of this group should be segregated in special classes and be given instruction that is concrete and practical. They cannot master abstractions, but they can

often be made efficient workers, able to look out for themselves. There is no possibility at present of convincing society that they should not be allowed to reproduce, although from a eugenic point of view they constitute a grave problem because of their unusually prolific breeding. (Terman 1919)

In Terman's 1919 book *The Intelligence of School Children*, the basic program for the twentieth-century racialized view of intelligence is laid out, and its echoes are familiar to this day:

1) Race and intelligence are linked in predictable and ranked differences between groups.
2) Practical or vocational education is recommended for the inferior races.
3) The eugenic solution for reducing the number of mental defectives is proposed.

The first two points are recognizable in today's terms, with the popular idea that whites and Asians as groups are more intelligent than blacks, while nonacademic programs are promoted for the inferior groups. It is the last point that may not be so familiar to a contemporary audience. The popular science of IQ testing was quickly applied to the growing strength of the eugenics movement, and by the 1920s the IQ test was considered sufficient to detect the "feebleminded," as described in chapter 4. We have been so socialized as a culture to the idea of the scientific neutrality of IQ testing that when this history is revealed to students for the first time they are shocked and often leave class shaking their heads in disbelief. They have all been tested, few have direct knowledge of their IQs, and many have harbored anxieties over the years as to whether their IQ is in the "normal" range. While most of the compulsory sterilization laws passed in the United States were applied to the inmates of prisons, hospitals, and geriatric and mental institutions, the fact that the United States was so close to what eventually unfolded in Nazi Germany is a chilling thought.

The proeugenist intelligence testers were so certain of their science and so enamored of their methods that they performed IQ tests on the dead, "discovering" that Sir Francis Galton, the founder of the eugenics movement, scored an IQ of 200, at the high-genius level. His score was sixty-five points higher than that of his half-cousin the mere near-genius Charles Darwin, who shared some pretty good company with Beethoven and Leonardo da Vinci at IQs of 135. The determination of the IQs of the dead was just about as objective as those of the living, since school grades, writings, and the evaluations of their contemporaries all figured into these precise calculations of intelligence.

Although Charles Darwin was not knighted for his revolutionary theory of evolution, which shaped modern biology and anthropology, his aristocratic cousin Sir Francis Galton was knighted, proving him to be one of Britain's "hereditary geniuses." Another of Britain's knighted scholars, Sir Cyril Burt, was elevated in 1946 for his studies that "proved" white superiority. Burt, the founder of educational psychology in Great Britain, argued that his studies demonstrated racial differences in intelligence. In 1961 and 1976 professors D. D. Dorfman of the University of Iowa and Leon Kamin of Princeton University noted that several extremely improbable statistics in Burt's published reports indicated that his data were highly suspect and might even be fabricated. Dorfman proved beyond a doubt that Burt had fraudulently manufactured his findings by placing the frequency of IQ scores used in his studies as perfectly distributed points on a curve of normal distribution, a perfect bell curve. Burt's "normal" curve mirrored Britain's class structure, with lower-class persons having lower IQs and professional classes having the highest IQs. Further, the numbers he reported in two scientific journals were exactly the same, although thirty years separated the two surveys.

As the world's first school psychologist Burt had a powerful influence on the newly developing field of educational psychology, especially the idea of the normal curve of intelligence of school children. For Burt and most of modern educational psychology the most common IQ is 100, and an equal number of children have IQs above and below that number, hence the predictable bell curve. The bell curve also came to be associated with "standard deviation" from an expected norm and influenced the educational practice of "curving" grades, with a predicted fat middle C range and with the same number of As and Fs, Bs and Ds. Few educators would question the principle of curving exams, but when the practice is contextualized within the history of IQ testing, Sirs Galton and Burt, and the fabricated bell curves of abilities, some may give the practice a second consideration.

Dorfman's exposé of Burt revealed that Burt had probably manufactured IQ scores that were presented and discussed as if they had been generated by testing people. Burt invented collaborators and positively reviewed his own books under false names. Burt's allegedly fraudulent findings were later defended as careless mistakes or wishful thinking, not purposeful duplicity (Fletcher 1991; Joynson 1989).

### Army Intelligence Testing on a Mass Scale; Yerkes; Educational Testing Service

Robert M. Yerkes, a leading proponent of eugenics and president of the American Psychological Association, was drafted by Henry Herbert Goddard and Lewis Terman to prepare mental tests for the U.S. Army. Alpha and beta tests were prepared—for the literate, English-speaking recruits and nonliterate, non-English-speaking recruits, respectively. Nearly two million army recruits were asked questions like the following:

1) The Rhode Island Red is a kind of: horse/granite/cattle/fowl
2) Cristie Mathewson is a famous: writer/artist/baseball player/comedian
3) Crisco is a: patent medicine/disinfectant/tooth-paste/food product
4) Habeus Corpus is a term used in: medicine/law/theology/pedagogy
5) The number of a Kaffir's[2] legs is: two/four/six/eight
(adapted from Chase 1980, 245)[3]

For any draftee with an American grade school education the alpha test was easy; however, the majority of army draftees in 1920 were not native born, and the specific cultural information required to answer questions such as those above assured that foreign-born, nonnative speakers would perform poorly. The now famous finding that the majority of army draftees tested at a mental age of fourteen years or less dogged the army for years, but not the testers. Yerkes maintained the IQ tests were culture free and were scientific measures of "native" (i.e., genetic) intellectual ability. Not much has changed—intelligence tests were given in English to Spanish-speaking children in California, in the 1980s, and 75 percent were found to have below-average intelligence.

Had logic been the master of this episode, the absurdity of the tests' results would have given way to some common sense. When the mayor of Chicago was classified as a moron in 1915, and the vast majority of America's voting citizens were evaluated at a mental age of thirteen years or less, and the IQs of northern blacks turned out to be greater than those of southern whites, reason might have prevailed. However, the social policy premise behind the massive testing of native-born and immigrant populations was the fear of the degeneration of the American populace, and the movement gained strength to "stem the tide of immigration" that would surely result in further decline. This effort was led by Henry H. Laughlin, who in 1920 was appointed "expert eugenics agent" of the House Committee on Immigration and Naturalization and set about limiting the immigration of non-Nordic, eastern and southern European groups. What is startling to many Americans is the fever pitch that eugenics-dysgenics hysteria reached in the United States throughout the decade of the 1920s and into the Depression years. This reached into the highest levels of government, at which it was not so much the science that was of interest to policy makers but the cuts in spending on social programs directed to the poor and immigrants that could be justified in the name of science. Soon the Great Depression would make necessary massive government programs to bring about national economic recovery, which would not be accomplished until the military buildup and labor mobilization that accompanied America's participation in World War II. By that time the world could see the logical end of a eugenics program in the form of Hitler's "final solution" for the Jews of Europe and his selective reduction of "dysgenic" populations like the Poles, Hungarians, Ukrainians, Gypsies, homosexuals, and disabled persons. It was not until twenty million were dead in the wake of the twentieth-century's Second World War that the wisdom of a eugenics approach to weeding out society's racial, ethnic, and class undesirables was fundamentally questioned.

It may seem a great leap to go from apparently simple intelligence tests to the European Holocaust, but the links in the chain are evident. From the development of "objective" tests of mental ability—to the labeling of individuals and then groups as "morons" or "feebleminded"—to the assertion that such defects are genetic or hereditary—to the social policy of reducing or eliminating such "dysgenic" populations—there are known and demonstrable historical linkages. However, this pernicious history is concealed, and some effort is required to bring it into the light of day for our examination. Each time an IQ test is administered, especially to a child at risk of discrimination on account of race, ethnicity, class, or language ability in English, the history of the testing movement should be examined anew for the light it might shed on the outcome of the testing.

## Survival of the "Objective" IQ Test

What is perhaps most surprising is the ability of the IQ test to survive the postwar period, especially after the revelations of the racist misuse of science at the Nuremburg Trials. I have a clear recollection of being administered IQ tests in parochial school in Philadelphia in the 1950s in the fourth and seventh grades. The tests were unannounced and the results were considered classified information that was not shared with parents or students. The purpose of administering the tests and the uses to which the results were put was never explained. Fundamentally, except where the tests have been challenged, this has changed little today. A shroud of secrecy still surrounds the development and administration of IQ tests, partly as a matter of professional protection in educational psychology and a strict code of confidentiality. Over the years of teaching the race and racism class, I have repeatedly made formal requests for copies of IQ tests currently in use; the latest attempt was during the public discussion and debate of *The Bell Curve*. Despite my credentials as an anthropologist expressing an interest only to examine the tests, my requests have uniformly been denied. The reasons typically cited for the denial are: 1) The Stanford-Binet and Wechsler Scale tests are administered under the supervision of a qualified clinician. 2) To obtain such tests one has to show credentials and often sign a confidentiality contract. 3) Public access would surely diminish the value of the tests. Why does this secrecy surround intelligence tests when the Scholastic Aptitude Test, the Graduate Record Exam, the Law SAT, and other tests that determine entrance to educational and life opportunities are in the public domain, and when preparation for taking the tests is widespread?

Allan Chase draws the historical divide between the old and the new scientific racism as taking place during the Second World War. The ferocity of the American eugenics Nazi supporters was held at bay by the fact that "superior," Nordic Aryans were fighting and killing British, American, and other allied soldiers. Aryan supremacy lost its luster while America fought the good war against fascism and racism in Europe, even while its own troops were segregated by Jim Crow institutions. American behavioral science responded with a more nuanced approach to intelligence testing. Testing in the 1930s was already showing that moving children with their families from rural, southern towns to urban areas resulted in higher average IQ scores, and that the immigration from southern cities to northern ones showed comparable increases. Intelligence seemed to have a cultural and class component, and the liberal critics of the tests seized on the environmental argument for intellectual ability. Even Lewis Terman admitted belatedly, in 1947, that income level and the numbers of books in a child's home played a significant role in the student's IQ scores.

It became essential then to find some new tools to reassert the genetic basis of intelligence and the scientific validity of the tests that measure this. The U.S. armed forces came to the rescue again. The postwar Armed Forces Qualification Test, as the revised "basic military mental test" screening for officers and "drones," showed two basic types: white men with superior minds and weak bodies, and black men with superior bodies and weak minds (Chase 1980, 433). It was this new round of mass ability testing that provided the "scientific" bases for arguing the genetic difference in intelligence between blacks and whites for those who opposed the legal desegregation of schools in the wake of the landmark *Brown v. Board of Education of Topeka Kansas* in 1954. It was also this baseline of "new" data that was used by Jensen, William Shockley, and Shuey in their 1969 anti–civil rights assault on Project Headstart and other government antipoverty programs aimed at "inner city" (i.e., minority and poor) children.

The most concerted effort to create a science of racially based intelligence surrounded the end of legal segregation of public schools in 1954, on what racial conservatives dubbed "Black Monday," when the *Brown v.*

*Board of Education* decision was handed down. Audrey Shuey's 1958 study of the old and new army intelligence tests and civilian mental test scores between the wars reached the conclusion that "native [genetic] differences between Negroes and whites is determined by intelligence tests" (Shuey 1966). This time mainstream psychology and anthropology stood formally against the revival of scientific racism, with each professional association passing resolutions against any scientific basis for continued segregation.

The Coleman study of 650,000 black and white American school children commissioned by Congress in 1964, ten years after *Brown v. Board of Education*. It showed little progress in narrowing the gap between black and white IQ scores and academic achievement. Of course, American schools were still largely segregated in 1964, as they remain today, although the report did highlight the importance of class and other "environmental" factors for both whites and blacks, more so than any previous large-scale study. What has rarely been questioned in this biological approach to the measurement of racial differences in intelligence is the highly biologically mixed nature of the populations of "blacks" and "whites" who are tested and measured as though they were discrete and pure groups capable of displaying distinctive differences.

The use of IQ and other standardized tests of intelligence became politicized in the early 1970s, with some cities, including Chicago, New York, and Los Angeles, limiting or banning them. The National Education Association in 1972 called for a moratorium on all standardized intelligence testing.

IQ tests are the primary means by which a determination is made of whether or not the death penalty will be sought by certain states for a person accused of a capital offense. In Arizona, for example, an IQ test score of 75 or above meant that a prosecutor could seek the death penalty. Eighteen states had prohibited executing the mentally retarded before June 2002, when the U.S. Supreme Court barred the use of the death penalty for retarded persons in all states. The problem with this ban is that the Supreme Court issued no guidelines to the thirty-eight states that have the death penalty as to how mental retardation is to be legally determined. Given past experience it is almost certain that the states will use IQ tests to establish arbitrary numerical boundaries between candidates who do and do not qualify for the death penalty (Greenhouse 2002).

Efforts to address the obvious cultural issues signaled by the different scores of blacks and whites have resulted in the creation of so-called culture-free or culture-fair tests. The "Black IQ Test" was devised by Dr. Alvin Pouissant of Harvard University mainly as a consciousness-raising device, and the Black Intelligence Test of Cultural Homogeneity (aka the BITCH Test!) has also appeared; however, neither has been widely administered nor taken very seriously. Other culture-fair tests have been designed around the analysis of shapes, or the cross-cultural use of the Draw-a-Man test—the latter widely regarded as a failure due to the range of cultural variation in the learned ability to draw, including the religious disapproval of representational art in some Muslim cultures. The few regularly used culture-fair tests, such as the Goodenough-Harris Drawing Test, or the Raven's Progressive Matrices, are still mainly used as supplements to the Stanford-Binet or Wechsler Scale measures of intelligence (Anastasi 1988, 309).

Many in the fields of education and testing have moved beyond the IQ test score and embraced the theory of "multiple intelligences" developed by Howard Gardner (1993). Gardner hypothesizes seven distinct intelligences—linguistic, musical, logical-mathematical, spatial, bodily-kinesthetic, and two types of personal-emotional intelligence. A balanced assessment of the ability of a child or adult is achieved by consideration of multiple variables, not a single variable, such as a test score.

Most students and their teachers will recognize the legacy of the power of the bell curve model in the "curving" of exam grades by teachers, with equal numbers of As and Fs and the largest number of average C grades in the middle.

### The College Board and the SATs

For more than a century the United States has invested in the belief that tests measure intelligence and that testing before college entrance is the main predictor of achievement and likely success or failure in higher education. As American higher education began to develop beyond the religious- and European-style classics-based education in the mid-1800s, it was nonetheless very class conscious. The idea of mass public higher education was a revolutionary idea when Russell Conwell of Temple University delivered his famous "acres of diamonds" speech in Philadelphia in 1884; in it, he spoke of the moral and intellectual potential of the common man.

The need for adequate preparation for college coupled with the growing demand for quality control led to a voluntary, nongovernmental response in the formation of the College Board in 1900 and the creation of the College Board Entrance Examination. A few prestigious colleges had already established preparatory schools to ensure that their academic standards would be met by their entrants—Hotchkiss for Yale University, Lawrenceville Academy for Princeton. The more practical approach was to develop an examination for the screening of qualified candidates, a test that came to be known as the College Board Entrance Examination. The original close relationship between secondary and postsecondary schools became even closer with the College Board exam. The major secondary school subject areas and appropriate syllabi were defined by the content of the exam, and secondary schools responded with greater standardization of high school curricula. The College Board Entrance Examinations were created by committees of examiners from private schools and consisted of three hours of essay questions. The exams were graded externally by private school teachers who did not know the students; the exams were held to a single standard of excellence or competence, rather than being compared. The last essay-based College Board exam was in 1941.

The College Board Scholastic Aptitude Test (SAT) was first administered in 1926 using an approach to "aptitude" very much akin to that of IQ test scoring; that is, the number resulting from the test indicates above-average, average, or below-average performance. SAT scores were expressed on a normative scale in terms of the mean and standard deviation of the candidates taking the test on a given day. The average SAT score was usually 500 on the mathematics and English language sections. As students from widely varying public school backgrounds began to seek opportunities in higher education an objective, non-essay-based SAT was developed to assess their readiness. The Educational Testing Service was established in 1948 to administer and operate the SAT.

Professor Carl Brigham of Princeton founded the Educational Testing Service of Princeton. A disciple of the racist French scholar Georges de Lapouge, who accepted the intellectual superiority of the Nordic race, Brigham was a eugenicist who advocated immigration restriction because of immigration's "clear effect on the decline of American intelligence"; he also "disproved" the myth of Jewish higher intelligence (Chase 1980). He was deeply involved with the development of the College Board and was the principal architect of the SAT. He admitted frankly in 1933 that the College Board's main function was "institutional control" through the enforcement of standards (Powell 1997, 13). On the liberal side, the SAT was championed by Harvard College's president Henry Conant, who saw it as a way to locate intelligent men from the lower classes to join Harvard's aristocratic elite.

This standardized test, with its questionable origins in racialized intelligence testing, developed into the main tool of assessing college readiness for all American high school students. A preliminary version of the SAT—the PSAT, designed for earlier administration, usually in the tenth grade—has been in general use since 1959. Another nationwide assessment instrument, the American College Testing Program (ACT) was developed in 1959 to assess readiness for public state universities, and has grown to be an acceptable alternative to the SAT.

The importance of the SAT in determining college admission has been declining since criticism of the test as having certain gender, racial, ethnic, and class biases has been raised. Increasingly colleges and universities—public and private, highly competitive and less so—have been rethinking the reliance on SAT scores as the strongest predictor of success in their institutions. They have also been moved to reduce the importance of the SAT score as some are troubled by state legislatures in California (in 1996) and Texas (in 1997), for example, that have banned the use of affirmative action in college admissions, and test scores consistently show performance gaps that disadvantage African Americans and Latinos (Gose and Selingo 2001, A-14). High school grade point average as well as other objective and subjective measures have been raised as important predictors of success in college, along with the numbers generated by the SAT. Questioning of the ability of the SAT to measure ability for persons whose first language is Spanish resulted in the creation of a Spanish-language version of the test, Prueba de Aptitud Académica (PAA), in 1973, designed primarily for use in Puerto Rico. Jane Mercer, a sociologist critical of the cultural biases of IQ tests, developed the System of Multicultural Pluralistic Assessment (SOMPA).

Criticism has stemmed from the consistent, relatively poorer performance on the SATs of blacks and Hispanics, especially those whose combined scores may average in the 800 range rather than the white average of about 1,000. The gap between the performance of whites and that of blacks and Hispanics barely budged between 1990 and 2000. Criticism has been the strongest from groups historically most affected by racial and cultural discrimination, primarily African American advocates, who charge that the test itself is biased, favoring white, middle-class information and values, a natural by-product of the makeup of the Princeton-based organization that continues to run the College Board. Moreover, these groups argue that expensive SAT preparatory classes, such as Princeton Review and Kaplan Educational Centers, are out of the reach of poor and minority students. Organizations such as the NAACP have sharply criticized the SAT for its bias, making it politically controversial. Colleges and universities are under pressure to consider SAT scores as only one variable in college admission, while, increasingly, higher education institutions do not request SAT scores, or indicate that the submission of scores is optional. Fair Test of Cambridge, Massachusetts,[4] offers information to the pubic that is critical of the conception and use of standardized tests and offers alternatives to parents and children who seek to bypass the powerful role that the SAT plays in determining college admission and the futures of young people. Fair Test annually publishes a list of colleges and universities that have eliminated or reduced SAT and ACT requirements for admission (in 1999 there were 281). Bowing to this pressure in 2002 the 175,000-student University of California dropped the SAT requirement for admission, which prompted the College Board to make a larger move toward revamping the SAT, promising to make it less biased by race and gender.

The SAT is a major business, producing $251 million in revenue from the 2.2 million high school students who take the test each year. The cultural bias of the SAT is suggested by the fact that students in the 1960s did better on the test—especially the verbal section—than today's students do. The NAACP has recommended reduction of the importance of SAT scores in college admissions. In response to these criticisms, in 2002 the SAT undertook reforms including a new writing test, addition of higher-level math problems, and elimination of the famous analogy word identifications. Predictable criticism came from *The Bell Curve*'s Charles Murray, who argued that the SAT was becoming too content based, linked to what is being taught in schools and therefore less of an aptitude test (2002). Without referring to the test's history of racial difference in "aptitude," he argued that black and Latino students in inner cities will be those most negatively affected by the changes, which will no longer measure their "raw cognitive processing power." Given the history this chapter has reviewed, we can conclude that the best that might be expected is that continuing further harm to racial minorities might be ameliorated by the reforms.

### Jensen's Criticism of Project Headstart as a Watershed Moment in the 1960s

Arthur Jensen's question posed in the *Harvard Educational Review*, "How much can we boost IQ and scholastic achievement?" predicts the failure of the Headstart Program to make a difference in IQ achievement of the poor and minority preschoolers served by the program. Jensen fundamentally questions that IQ differences are the result of environmental differences or the cultural bias of the tests themselves. Jensen defines IQ as that which can be measured by tests of higher mental processes, as all of his racialist predecessors contended, and he assesses the degree to which intelligence is influenced by genetic factors, arguing that the "heritability" of intelligence is high. He claims that racial and social class differences are not sufficiently explained by environmental differences but are attributed to genetic differences. Also, like his predecessors Francis Galton and a host of eugenicists and social Darwinists, Jensen questions the efficacy of educational programs intended to boost mental performance and IQ. The influence of such programs is small or insignificant, suggesting that "extreme environmental deprivation can keep a child from performing up to his genetic potential, but an enriched educational program cannot push the child above that potential" (Jensen 1969, 2). Finally, he declares the failure of compensatory education (like Headstart), concluding that such efforts are misdirected and in effect a waste of taxpayer money.

Reading through Jensen's article one finds a familiar cast of characters whose work is cited favorably, such as Lothrop Stoddard, Sir Cyril Burt (ten cited works by this man whose work on class and intelligence in the United Kingdom was found to be fraudulent), and Sir Francis Galton himself (1969, 22). Jensen even recycles Galton's "g" factor to ensure quality education for the truly gifted. Bell curves liberally illustrate Jensen's points about the normalcy of inherited intelligence differences.

On the matter of racial difference in intelligence Jensen builds on the older idea of the inferiority of Negroes as a group and distinguishes between individuals and populations. Allowing for the existence of some talented members of certain racial groups, Jensen nonetheless observes an evident disproportionate representation of particular racial groups at the lower (Negroes in the United States) and upper (white U.S. schoolchildren) ends of the bell curve. Negro intelligence is measured by at least one standard deviation (fifteen IQ points) below average white intelligence. Jensen asserts that equal ability between Negro and white children has never been proved (1969, 82–83). As races differ by phenotype, Jensen argues, they surely differ by abilities, which are part of their genetic programming, the result of population inbreeding. Finally Jensen argues that the specter of "possible dysgenic trends" is real if the less intelligent breed too much, leading to the possible decline of the national IQ. Jensen sounds the dysgenic alarm, citing evidence that children from large families, such as poor white and lower-class Negro families, have lower IQs. Diversity of mental ability, he argues, is a fact of nature, and uniform, equal education for all should fundamentally be questioned.

After the publication of Jensen's article, headlines all over the country read, "IQ, God-given or Man-made?"—"Intelligence, Is There a Racial Difference?"—"Born Dumb"—"Can Negroes Learn the Way Whites Do?" Jensen's article was summarized and approved several times in the *Congressional Record*. Arthur Jensen was a professor of educational psychology; William Shockley, a Noble laureate who invented the transistor, spent the rest of his life advocating eugenical sterilization of low IQ individuals; and Dr. Audrey Shuey is best known for *The Testing of Negro Intelligence* (1966).

## Galton Revival with Publication of *The Bell Curve* (1994)

*The Bell Curve* is subtitled *Intelligence and Class Structure in American Life* and is really about race and ethnicity, intelligence and success in America. With a very deep bow to Sir Francis Galton, the book's authors,

Richard J. Herrnstein and Charles Murray, follow the well-trod path
begun by Galton in *Hereditary Genius* in 1869; they use measures of intelligence to grade performance in society by race and class. They accept the
basic heriditarian belief that humans differ in intelligence, that this difference can be measured by tests, that IQ tests are the best measure of intelligence, and that IQ is 40 to 80 percent inherited as a cognitive trait.

Using IQ tests primarily, as well as other measures of intelligence, the
authors compare the performance of black and white men and women,
judged on a scale from "very bright" to "very dull," in terms of their performance in jobs, welfare, crime and imprisonment, and educational and
professional advancement. Herrnstein and Murray attempt to show that
"dull" whites are not a part of the "cognitive elite" and that their numbers are greater on the welfare rolls and their children perform less well
in school and cause more problems. They judge "ethnic differences" in
intelligence, comparing the intelligence of Asians, blacks, and whites.

Breaking with decades of similar racially interpreted measured intelligence, they conclude that East Asians (e.g., Chinese and Japanese),
whether in the United States or in Asia, score higher on intelligence and
achievement tests than do white Americans (the authors don't include
European statistics, although they are available). The difference in overall
cognitive ability between races is measured at as much as ten points on
average (Herrnstein and Murray 1994, 269). This new finding suggests
that the usual descending order of intelligence by race of Caucasian, Mongolian, Negro was adjusted in the late twentieth century, with Asians surpassing white Americans for the first time. Herrnstein and Murray
answer yes to the question they pose to the reader, "Do Asians have
higher IQs than whites?" The authors do not explain this remarkable biological advance for a trait they hold to be 40 to 80 percent inherited.

European American and African American group scores are compared,
with the historical fifteen-point difference between blacks and whites said
to have narrowed by perhaps three points; this is said to be more a result
of the shrinking numbers of very low scores than a dramatic increase in
high scores. The authors answer no to the question of whether the differences in test scores are due to differences in socioeconomic status or the
cultural bias of the tests, the main sources of criticism (Herrnstein and
Murray 1994, 286–95). In a section treating Latino-white differences in
intelligence and achievement, they show that Latinos with high cognitive
ability have as good a chance of success as whites with similar ability.
Herrnstein and Murray fail to distinguish light- and dark-skinned Latinos
and discuss the subject of Latino performance without mentioning language. Their overall conclusion, in the tradition of Galton, Stoddard, Burt,
and Jensen, is that genetic differences in intelligence are ignored at our
peril as a nation, that "dysgenic pressures in America" have been evident

since the early 1990s with declining SAT scores, and that social-behavioral problems in society may well be linked to the lower cognitive abilities of certain "ethnic" groups. The authors also conclude that reliable, inexpensive methods of raising IQs among low-scoring populations are not feasible. Not surprisingly, they are critical of affirmative action programs in education and employment and are advocates of meritocracy. Equality is an ideal that cannot be matched by social or cognitive realities. It is important to point out that *The Bell Curve* study was prepared in part for the American Enterprise Institute as advisory to politicians desiring to have academic justification for conservative social policy recommendations. *The Bell Curve* was a commercial success despite its controversial conclusions, and it was much discussed in the electronic and printed media. In short, it was taken seriously.

## RACE, INTELLIGENCE, AND ACHIEVEMENT TESTING

Beyond the issue of race, ethnicity, and achievement testing in the United States is the fact that the performance of Americans as a national group is well below the scores of comparable developed nations and high-achieving Asian countries. These results are puzzling in light of the fact that the United States dominates the realm of technological innovation and scientific research. And American performance is low despite the fact that IQ scores are supposedly rising in the United States and around the globe, causing frustration to educators and policy makers trying to make a predictable science out of such testing. The so-called Flynn effect, described as "the rising curve," is an increase of about three points per decade over the past sixty years in the overall average of IQ scores in nations for which data exist. The political scientist James R. Flynn himself disavows this effect, saying that is implausible that humans are progressively getting smarter and are on the whole more intelligent than their grandparents' generation. Despite such powerful data suggesting the lack of objectivity in testing over time so far, few have suggested eliminating the tests as any kind of reliable guide.

The idea that intelligence is reducible to a single number measured by a test administered on a given day in a person's life has been seriously challenged. This idea has generally been eclipsed by a more complex view of intelligence as a multifaceted quality or set of abilities. A triple model of intelligence has been developed by psychologist Robert Sternberg, suggesting that there are three kinds of intelligence: analytic (what IQ tests measure), creative, and practical. Kenyan children, for example, score very high on the practical ability to identify medicinal herbs and score lower on IQ tests, while a reverse of this finding characterizes U.S. children's performance, thus underscoring the important variable of culture. In his best-seller *Emotional Intelligence* Daniel Goleman argues that empathy, self-control, persistence, and other skills involving personal affect are more important in life than IQ scores (Johnson 1998).

Neither the SAT nor the IQ test is a predictor of competence and success in many domains of real life. Both are so tainted historically by racialism and racism as to make them permanently suspect as reliable indicators of ability, achievement, or the potential contributions an individual may make in the world.

In 2003, under intensifying criticism of the racial gaps in SAT scores, the College Board attempted reform yet again with a parallel test that measures "other than cognitive ability," including creative ability, intended to close the gap between whites and racial minorities. The future of the SAT test is a race between those who seek to amend it so that the racial gap is closed and those who seek to eliminate it as the sole basis for the determination of college admission.

## SUMMARY

Mental testing has not been objective in theory or practice since its beginnings in the nineteenth century. Racial, ethnic, and class bias permeate its history, along with an anti-immigrant sentiment. Moreover, the "objective" measure of racial ability and intelligence has been linked to eugenical theories and practice that have resulted in social policies advocating the reduction or elimination of dysgenic elements—the lowest racial, ethnic, and class segments of society. These ideas have flourished and been implemented at times in England, the United States, and Germany.

The history of intelligence testing is closely tied to achievement testing and is tainted by this association. The consistently lower performance of racial minorities in the United States, especially African Americans and Hispanics, can be explained only by: 1) their innately inferior abilities; 2) the racial and class bias of the tests themselves; 3) the failure of the public schools; or 4) racism and social-class inequality affecting income, neighborhoods, and schools. The last factor is certainly the most compelling, yet it is often the least addressed. Democratic ideals in American education tend toward rejection of the first, second, and fourth explanations, so the focus on "fixing" these scores has been on the improvement of the public schools that minorities attend. However, concerted efforts from parents and educators to eliminate the testing have been gaining ground (Hilliard 1995). Understanding the history of mental testing and its various applications informs this important debate about intelligence, race, opportunity, and success in democratic societies.

## NOTES

1. The highly respected work by Allan Chase *The Legacy of Malthus* (1980) argues persuasively that Malthus is the founding father of scientific racism. His *Essay on the Principle of Population* (1798) is based on a fear of overpopulation from the poor outproducing the rich. It argues against any special measures that might ameliorate poverty and result in the survival and reproduction of the poor. However, since race is more implicit in Malthus's writing, I defer to the more explicit evocation of race by Gobineau and Galton. The section titled "Race and the Measurement of Intelligence" relies heavily on Chase's comprehensive research on the subject.

2. "Kaffir" is a racist term employed by South Africans for Africans that is derived from Arabic and means "heathen" or "unbeliever."

3. Correct answers: (1) fowl, (2) baseball player, (3) food product, (4) law, (5) two.

4. FairTest, of the National Center for Fair and Open Testing (342 Broadway, Cambridge, MA 02139), is an advocacy organization working to end the misuses of standardized tests.

## REFERENCES

Anastasi, Anne. 1988. *Psychological Testing*. 6th ed. New York: Macmillan.

Boas, Franz. 1920. *Race, Language, and Culture*. New York: Macmillan.

Brace, C. Loring. 1999. "Beware Bigot Brigade." Letter to *Anthropology Newsletter*, March, 2.

Chase, Allan. 1980. *The Legacy of Malthus: The Social Costs of the New Scientific Racism*. New York: Knopf.

Firmin, Anténor. 1885. *The Equality of the Human Races: Positivist Anthropology*. Translated by Asselin Charles and introduced by Carolyn Fluehr-Lobban. New York: Garland, 2000.

Fletcher, R. 1991. *Science, Ideology, and the Media*. New Brunswick, NJ: Transaction.

Fluehr-Lobban, Carolyn. 1994. "Race and Objectivity in IQ Tests." *Providence Journal*, November 6, A20.

Galton, Francis. 1869. *Hereditary Genius*. London: Macmillan.

Gardner, Howard. 1993. *Multiple Intelligences: The Theory in Practice*. New York: Basic Books.

Gobineau, Arthur. 1853–1855. *Essai sur l'inégalité des Races Humaines*. 4 vols. Repr., Paris: Belfond, 1967.

Goddard, Henry Herbert. 1917. "Mental Tests and the Immigrant." *Journal of Delinquency* 2, no. 5 (September), quoted in Chase, *Legacy of Malthus*, 233–34.

Gose, Ben, and Jeffrey Selingo. 2001. "The SAT's Greatest Test." *Chronicle of Higher Education,* October 26, A10–15.

Greenhouse, Linda. 2002. "Citing 'National Consensus' Justices Bar Death Penalty for Retarded Defendants." *New York Times,* June 21, A1, A14.

Haller, John S. 1971. *Outcasts from Evolution: Scientific Attitudes of Racial Inferiority, 1859–1900.* New York: McGraw-Hill.

Herrnstein, Richard J., and Charles Murray. 1994. *The Bell Curve: Intelligence and Class Structure in American Life.* New York: Free Press.

Hilliard, A. G. 1995. "Either a Paradigm Shift or No Mental Measurement." *Psychological Discourse* 26, no. 10:6–20.

Hunt, Sanford B. 1869. "The Negro as a Soldier." *Anthropological Review* 7:42–52.

Jensen, Arthur R. 1969. "How Much Can We Boost IQ and Scholastic Achievement?" *Harvard Educational Review* 31, no. 1:1–123.

Johnson, George. 1998. "Tests Show Nobody's Smart about Intelligence." *New York Times,* "Week in Review" section, March 1, 1, 16.

Joynson, R. B. 1989. *The Burt Affair.* New York: Routledge.

Kroeber, A. L. 1948. *Anthropology: Biology and Race.* New York: Harcourt, Brace and World.

Lapouge, G. V. de. 1909. *Race et milieu social: Essai d'anthropo-sociologie.* Paris: Rivière.

Lemann, Nicholas. 1999. *The Big Test: The Secret History of the American Meritocracy.* New York: Farrar, Straus and Giroux.

Lieberman, Leonard. 2001. "How 'Caucasoids' Got Such Big Crania and Why They Shrank." *Current Anthropology* 42, no. 1:69–95.

Morton, Samuel. 1839. *Crania Americana.* Philadelphia: J. Penington.

———. 1844. *Crania Aegyptica; or, Observations on Egyptian Ethnography, Derived from Anatomy, History and the Monuments.* Philadelphia: Transactions American Philosophical Society, 9.

———. 1849. "Observations on the Size of the Brain in Various Races and Families of Man." Philadelphia: Proceedings of the National Academy of Science.

Murray, Charles. 2002. "SAT Reform Fails the Needy." Editorial, *Wall Street Journal,* July 13.

*On Campus.* 2002. "College Board Will Revamp the SAT." Vol. 21, no. 8 (May–June): 2.

Onslow, H. 1920–1921. "Fair and Dark." *Eugenics Review* 7:212–17.

Powell, Arthur G. 1997. "Student Incentives and the College Board System." *American Educator* 21, no. 3 (Fall): 11–17.

*Providence Journal.* 1999. "Brain Collection Proves Embarrassing for Museum," May 30.

Quetelet, Lambert A. Jacques. 1842. *A Treatise on Man and the Development of his Faculties.* Translated from the French by R. Know and T. Smibedrt. Edinburgh: Chambers.

Rushton, J. Philippe. 1995. *Race, Evolution, and Behavior.* Special abridged ed. repr., Somerset, NJ: Transaction, 1999.

Shuey, Audrey. 1966. *The Testing of Negro Intelligence.* 2nd ed. New York: Social Science Press.

Sorokin, Pitirim. 1928. *Contemporary Sociological Theories*. New York: Harper and Brothers.

Stoddard, Lothrop. 1922. *The Revolt against Civilization: The Menace of the Under-Man*. New York: Charles Scribner's Sons.

Terman, Lewis M. 1916. *The Measurement of Intelligence: An Explanation of and a Complete Guide for the Use of the Stanford Revision, an Extension of the Binet-Simon Intelligence Scale*. Boston: Houghton Mifflin.

———. 1919. *The Intelligence of School Children: How Children Differ in Ability, the Use of Mental Tests in School Grading, and the Proper Education of Exceptional Children*. Boston: Houghton Mifflin.

# 6

# Whiteness and White Privilege
# in the United States

The discovery of personal Whiteness among the world's peoples is a
very modern thing—a 19th and 20th century matter indeed.

—W. E. B. Du Bois, "The Souls of White Folks"

Whiteness in America is normative, and for the present time whites
are still the numerical majority. Whiteness has been historically
defined as not being black, or brown, or Asian, and is associated with
"being American." Whites have also been historically positioned in a
place of dominance. Without its racial others whiteness cannot exist.
Moreover, whiteness is "at the vortex" of America's race problem (Lopez
2000, 632), although it is not recognized as such.

Whiteness is a benefit conveyed at birth without being earned. It carries
a positive identity without negative racial stereotyping—that of being a
good neighbor or citizen without having to prove oneself. There are
numerous examples of nonwhites in the United States being thought of
as less American or as "others," such as the treatment of Japanese Americans in World War II as aliens, or the concept of Chinese Americans living
in American Chinatowns being exotic. Until recent times America was
represented abroad as a white country. The concept of a multicultural and
multiracial America is a recent creation. The demographics of race in
America are changing rapidly and dramatically, with predictions that by
2050, or before, whites in the United States will no longer be a numerical
majority.

Since being white is the norm, whiteness is invisible to whites. Since
whiteness is invisible, the privileges that are conveyed by it are also invisible, unrecognized, and unacknowledged. An important part of this chap-

ter is an examination of white privilege and its acknowledgment with a sense of accountability, which is key to an improvement of the discourse on race in America and to the construction of a racially equitable society.

## THE SOCIAL CONSTRUCTION OF WHITENESS

Like all else regarding race, whiteness is socially constructed. Theoretical awareness and the analysis of whiteness is part of a broader postcolonial discourse that began in the decades after the Second World War and the waves of African and Asian independence; this discourse focused on anticolonialism and antiracism as global phenomena. Whiteness in America has been historically constructed along a black-white binary, as "not being black." The American one-drop rule—that one drop of African blood renders a person "black"—did not permit the identification of a mixed-race middle group, like the Creole populations of the Caribbean or so-called mulattoes, although phenotypic differences among "blacks" and "whites" are evidence of extensive racial mixing. The logical extension of the one-drop rule to blacks—that a drop of European blood conveys whiteness—has never been an acceptable option in the United States, although the ideal of "whitening" is normative in the Caribbean and much of Latin America. The American one-drop rule has been in one direction only—to darken, not to lighten—in marked contrast to America's closest neighbors in the Western hemisphere.

The black-white binary has blunted racial discourse in America, forcing individuals to identify as one or the other. Simplistic black-white opposition has resulted in confusion and even alienation among lighter- and darker-skinned members of the same family. American literature and folklore are replete with cases of "passing" as white and disguising African heritage in an effort to achieve the benefits of white identity. In the landmark Supreme Court case in 1896 *Plessey v. Ferguson*, which erected the "separate but equal" doctrine, Plessey argued that because he appeared white he should be able to ride in the white section of the New Orleans streetcar. The Supreme Court disagreed and reaffirmed the one-drop rule, thus making legal segregated facilities and institutions nationwide, and especially the Jim Crow segregation that became infamous in the South. The civil rights movement began as an effort to overturn Jim Crow and legal segregation.

European immigrants—even those who were racially despised in their own lands, such as the Irish in the United Kingdom or the Jews in Eastern Europe, quickly learned the advantages of being white in America. Recent studies of how the Irish and Jews became white have aided in a critical reflection about this history. In early American history poor indentured whites nonetheless were beneficiaries of being white and were able to achieve class mobility, while being black in America was correlated with slavery and a state of permanent black inferiority.

A problem is that "whiteness" has been defined by racially conscious whites. Black, American Indian, or other constructions of whiteness would look quite different (hooks 1991). Moreover, if whiteness is a part of historic decolonization after the Second World War, then conscious whites and persons of color should be on the lookout for the new forms that racism will take as the United States engages in its own era of empire and neocolonization.

## INVENTING WHITE PRIVILEGE

Because of the normative construction of whiteness, whites have the privilege of not viewing the world through a "race filter," and as a privileged group they define the social norm. This allows whites to ignore their own race, or to dismiss it as a significant factor in their successes or failures. Privilege permits numerous advantages for whites at the expense of America's racial others, including the option to speak out or remain silent regarding their own privilege and the oppression of others (Wildman and Davis 2000). Without recognition of privilege and the oppression to which it is tied, there is little hope of progress being made toward racial equity. Whiteness has been embraced by both historical European elites and newer immigrants who assimilate or "pass" as white as a normative and invisible identity of "being American." A significant and perhaps unique American characteristic of whiteness is its lack of a class consciousness. Rich and poor whites are still white. The phrase "white trash" can be used by some whites to wound other whites, but this insult is intended to suggest poverty rather than race, with "trailer park" often being a part of the message. This is the result of the black-white binary, which is driven by race without being class sensitive.

Today poor and disadvantaged whites still benefit from white privilege, and no matter how desperate their economic situation, they still may be grateful that they were not born black. In *Worked to the Bone* (2001) Pem Davidson Buck argues that from as early as 1720 in Virginia white privilege was invented to prevent rebellion among poor landless whites. White privilege was intended to prevent them from allying with enslaved African laborers, with whom they had a natural alliance in their economic oppression by elites. Many poor white settlers in America of the 1700s were landless, as many as 40 percent of all whites. Those whites who were in debt, illegitimate or orphaned, or homeless as well as landless were subject to being bought and sold and indentured, and some were referred to as "slaves" (Smedley 1993, 105). The problem of rebellion against the elites of the colonies was initially solved by extending credit, in return for which landless whites deferred to and supported the rich in a quasi-feudal system of relations. But America was not a feudal society, and poor whites rebelled.

Before 1670 all free men, African and European, had the vote, but, fearful of the majority who were "poor, indebted, discontented and armed," the Virginia legislature took away the voting rights of landless men. In what came to be known as Bacon's Rebellion, poor, landless men—regardless of race—rose up against the elites to force land redistribution and regain the vote. In these early days of the settlement of America, as troublesome as fighting Indians to take possession of their lands was the problem of elites gaining legitimacy and controlling the growing underclass as wealthy landowning families were consolidating their growing power and control. Periods of indenture were extended as a stopgap measure, but as more indentured men gained their freedom they demanded land. Enslavement of these Europeans would have cut off the flow of new immigrants to the colonies. The solution was to divide the unfree laborers of African and European descent.

Intermarriage of white women with Africans or Indians was the first thing to be punished and then banned by the end of the 1600s. Indenture with the possibility of eventual freedom was the privilege of whites, while slavery was defined as black. Control of white women's reproduction was essential to the separation of races, with children acquiring the status of their mothers and not their fathers; this freed propertied white men from responsibility to their children born to indentured or slave mothers. Built into the increasing separation of races and exploitation of blacks and whites was the use of force and coercive measures that penalized not only intermarriage, but socializing between the races and other equitable treatment of the races. Torture and terror awaited those who broke the increasingly rigid racial code of behavior that was established by the early 1700s.

White privileges were established, and multiple privileges encouraged whites to identify with the big landowners and slave owners as fellow "whites"; whites were also aware that those elites controlling the economic, political, and judicial protected the benefits of being white. The early privileges afforded poorer whites were material and social:

a) Whites alone could bear arms and possess the right of self-defense.
b) Whites but not Africans had to be given freedom at the end of their indenture.
c) White servants could own livestock; Africans could not.

d) Whites were given the right to discipline (whip) blacks, even those they did not own.
e) White men were given the right to control "their" women, while enslaved blacks were denied the right to a family at all.
f) Whites were given lighter tasks as servants; white women were given the right to substitute black labor for their own. (Buck 2001, 26–27)

As the colonies developed from east to west, privilege in status was supplemented with the offer of land to whites as an incentive for the role they were to play in Indian removal and African subordination. These whites became in effect a buffer class between the richer elites and the American Indians, Africans, and poor, landless whites whose exploitation was in need of control. But the majority of whites remained land poor or landless, and they resented the wealth and position of the land-grabbing aristocrats. The privileges afforded them were not sufficient. At the next stage the richer elites staved off rebellion by poorer whites by offering them the vote, thus granting them the illusion of a stake in government.

Thus, long before American independence, European and African laborers were divided by race, and their solidarity was broken, with the effect that the elites could guarantee a steady flow of controllable, slave African labor that would not ally with an only slightly better off group of controlled European labor (Buck 2001, 26). White privilege was invented to drive a wedge between African and European laborers. Thus, the oppression of one group is organically tied to the privilege of the other.

The history of America after independence is better known. In critical history courses students are taught that the birth of the republic empowered propertied white males and excluded all women, enslaved persons, and Indians. The southern plantation economy was dependent on slave labor for its wealth and immense profitability. The Civil War determined that the industrial North would prevail against the agrarian South. Reconstruction of the United States was anything but, and legal segregation in the South—Jim Crow, with is separation of the races in virtually all spheres of life—and de facto segregation in the North fixed the American racial paradigm for the century that passed from the end of the Civil War in 1865 to the civil rights legislation of 1964. In the post–civil rights period improved equality in law has not been matched by full equality in society, and the legacies of slavery and race remain profound in America. And the white privilege so intimately tied to the denial of black and Indian rights is unacknowledged and unexamined.

Another, less well-known American case involves the youngest state, Hawaii, and its late nineteenth-century demographic change after the suppression of indigenous royal rule. Portuguese immigrants were originally considered brutish; however, when the U.S. government wanted to increase "white" representation on the islands, the Portuguese became white. They quickly came to be considered civilized and white, according to one document, because they used soap.

In 1835 and 1840 Alexis de Tocqueville published the two volumes of *Democracy in America*, pointing out the fundamental and unresolved contradiction in the United States whereby whites enjoy full freedom at the expense of blacks. His words are relevant to this day.

It is a telling anthropological point that two of the most important classics on American race relations directed toward the responsibility of

---

## Alexis de Tocqueville on the Races in America in the 1830s

- The most formidable of all the ills that threaten the future of the Union arises from the presence of a Black population upon its territory. The Whites and Blacks are placed in a situation of two foreign communities. These two races are fastened to each other without intermingling; and they are unable to separate entirely or combine.
- The Europeans chose their slaves from a race differing from their own, which many of them considered as inferior to the other races of mankind. You might set the Negro free, but you cannot make him otherwise than an alien to those of European origin.
- White Americans first violated every right of humanity in their treatment of the Negro. But with his liberty, he will acquire a degree of instruction that will enable him to appreciate his misfortunes and to discern a remedy for them.
- If the Negroes are to be raised to the level of freedom, they will soon revolt at being deprived of almost all of their civil rights. And as they cannot become the equals of the Whites, they will speedily show themselves as enemies.

If I were called upon to predict the future, I should say that the abolition of slavery will, in common course of things, increase the repugnance of the White population for the Blacks. The danger of a conflict between the White and the Black inhabitants perpetually haunts the imagination of the Americans, like a painful dream (quoted in Hacker 1992, 216).

whites in the resolution of the "race problem" have been written by non-Americans, Tocqueville and Gunnar Myrdal. A century after Tocqueville's prophecy, Myrdal, a Swedish scholar, published in 1944 *An American Dilemma: The Negro Problem and Modern Democracy*, in which he argues that race in America is like caste in India, and that black people in America cannot escape their birth.


## WHO IS WHITE?


The determination of who is "white" in America has been driven by biological models of race as much as the determination of who is black, or who is Indian. The logical extension of the one-drop rule to blacks—that a drop of European blood conveys whiteness—has never been an acceptable option in the United States. The American one-drop rule is a simple, albeit nonscientific, way of determining "blackness." Since whiteness has been defined and constructed in terms of "not being black" a white-nonwhite racial construction is familiar even today. The value of possessing white identity is self-evident in a society that separates and devalues blackness or darker hues of humanity. Rigid rules backed by laws and courts had to be instituted to clarify and delineate the lines of separation in the black-white binary. The state of Louisiana offers a case in point.

As discussed in chapter 2 in 1970 a Louisiana statute made one-thirty-second "Negro blood" the dividing line between white and black. This interpretation actually reformed the wording "any trace" of Negro blood—the one-drop rule—to a numerical fraction, one-thirty-second, or one great-, great-, great-grandparent. Since America did not allow racial construction "in the middle," as other New World societies did, it never legally recognized its Creole populations. Creoles in Louisiana are white, as well as brown and black, and their ambiguous identity mirrors America's racial formation since the end of slavery.

In *White by Definition: Social Classification in Creole Louisiana*, by Virginia Domínguez (1994), describes a living Creole population—black, brown, and white—as a recognized group of people of mixed ancestry descended from enslaved Africans and French or Spanish colonial ancestors. Some Creoles of predominantly white ancestry became "Cajuns" and "crossed over" to become one of the definitive white groups of Louisiana. Documented by city records in 1805, about 25 percent of New Orleans "white" households were made up of a white male and a woman of color (Domínguez 1994, 198). While Cajuns became white, many other Creoles passed over into non-Creole black communities, mainly outside of the city. The clear racial rule was that Creoles admitting African ancestry held lower status, while demonstrable European ancestry raised economic and social status.

The phenomenon of "passing" is still a sensitive but lively subject in New Orleans and elsewhere in Louisiana. As when the colored of South Africa occasionally passed for white, doing so in Louisiana meant moving away, denying Creole ancestry, and living in segregated communities as white. White Creoles are reported to obsess about racial purity (Domínguez 1994, 203), and when ancestry is brought up only the white ancestors are named. Some mixed-race Louisianans self-identify as Indian and deny any Creole or African heritage.

The preservation of whiteness and the rigid racial lines separating blacks and whites were backed by the U.S. Supreme Court. Antimiscegenation laws, prohibiting interracial marriage, were not made unconstitutional until 1967 (*Loving v. Brace*). Until 1973 in North Carolina, 1967 in Maryland, 1978 in Tennessee, and 1969 in Texas intermarriage between whites and "persons of Negro blood to the third generation" was prohibited. Florida, Mississippi, Missouri, and South Carolina prohibited marriage between whites and persons of more than one-eighth Negro blood. Alabama, Arkansas, Georgia, and Virginia prohibited marriage between whites and Negroes, mulattoes, or persons with any ascertainable trace of Negro blood (Domínguez 1994, 269–70). Alabama was the last to repeal its statute, in 2000. Similar statutes existed in California from 1880, adding a prohibition of marriage between whites and Mongolians as well as Negroes or mulattoes. It was not until 1959 that these provisions were deleted, and after 1961 marriage licenses in the state were not to include any identification of race or color (Domínguez 1994, 271).

Southern Jim Crow segregation and antimiscegenation laws have cast racism in America as a southern problem, while northern liberals remain in denial that they or their communities have a problem with race. But the closeness of life between whites and blacks in the South makes it a region where racial transformation has greater potential, and in the decades following the civil rights era, progress in the South has been dramatic, creating in effect a "new South" for blacks and whites.

The story of Louisiana white Creoles reveals the importance of the preservation of whiteness in America. White Creoles who can pass do so; they abjure menial or manual labor; if poor they invoke white ancestry as a source of prestige; they create clubs that restrict membership; they found chapters of national genealogical societies in New Orleans that support their claims to aristocracy (Domínguez 1994, 236); and they reaffirm this identity every Mardi Gras with exclusivist "krewes" that parade and ride in lavish floats. White hierarchies are affirmed by influential krewes, and racial endogamy (marriage within race) is aided by the continuing popularity of segregated "debutante balls."

## WHITE SUPREMACY AND RACIST TERRORISM

Innocence of being involved with the Ku Klux Klan (KKK) is an often-used defensive response by whites in proclaiming that they are not racist. Public dissociation from the KKK, America's oldest terrorist organization, is employed as proof that a white person is free of racial bias. Confronting America's racist history is a part of the national dialogue of "truth and reconciliation" that may eventually lead to racial healing. Of course, like the debate over reparations for slavery, many such conversations are non-starters due to a fundamental denial of the country's racial history and polarization along racial lines. One of the most difficult and painful chapters of American history to confront is that of white lynching of black people.

Following Reconstruction, from the 1870s to the late 1940s, thousands of black men and women were brutally tortured and murdered, especially in the South. Beyond the brutal images is a historical and sociological story subject to analysis. W. Fitzhugh Brundage's study *Lynching in the New South: Georgia and Virginia, 1880–1930* (1993) compares lynching in two southern states with differentiated histories. Georgia was more violent and brutal than Virginia, with a total of 460 lynching cases (19 of which were of whites), while Virginia witnessed a total of 86 lynching in the same period (16 of which were of whites). Virginia managed its post-Reconstruction maintenance of the status quo of black-white relations with a minimum of racist violence, while Georgia exhibited a long and continuous history of racist mob violence.

Brundage's methodology reached beyond the national press coverage of these lynching cases into the local communities; he visited these communities and read the dominant white press and local black press coverage of the events. Lynching was not invented in America, but was probably brought to its shores from Ireland; however, its racist expression in this country is unique. Before Reconstruction and its aftermath lynching was a part of a much larger mob violence that regulated illegal activities, such as moonshining, vagrancy, and alleged white rapists. The revival or reinvention of lynching as "whitecapping" or KKK "night riding" is the most recognized form, yet it was not universally approved among southern whites. In fact Klan actions deeply divided whites as they vied with one another for economic control of the "new South."

White vigilante posses were comprised of neighbors, relatives, or witnesses to an alleged crime; the swiftness of their summary justice differentiated posses from private or terrorist mobs, as they were usually organized spontaneously immediately after the discovery of a crime. Most victims were executed within a few days of their alleged offense. Unlike private terrorist mobs that divided white opinion, posses enjoyed a high degree of popular white support for their swift "justice" in aveng-ing assaults on whites. Mass mobs, of from sixty to four thousand indi-viduals, often including women and children as witnesses, were the most dramatic expression of communal white violence against blacks. They were reserved for victims accused of the alleged crimes of rape, attempted rape, and murder. As such they displayed greater brutality and degrada-tion than simple illegal executions. These mobs displayed considerable organization and planning, needed to overcome jailers and storm jails.

Brundage sees the ritualized nature of this specifically southern racial violence as heavy with symbolism. Hangings often took place at the site of the alleged crime or in black neighborhoods; victims were given the opportunity to confess and pray; the victim was then hung or shot; and custom demanded that all members of the group or mob partake in the murder or mutilation of the victim by stabbing or firing into the corpse. This grisly, final element in the ritual explains why corpses were riddled with hundreds of ammunition rounds or knife wounds. Culminating the ritual, signs were hung on the corpse explaining the "justified" cause of the lynching, with warnings to others who might have offended the southern white "code of honor." That the bodies of victims were fre-quently left hanging or on public display for hours or even days after the lynching gives evidence of the minimally passive, and often active com-pliance of local white authorities. So terrorized was the local black popu-lation that some families or neighbors were fearful of retrieving bodies for burial, especially after lynchings by mass mobs, or of reporting the gruesome detail in the local black press.

The ideology of white supremacy and defense of white "honor" that underlay the perpetuation of this extreme of racial violence was coupled with the pervasive belief in black criminality, an idea that has hardly van-ished from the American scene. A clear hierarchy emerged in the degree of white supremacist "justice" that was meted out for alleged offenses by blacks. Minor transgressions, such as "wild talk" or "uppity talk" graded into alleged sexual crimes against white women and ended with the worst offense, alleged murder of whites, especially white women or law officers. Lynching not only performed the crucial task of reinforcing white supremacy, but it also reinforced white patriarchy in its defense of the honor of white women. This may help to explain why white women and children were present at and participated at lynchings.

Brundage's study dispels more than one myth; besides showing that most lynching was not carried out by Klansmen, he shows that while sex-ual issues and race mixing were often elements in justifying these mur-ders, sexual crimes were not the defining feature of lynching. The definitive character of lynching was the maintenance of the post–civil war status quo and the insurance that white superiority and black inferiority were preserved.

This point is clearly and definitively made in an analysis of the "geography" of lynching in both Georgia and Virginia. It is clear that the vast preponderance of lynching in Georgia took place in the economically unreconstructed cotton belt counties of central and south Georgia, with the northern Piedmont and south coastal areas accounting for only 32 of the total 490 Georgia cases of lynching. Whites clinging to "king cotton" and struggling to maintain plantation relations were confronting violently blacks who struggled to redraw the social and economic boundaries. Whites replaced slavery with sharecropping, which allowed them control of the production and marketing of crops without loss of their authority; where the old order was disturbed by "wild-talking" Negroes—black men who dared attempt normal social interaction with white women or confronted white authority in numerous other ways— racist violence, terror, and lynching were the preferred tools of repression. Overwhelmingly, white southerners either acquiesced silently or supported mob violence until the first decades of the twentieth century. Their silence in the face of brutal criminal acts that enforced an extralegal racist "justice" demonstrates the degree to which they recognized the value of their white privilege.

Lynching in Virginia was different and dispels the myth that the number of lynching cases is proportional to the number and density of the black population. Georgia and Virginia had comparable percentages of black and white populations but had vastly different experiences regarding lynching in numbers and in kind. White Virginians turned away from the plantation-sharecropping model and moved on to a more "modern" model of the use of casual day labor, while they also diversified their economy; thus they were able to maintain racial boundaries without the mob violence that reigned in Georgia. Lynching peaked in the 1890s as the old order passed, and with the new employment of blacks and whites in the mines and mills a surprising degree of racial harmony prevailed. The antilynching, antilawlessness crusades began earlier in Virginia, culminating in an antilynching law in 1928 that sought not so much racial justice or enlightenment as the restoration of social order.

Antilynching movements in Georgia were sporadic and largely unsuccessful, and by 1910 lynching was still accepted, while black survival was a crowning achievement. The gradual economic development of Georgia, with increasing urbanization and industrialization in the early decades of the twentieth century, marked the turning of the tide. With the birth of organized black resistance, such as the NAACP, and the growth of a white middle class with some enlightenment attempting interracial organization, such as the Committee on Interracial Cooperation in Atlanta, a new

Figure 6.1.   Whites pose for picture after lynching of an African American man,
Marietta, Cobb County, Georgia, ca. 1920s. Courtesy of the Georgia Department of
Archives and History.

social order emerged that cleaned up the shameful, lawless business of lynching. Lynching evolved into new forms of state-backed racial violence and white justice whereby the ritual of the courtroom replaced the ritual of mob violence.

Lynching is a diagnostic feature of American racism that, when interpreted in light of vested interests in whiteness, can be seen as a necessary tool of the continued dominance of whites and oppression of emancipated blacks after the Civil War. People who view pictures of lynchings may focus not on the black victims but on the faces of the proud and belligerent whites; looking at such pictures is an excellent method of getting whites to talk about their history of dominance and privilege. Where, one might ask, were the good white folks—the preachers, the teachers, businesspeople, and civic leaders—whom morality and justice would have called to name the names of the perpetrators and to raise a call for bringing them to justice? The white faces in lynching pictures, when closely examined, hold up an unflattering image of whiteness, not of whites, as an ideology of self-righteous vigilantism intent on the preservation of its dominance and of black subordination.

## HOW THE IRISH AND THE
## JEWS "BECAME" WHITE

"Becoming white" is now a recognized feature of American immigrant history. The Irish were viewed as a reviled ethnic, racial, class, and religious group by the ruling and dominant English in their homeland. As immigrants to America in the era of the Civil War and the post-Reconstruction period, they vied with blacks, especially in the teeming cities of the growing industrial North. English aristocratic prejudice was inherited by the most successful rich elites of the United States, who were from the British Isles but not from Ireland. That the Irish were Catholic added to this prejudice. The new Irish immigrants were placed in a competitive position with indigenous blacks and other new immigrants and were racially cast as inferior, so they needed a route to becoming American that neutralized or recast the racial issue.

Irish racial and intellectual inferiority was compared to that of Negroes. In Ireland under English Protestant rule Catholic Irish were the victims of discrimination that most would recognize as racial. The average English worker looked down on the Irish in the same way that poor whites in the American South looked down on African Americans (Ignatiev 2004, 606). In the early years of their immigration Irish lived in conditions of poverty in urban tenements that were held to be places of crime and drunkenness. One "solution" proposed for dealing with the "Negro problem" was to hire an Irishman to kill a Negro and hang him for the offense! Faced with two choices, of either allying with newly emancipated blacks or becoming in effect white and American, the Irish chose the latter. Irish entertainers enthusiastically took up the minstrel tradition, mocking blacks and making buffoons of them, as proof of their not being black.

By gaining the right to vote while free Negroes were losing it in the post-Reconstruction period; by supporting the Democratic Party (not the party of Lincoln, the Republicans, but the party of the slaveholders); and by competing against free blacks for jobs, the Irish were admitted to the privileges of whiteness (Ignatiev 2004, 606). As proof of loyalty to their adopted country the Irish gravitated to the newly formed police and fire departments of the mid- to late nineteenth century, eventually dominating in their ranks. They formed some of the first trade unions as Irish associations that later excluded blacks from membership. They were drawn to the largely white Democratic Party—as the Republican "Party of Lincoln" was the preference of emancipated blacks well into the twentieth century—and entered mainstream American politics, becoming some of its most colorful practitioners.

As an important parallel to the Irish story of assimilation to whiteness in America, Karen Brodkin Sacks has written "How the Jews Became White Folks" (Sacks 1994, 78–102; Brodkin 1998). Jews were reviled and discriminated against in communities throughout eastern Europe and Czarist Russia. They were segregated in European cities where the term "ghetto" was first applied to their separate communities rather than to American black or Hispanic urban communities. Jews were cast as conniving businesspeople, stereotyped with Semitic features, and degraded as the killers of Christ; Jews were also blamed for the great plague that killed millions of Europeans in the Middle Ages.

This anti-Semitism inherited from European prejudice was prevalent in America prior to World War II, whether in higher education, the professions, or in arguments by advocates of scientific racism. Eastern European Jews were less intelligent according to standardized IQ tests administered to immigrants at Ellis Island and in public schools. Exclusion of Jews from Ivy League schools and from private clubs was commonplace and unchallenged. In the American South some of the few examples of interracial association and alliance were between African Americans and Jews.

The aftermath of the Second World War began the transformation of Jewish identity and mobility, as Jewish people flocked to college, opened small businesses, and moved to the newly developed suburbs of the great cities of the North. According to Sacks, their transformation was from "Euro-ethnics" into whites through this new middle-class status and suburban cultural assimilation. Slow to recognize changing racial identity, as late as 1987 the U.S. Supreme Court ruled that Jews and Arabs could sue for discrimination because they are not white.

Although anti-Semitism fell from fashion after World War II, personal revelations of the anti-Semitism of president Nixon and the first George Bush reveal its retention among the American "blue blood" elite, who kept other American Euro-ethnics, especially others of eastern European heritage, out as well. (The term "blue blood," meaning "aristocratic," probably is derived from the visible blue veins of fair-skinned elites.)

The postwar GI Bill of Rights was probably the most massive affirmative action project in U.S. history. A college degree was no longer an upper-class privilege, as eight million white GIs took advantage of the program. White workingmen left the assembly line to become professional doctors and lawyers; this workforce was replaced by Latinas and African American women in the 1950s and 1960s, and by immigrant women after 1970 (Sacks 1994, 64). As racial quotas in medical schools fell, Jewish enrollment skyrocketed—in Boston figures jumped from 1 percent to 16 percent in pre- and postwar numbers of doctors. Racist violence against blacks occurred not only in the South but in Philadelphia and Chicago as well, as a way to demobilize their labor, mobilized during the war. African American GIs were almost completely shut out from the benefits of the GI Bill as they flooded into northern cities where black segregation was fully enforced, as it had been when they served in segregated armed service units during the war.

Suburbanization, symbolized by Levittown outside of New York City, was hugely aided by cheap Federal Housing Authority loans, and blacks were closed out once again, creating "lily white" suburbs that remain mostly segregated to this day. Jews, backed up by myth that they "pulled themselves up by their bootstraps" as they became professionals, technicians, salesmen, and managers, were in fact becoming white. Meanwhile, according to Sacks, the government offered African Americans "the cement boots of segregation, redlining, urban renewal, and discrimination" (1994, 97).

Whiteness, like all else with race in America, is dynamic. The contemporary changing face of whiteness includes certain lighter-skinned Latinos as the next candidates for becoming white, such as Cuban Americans, especially as their power and influence has been linked to American foreign policy toward Castro's Cuba. The Japanese were elevated as "honorary whites" during apartheid times in South Africa so that they could stay in white hotels and enjoy the amenities afforded to whites while conducting business. The Japanese economic miracle has impressed contemporary American society as well. Asian Americans have been labeled the "model minority," meaning that they behave like whites— therefore they too could be candidates for "becoming white." By contrast, according to Nigerian-born anthropologist John Ogbu's (2003) study of the racial disparity between white and black students in an affluent suburban high school, despite their similar class backgrounds, black students failed to perform at the same levels as whites. In addition to factors such as white teacher expectation and a lack of recruitment of blacks to honors programs, a key cultural factor was that "acting white" was not cool among these suburban, affluent black students. The evident nonassimilation of blacks into white culture meant that "talking white" was stigmatized, and that some black students were acting out "ghetto" stereotypes, since that is what is expected and what it means to be "black" in American society.

## WHITE PRIVILEGE AS AN EVERYDAY
## FACT OF AMERICAN LIFE

White privilege is the unearned and unacknowledged benefit conveyed by being white in America. It is probably the single most important obstacle to the construction of a racially just and equitable society that remains largely unaddressed. Consciousness of white privilege was pioneered by Peggy McIntosh, whose now classic 1988 article "White Privilege: Unpacking the Invisible Knapsack" explores basic, unconscious arenas of privilege that benefit whites, such that they need not concern themselves with everyday facts of life that people of color find problematical or need to worry about most or all of the time. Some examples are listed here:

1) I can live anywhere I choose without worrying that my neighbors will move away if I move in.
2) I don't have to worry when shopping or driving that I will be racially profiled.
3) I can arrange to protect my children most of the time from people who might not like them.
4) I am never asked to speak for all of the people in my racial group.
5) I can choose blemish cover or bandages in "flesh" color and have them more or less match my skin.

McIntosh distinguishes between "earned strength" of achievement irrespective of race and "unearned advantage, or power conveyed systematically," as in the ascribed value of whiteness (1988, 78). Privilege by virtue of one's birth helps to move a person forward, such as being the daughter of the boss or the son of an established actor. The sociologist Andrew Hacker asked his white students to project, as a class exercise, how they would live out their lives as blacks. If they discovered that the government had misclassified them as black, Professor Hacker asked, how much financial recompense would they ask of the government? Their estimates in the early 1990s of between $250,000 and $50 million reveal the high value they placed on their white privilege (Hacker 1992, 32–33).

Silence about privilege is itself a function of privilege, and it has a chilling effect on political discourse, while conversations that focus strictly on oppression—without considering privilege—are incomplete and reinforce the structured invisibility of privilege. Understanding the ascribed, unearned, and unacknowledged benefits of white privilege is key to advancing the dialogue on race in America. Without an acknowledgment of white privilege whites can claim innocence of any knowledge of racial profiling, because they do not see it or experience it, or even discuss it. The problem of solving racism thus falls onto the shoulders of the victims, since the beneficiaries do not recognize, confront, or develop any accountability for their privilege. Likewise, whites can live their lives free of any guilt (that might result from their acknowledgment of white privilege), reasoning that individually they were not responsible for slavery, reconstruction, lynching, or any other crimes or legacies of racism.

## TEN REASONS WHY THERE IS RESISTANCE TO DISCUSSING WHITE PRIVILEGE: CLASS EXERCISES

(Developed by students Bridgid Lee Brady, Deneia Fairweather, Marco McWiliams, Joyce Stevos, Edicta Gruillon, Cynthia Williams, and Robert Borges in my spring 2004 seminar in *Critical Race Theory* in response to a "whites only" scholarship that was awarded at a local university by its College Republicans, a group supported by Young Americans for Freedom.[1])

1) Whiteness is normative and invisible, and therefore *denial* is a major source of resistance.
2) It is easier to blame racial "others" than to confront one's own history and responsibility.
3) Resistance to talking about white privilege deflects the spotlight from the core issues of racism and white privilege.
4) Discourse about white privilege is often personal and individual and devolves into white guilt rather than collective accountability, and as a result the conversation "shuts down."
5) The myth of a color-blind society in which race does not or should not matter prevails without challenge.

6) The "color-blind" society is articulated as a moral position reinforcing the innocence of whites and thus any responsibility whites have for continued racism.
7) Any compensatory action, such as affirmative action, is viewed by whites as unfair "reverse discrimination" and is a source of anger, even outrage against the perceived racial minority beneficiaries.
8) Accountability for one's actions or history of collective actions is not a social or political priority in America.
9) The projected demographic that whites will become a numerical minority in 2050 is a source of fear for the white majority that they are ill-equipped to address.
10) Whites have little incentive to talk about their privilege, for acknowledging its importance would lead to changed behavior.

As a counterweight to the power of the last argument, that whites have no need or desire to discuss their privilege, the multiracial group of students in the seminar developed the following reasons why whites would actually benefit from addressing white privilege. They chose to focus on the highly visible and racially divisive issue of affirmative action.

## ACKNOWLEDGING WHITE PRIVILEGE AND SUPPORTING COMPENSATORY ACTIONS, SUCH AS AFFIRMATIVE ACTION, AS A MATTER OF SELF-INTEREST FOR WHITES

Privileged whites have benefited from affirmative action, such as George W. Bush, whose family wealth and connections to Yale ensured his admittance, despite a relatively poor academic performance. Affirmative action admissions for rich whites have not been about test scores and grades but have stemmed from their class and race privilege.

1) White women have been the biggest beneficiaries of affirmative action, while many white veterans and disabled persons have also benefited. Would anyone want to eliminate access ramps or veterans' benefits as undeserved "handouts?"
2) Affirmative action guarantees access and opportunity, not graduation. Has not America been the land of opportunity for whites? Why not accept that history of privilege and extend it to disadvantaged minorities?
3) Following the implementation of affirmative action guidelines, the number of black male PhDs has declined, so affirmative action is not a blanket cure for racial discrimination.

4) Whites who are educated in diverse schools have an added value to their degree: employers prefer them for their learned ability to work on familiar and equitable terms with a diverse workforce. This may be especially true of companies that have been sued for violations of affirmative action guidelines.

5) One student said that whites have a responsibility to "pay" for their privilege of whiteness, and that the initial payment is to give up their silence and speak out against racism and white privilege in the interest of creating a just society.

Following McIntosh's lead, the students developed the following statements of white privilege in regard to affirmative action:

1) "I don't have to worry about perceived advantage or race discrimination when I check the white/Caucasian box on an affirmative action form."

2) "In a college classroom I don't have to worry that I will be viewed as an affirmative action admit."

3) "I don't have to worry that I will be reclassified or misclassified as black or Hispanic as a mixed-race individual."

4) "I have the freedom to speak about race without being stereotyped as speaking on behalf of all members of my 'race.'"

Such exercises are easy to replicate in class and can serve to open a dialogue in which fears as well as hopes that white students may have about race and their future can be brought up and addressed rationally, often emotionally, and especially morally. If present in the class, students of color will be very pleased to hear the issues discussed and will likely join the conversation with their own ideas about finding common ground in America's struggle for a just, color-blind society. Nonetheless, this conversation needs to take place whether the class is racially homogenous or diverse.

## CONFRONTING THE HISTORY
## OF WHITE RACISM

Facing the painful and uncomfortable history of acts of white racism and brutality is a necessary part of the work toward transforming race relations in America. In the case of lynching there is an unbroken chain of brutal murders from Reconstruction until the late 1940s. Most agree that the brutal murder of Emmett Till in 1955 and the dragging death of James Byrd behind a truck driven by three white youths in Jasper, Texas, in 1998 were in spirit and in form acts of lynching. The reaction of the good folks of Jasper was predictably divided into black and white as disgrace fell on the community—much like the shame that finally ended the epidemic of lynching in the southern United States and elsewhere.

The last mass lynching in Walton County, Georgia, in 1946, has been chronicled as a shameful memory. George Dorsey, a black veteran of World War II who had served in the Pacific and returned home with three medals, apparently had forgotten his place back home and was accused of flirting with white women. Moreover, Dorsey had gone to the county jail to bail out his brother-in-law Roger Malcolm. After they left the jail the two black men were dragged out of the car of Malcolm's white attorney by a gang of twenty white vigilantes, who kidnapped their wives as well; both men and their wives were lynched. In the age-old pattern no one was ever convicted or even charged with the murders, although the identities of the whites would have been well known, since bragging rights were a part of their brutal act. Some fifty years later an account of the mass lynching was written by a white woman who interviewed blacks and whites with a memory of the event. As in Jasper, Texas, and in every other lynching, memory was divided between blacks, who recalled the lynching as the most horrific thing that ever happened in the county, and whites, who recalled it primarily as an annoyance (Caldwell 2003; Wexler 2003).

## PRAISING THE HISTORY OF BLACK-WHITE UNITY

There is an important history of antiracism and white-black solidarity that is often overlooked in the polarized state of American race relations. From the earliest years of America's involvement in the slave trade slavery had white opponents as well as defenders. In the state of Rhode Island and Providence Plantations (still the state's official name) the Brown family included four brothers who became entrepreneurs in the slave trade—including John Brown, whose fortune grew from the trade and his other enterprises and laid the financial foundation for the establishment of Brown University. After the disastrous slaving voyage of the *Sally*, in which 143 slaves perished, the financial and human toll led John's brother Moses to condemn the trade and become a lifelong abolitionist and Quaker. He filed suit successfully against his brother John, who continued the trade after it became illegal in the state and republic. Forced to stop openly trading in slaves by legislation abolishing the trade in 1797, John Brown became the first American tried under the law's provisions. In 1800, as an elected representative to Congress, he cast one of the few votes against broadening the 1797 law, and he continued to aid slaving interests. He turned his attention to holdings in the Caribbean, especially in Surinam, and continued to advocate for the legality of the trade (Rhode Island Historical Society 2003).

Quaker opposition to the slave trade was consistent throughout early American history, but several non-Quaker founding fathers and mothers also opposed slavery, finding it inconsistent with American self-proclaimed liberty. These include both John and Abigail Adams and Thomas Paine. From the early decades of the nineteenth century the Abolitionist movement grew as a white-black alliance as well as a female-male one. The New England region and the state of New York developed into virtual hotbeds of radical religious and political thought that fundamentally challenged the slave system; abolitionists in these areas built networks that provided practical support to the system's opponents. The young, newly self-emancipated slave Frederick Douglass fled to Massachusetts and then settled in Rochester, New York, where he knew he could count on the moral and financial support of local whites, including the antislavery societies and abolitionist philanthropists, such as Gerrit Smith of Peterboro, New York.

Abolitionists and their supporters deplored America's immoral yet legal support of slavery, perhaps best symbolized in the well-known Dred Scott decision in 1857 in the U.S. Supreme Court, which held that "a black man has no rights that a white man is bound to respect." The best-known white radical abolitionist was another John Brown, very different from the Rhode Island John Brown, whose 1859 attack on Harper's Ferry, Maryland, was an effort to foment an uprising that would overthrow the republic's slave owners, especially in the South. Brown's "Provisional Constitution and Ordinances for the People of the United States" was nothing less than a plan for the government of a nation of liberated slaves by "amendment and reform" of the government of the United States; in short this was a revolutionary movement for the emancipation of blacks led by a white man. Small wonder that John Brown was alleged to be insane and that he was hung for his treasonous act. The preamble to John Brown's provisional constitution is still stirring:

> Whereas slavery, throughout its entire existence in the United States, is none other than a most barbarous, unprovoked, and unjustifiable WAR of one portion of its citizens upon another portion; the only conditions of which are perpetual imprisonment, and hopeless servitude or absolute extermination; in utter disregard and violation of those external and self-evident truths set forth in our Declaration of Independence: Therefore,
>
> We, Citizens of the United States, and the Oppressed People, who, by a recent decision of the Supreme Court are declared to have no rights which

Figure 6.2.  Black-white unity—abolitionist Frederick Douglass and New York patron Gerrit Smith, Madison County, New York, 1850.

the White Man is bound to respect; together with all other people degraded by the laws thereof, Do, for the time being ordain and establish for ourselves the following PROVISIONAL CONSTITUTION and ORDINANCES, The better to protect our Persons, Property, Lives, and Liberties; and to govern our actions. (Brown 1969)

Standard American history books treat the radical abolitionist John Brown as a fanatic or as deranged. His military plan to overthrow the slave states and establish an "amended" republic was not supported by the majority of his sympathizers, including Frederick Douglass. But Brown's radical view that an unjust political and social system must be fundamentally revised in the United States could still find its supporters today.

The foundation of the feminist movement, with its historic declaration of the rights of women in Seneca Falls, New York, in 1848, was a direct outgrowth of the abolitionist movement. This was symbolized by the presence of white and black men, including Frederick Douglass, as signers of the declaration and of black and white women at the historic congress. Ever able to play the race card exquisitely, the U.S. legal emancipation of enslaved black people brought suffrage to black men with the passing of the Fourteenth Amendment, but not to any woman, irrespective of race. The multiracial abolitionist movement was fractured, and white women fought largely in racial isolation for women's right to vote, which was not achieved until decades later, in 1922.

The NAACP, the oldest civil rights movement in the United States and probably in the world, was founded in 1909 in New York City by an interracial group of citizens who had grown greatly concerned by increasing violence, including lynching, against black people in all parts of the country.

This white-black alliance was powerfully restored during the civil rights movement of the 1950s and 1960s, when men and women, black and white, joined arms and pronounced in song and deed "we shall overcome" racism and discrimination. The most famous white martyrs of the civil rights era include Viola Liuzzi, a civil rights activist from Detroit who was murdered in her car in 1965, and James Goodwin and Michael Schwerner, who were registering black voters in the freedom summer of 1964 and were murdered in Philadelphia, Mississippi, together with African American activist James Chaney and were the subjects of the film "Mississippi Burning." The 2005 manslaughter conviction of their KKK killer, Edgar Ray Kellen, took forty-one years to achieve. These white and black civil rights heroes and heroines are revered symbols of interracial struggle reminiscent of the male-female and black-white composition of the nineteenth-century abolitionist movement, which spawned the struggles for black and female emancipation. The civil rights activists of the 1950s and 1960s, in turn, laid the groundwork for the women's and other human rights movements of the subsequent decades.

## THE IMPORTANT ROLE OF WHITE WOMEN

African American feminist bell hooks (2001) has written about the unself-conscious racism that white feminists can manifest in their relations with women of color, even as they seek to undo patriarchy and combat racism. During the "second wave" of American feminism in the 1970s the pervasive nature of white supremacy made unity between black and white feminists nearly impossible, although white feminists desired this alliance. A focus by white women on eradicating white supremacy, hooks argues, is the best way to forge this alliance; instead white women wanted black women to join them.

White women have been the chief beneficiaries of affirmative action; thus they have reaped the largest rewards of the legacy of the civil rights era, but without acknowledging their debt to the prior struggles of African Americans. Conscious white women are aware of the gender discrimination they have suffered or that which their daughters may suffer. Thus, they have a greater potential sensitivity to the myriad tasks of accountability for white privilege. White women who focus solely on their oppression as women generate incomplete accounts of oppression when they fail to explore the role white privilege plays in the subordination of their sisters of color (Bailey 2003, 314).

White women's lives are shaped by race in the same way that gender shapes men's and women's lives. White people are "raced" just as men are "gendered." Whiteness is a location of structural advantage and race privilege. Whiteness is a standpoint from which white women can observe themselves. Whiteness refers to a set of cultural practices that are usually unmarked and unnamed (Frankenberg 2003). Ruth Frankenberg is critical of white feminists who have failed on the race question. As an anthropologist she explores questions of feminism and race through the lives of women of color and of those of multiracial working-class women.

The multicultural dominant paradigm of today—while having some impact in education and mass media—has not yet transformed daily thought and practice. In the face of continued structural and institutional white leadership multiculturalism is built on classical color-blindness and avoidance of the realities of power relations and race. White women can assist in the struggle for racial justice by seeing their recent gains as, in part, resulting from white privilege. They can further the discussion by expressing gratitude to the original civil rights movement based on race, and by asserting that until all women, irrespective of race, are treated with fairness and equity the feminist movement is incomplete and insufficient. Some white feminists do recognize these facts, but their view has not been mainstreamed in predominantly white feminist organizations, such as the National Organization of Women. White feminist teachers can help by centering race and white privilege in their lessons about American history and society. They can point to many important struggles—the nineteenth-century abolitionist movement and the twentieth-century civil rights movement—that witnessed powerful and successful alliances between white and black men and women.

## THE IMPORTANT ROLE OF
## WORKING-CLASS WHITE MEN

It can be argued that the most privileged persons in American society are white males. Further, it could be argued that white males would perceive that they have the most to lose in acknowledging the privilege with which they are endowed at birth. McIntosh relates that she has met very few males who are truly distressed about unearned male advantage and conferred dominance (1988, 136). The most potentially conscious white males in American society are those whose origins are in the working class. These males understand class privilege and can easily comprehend why they are not able financially to attend the "best" schools, that is, the most expensive Ivy League universities. And they can clearly grasp that they or their friends may have had to delay postsecondary education until they could afford it, or finance their education through loans or a period of military service. Working-class white males are seeking the American dream of upward mobility and may not have the incentives to acknowledge their relative privilege over men of color who are seeking the same American dream. Some white males have elected to challenge the "reverse discrimination" that they allege affects them due to affirmative action "quotas." The argument that such quotas are real has fueled anger, resentment, and even outrage among white males, who may find a convenient scapegoat in blaming African American or Latino males for their disappointments or failures to get into the schools they desire or the jobs they seek. A major case in point is that of Allan Bakke, who filed the first "reverse discrimination" case in California as a result of his failure to be admitted to medical school at the University of California, Davis, in 1975. In 1978 the U.S. Supreme Court agreed with Bakke that he had been a victim of race discrimination and ordered the University of California to admit him, thus giving legal sanction and social legitimacy to the claim of discrimination against white males.

The facts of racism consistently reinforce the economic effects of white privilege. Nearly 40 percent of black children live below the poverty line, with only 15 percent of white children living in families below the poverty line. Of all persons living in poverty 8.8 percent are white and 31.9 percent are black. Moreover, the income of white families is increasing more quickly than that of blacks. Black and white women's earnings are close ($900 for black women to $1,000 for white women in 1990), reflecting the continuing prevalence of sexism; however, black males earn only $731 to $1,000 for white males. Overall, the unemployment rate of all blacks historically is three times that of whites; the black unemployment rate was 11.3 percent to 4.1 percent for whites in 1990 (Hacker 1992, 103). These "bottom line" figures are difficult to dispute, except with old racialist and racist arguments about innate differences between races in capability and achievement.

## CULTURAL DIMENSIONS OF WHITENESS

Noel Ignatiev argues that there is no such thing as "white culture" (2004, 607). There is Italian culture, Polish, Irish, German, and Applachian culture; there is youth culture and drug culture and queer culture; but whiteness is nothing but an expression of race privilege. It has been said that the typical white American male spends his childhood as an Indian, spends his his adolescence as an African American, and becomes white only when he reaches the age of legal responsibility.

The field of "white studies," which developed during the 1990s, is often focused on working-class whites and thus is more about class than race. Some working-class whites who openly express their white identity are actually expressing old forms of white supremacy, and such groups can become recruiting grounds for white power, neo-Nazi, or racist skinhead movements. Such movements attempt to recruit poor urban and rural whites, recognizing that for them race pride can substitute for a lack of economic success in competitive capitalist America, where they should be more successful as a result of their whiteness. Historical racism and white privilege have blunted the natural solidarity that working-class whites have with working-class blacks, Latinos, and other racial minorities.

White ethnic studies—Polish, Irish, Italian, or others—enjoyed some currency during the 1980s as white ethnicity and race competed for academic attention. For a brief period Puerto Ricans, Mexicans, blacks, Hawaiians, American Indians, and other racially classified groups were treated as "ethnics" comparable to white ethnics. "Ethnic studies" nearly eclipsed black, Latino, and Asian studies for a time, but carried little intellectual weight into the twenty-first century.

In popular culture whiteness is viewed as a nonidentity, and some young whites are frustrated by diversity or multicultural events at their schools; they feel left out as African American, or Latino, or a variety of Asian cultures are celebrated. With their invisible whiteness and corresponding privilege they want a place at such diversity events. Creative teachers will find ways to examine white-minority relations in a positive light, such as in the abolitionist or civil rights movements, or extol the struggles of white ethnic groups while acknowledging that white privilege was a part of the success they achieved.

In popular vernacular among youth the terms "white-bread" and "Kleenex" have come to symbolize blandness or something ordinary, thus reinforcing the normative nature of being white in America. "White girl" and "white boy," when uttered to a white person by a person of color, can be words that wound or provoke by bringing a power dimension into the encounter. The term may be as a put-down or a type of mocking behavior that reverses past practice, in which racist epithets were used by whites against blacks. Examination of these linguistic epithets, their current and past use, provides fertile ground for classroom discussion.

Whites experience their whiteness when they find themselves in settings where minorities are a majority, such as in a black or Hispanic neighborhood, or in a historically black school, church, or other social group. This may be a rare event due to American segregation, but it can be a profound experience that leaves lingering positive or negative feelings. Discomfort levels can be high when whites find themselves a minority in these groups and can be evident in body language or speech, as with politicians who must go to historically black churches to gain votes. President Bill Clinton got high marks for his evident comfort level with blacks and his choice of Harlem for his postpresidency office. Tour groups of African American churches on Sunday mornings may be more likely to include Japanese or Germans than white Americans. White church ministers are beginning to understand that they need to reach out more to their fellow Christians in black churches, but Sunday morning is as segregated today as when Dr. Martin Luther King Jr. described religious segregation in America in the early 1960s.

## POPULAR CULTURE: WHAT WHITE PEOPLE HAVE TAKEN FROM BLACK PEOPLE

Some whites in American popular culture have been accused of "ripping off" black culture, as illustrated in the history of white rock and roll, which is heavily derived from African American blues and gospel music. Elvis Presley was the megastar of rock and roll, while great blues musicians remained obscure. As a result of the black-white binary functioning in culture as well as society, black and white artists have developed largely segregated audiences with historically few "crossover" artists able to appeal across racial lines. Contemporary hip-hop culture represents a break with this history and has been remarkable for the amount of racial crossover in performing artists and in audiences.

In *Everything but the Burden* (2003) Gregory Tate examines the domain of popular culture, focusing on the long-standing white expropriation of black culture—from jazz, to blues, to rock and roll—without accreditation. White musicians Paul Whiteman and Benny Goodman were the respective "king of swing" and "king of jazz"; Elvis Presley became the "king of rock and roll"; and Eric Clapton became the "world's greatest blues guitar player." The language of cool was derived from urban African American speech, prompting Tate to ask the question, "Why does everyone love Black music but nobody loves Black people?" (2003, 5).

## HIP-HOP CULTURE: HOW YOUNG WHITES AND BLACKS FIND COMMON GROUND

Contemporary rap is embedded in African American culture and speech, and white rap artists such as Eminem are controversial. Hip-hop has been remarkable for the amount of racial crossover that has occurred in the genre. Just a few samples of hip-hop lyrics or "spoken word" poetry from conscious youth can reveal a deep involvement with the issues of race and racism.

The following spoken word poem was written by Hannah Resseger, a student in my seminar on Critical Race Theory and spoken word artist locally known as "B-mor7." The poem was written in response to the "whites only" scholarship that was established by the College Republicans at a local university as an attempted satire of affirmative action, and is printed here with her permission.

Hip-hop culture and the racially sensitive and politically conscious lyrics of rap music are positive contemporary forces. They allow white and black youth—as well as youth of other racial backgrounds—to meet on a common ground in an atmosphere of antiracism and universal humanism.

## THE FUTURE OF WHITENESS IN THE TWENTY-FIRST CENTURY

Whiteness in America, like all else regarding race, is in a state of change. Whites do not see themselves as racist, nor are the overwhelming majority of whites active racists; that is, most whites do not engage in overtly racist acts intended to verbally or physically harm "minorities." Because most whites do not carry out these actions they excuse themselves from responsibility for the improvement of race relations. Passive racism may be understood as not carrying out acts of active racism, but taking advantage

## "White Privilege and Affirmative Action"
### Spoken word poem by Hannah Resseger, March 2004

Black faces in high places doesn't necessarily mean equality of the
   races
If you got white skin then you got white privilege
We all live in a white supremacist village
Don't forget patriarchal capitalist pillage
Will you struggle or conform to the illness
Turn your back on prisoners, social or political
While true criminals reign supreme and you don't ridicule
Driving while black, or traveling while arab under attack
The weight of your skin when it's tan, brown, or black
Or the privilege you're in, when your skin is called white
The oppression we sow and reap when it's ripe, it's not right
And I know this ain't how it's supposed to be
So what we gonna do to change this calamity?

I'm here to break the cycle of blaming the victim!
You say scholarship should not be based on race . . .
I agree
If we lived in a perfect place
But we don't
So don't let that money go to waste
When you could hand over those five g's to me
Cuz I'm white and I'm disadvantaged, right?
Or so you say, matter of fact
I know a place to put that money
You say to those who need it, how 'bout ghetto youth who don't
   have funding
Why are they struggling?
Who gets the silver spoon in mouth and who gets the gold
who is born with nothing but a piece of coal
Let's propose a toast
To hypocrites who take what they can and then condemn
the same institutions that benefited them
Affirmative action
Not the best solution
But what would you suggest
Benefits white women, more than any others so what do you
   profess?

You say it handicaps whites
when really it has helped the handicapped get more jobs and
    rights
How dare you say this system blocks whites and takes their places
Look at history and present day oppression of all non-white races
Yeah, we all human, one race, body soul and mind
But history has constructed something different so let's not be
    blind
When light becomes right and dark becomes wrong
How can we reverse this curse
And all become strong?
Follow along I know it might seem strange but the lighter you are
    the bluer ya veins and
when flesh bleeds guess we all bleed the same.
So let's come together and create more changes
To uplift and elevate these complex situations.
If you're white use ya skin for the advantage of the disadvantaged
Step out of ya skin for a day and see how others manage.

of the privileges of being white when the fact of whiteness is the protected norm. For the most part whites in the contemporary United States
perceive themselves as part of a distinctly different, color-blind, sympathetic generation that has learned to look beyond the "color of the skin"
to "the beauty within" (Gallagher 1997, 6). This is especially true of youth
in America, who see their parents' generation as having problems with
race but not their own. This is another example of American denial. In
fact, whites have a vital role to play in the healing, reconciliation, and
reconstruction of race and racism in America.

## WHITES PARTICIPATING IN AND ADVANCING
## THE DIALOGUE ON RACE

Whites may—and should—study race, including their own. But what if a
white person wants to do more than study and become an agent of
change? Some authors suggest that whites reflect carefully on their own
privilege and begin the difficult process of giving it up as a key to the
transformation of race relations that many seek (Delgado and Stefancic
1997, 605). That process is made all the more difficult because of the major
points made in this chapter:

1) Whiteness is the norm and is therefore invisible.
2) White privilege is intimately tied to whiteness.
3) Most whites do not engage in overt acts of racism and are innocent of any guilt in race relations, and therefore they believe they have no role to play in their improvement.

White people tend to view intent as an essential element of racial harm (Flagg 1997, 630), while nonwhites view racial harm as a fact of history and everyday life. Whites may be willing to acknowledge that wrongs occurred in the past, but they proclaim innocence in the present moment and want to begin the process of racial reconciliation in the present moment—when, supposedly, no one is a racist and whites do not intend to cause racial harm. When whites do cause harm nowadays—such as in the brutalizing and torture of Abner Luima by members of the New York police force, or the dragging to death of James Byrd in Jasper, Texas—most whites are quick to condemn such acts but shy away from a discussion of the underlying issues that allow them to occur. Few whites take any action.

In both structure and content whiteness stands between society's present injustices and any future of racial equality (Lopez 2000, 632). Thus the key to advancement in race relations is an active role by whites. Rehistoricizing whiteness and Americanness requires the analysis of multiple histories of assimilation, appropriation, and exclusion that shape the cultural fields that white Americans inhabit. It requires engagement with whiteness and Americanness as powerful spaces rather than seeing whiteness and Americanness as "cultureless, culturally neutral, or culturally generic terrain" (Frankenberg 2003, 75). The categories of race and culture need to be reexamined; we need to insist on antiessentialist concepts—getting beyond concepts of blacks as athletes or entertainers alone; or Hispanics as violent; or Asians as highly intelligent—while emphasizing that these essential racial concepts are made real within relationships of power.

Several critical scholars argue that whites should attempt to dismantle whiteness as it currently exists. Whites should renounce their privileged racial position, not simply out of guilt or any sense of self-deprecation, but because this mythological construct stands at the vortex of racial inequality in America and is one of the most important keys to its end. The perceived value of whiteness to whites will probably insure the continuation of white racial superiority (Frankenberg 2003, 75), unless today's generation of youth proactively undertake this reconstruction of race. This means not only a radical critique of historical white dominance, but a fundamental change in social practice; it means building a new society from the ground up that is acutely conscious of race while seeking to transform institutions of racial dominance. This means active antiracist work on multiple fronts—from public criticism and rejection of racial profiling as biased and undemocratic to the promotion of active interracial social mixing that builds familiarity and trust among different racial and ethnic groups.

Our culture tends to repress any discourse surrounding race or racism. Although we live in a highly racialist and racist society we are not provided, nor do we construct, a safe space to discuss race. Just about the worst thing that a white can be called is a racist. White Americans spend more time trying to avoid the label of "racist" than addressing the underlying issues of race (Wildman and Davis 2000). Instead of avoiding the label of "racist" whites can vigorously and morally embrace the role of "antiracist" as America performs the hard work of acknowledging its past and constructing its future. This investment in the active construction of an equitable, multiracial future for America will reap rewards not only domestically but internationally as well.

## NOTE

1. I express gratitude to Paul Khalil Saucier for his constructive comments in reading a draft of this section.

## REFERENCES

Bailey, Alison. 2003. "Privilege: Expanding Marilyn Frye's 'Oppression.'" In *Oppression, Privilege, and Resistance: Theoretical Perspectives on Racism, Sexism and Heterosexism*, edited by Lisa Heldke and Peg O'Conner, 301–16. New York: McGraw-Hill.

Brodkin, Karen. 1998. *How Jews Became White Folks and What That Says about Race in America*. New Brunswick, NJ: Rutgers University Press.

Brown, John. 1969. *Provisional Constitution and Ordinances for the People of the United States*. Preface by Boyd B. Stutler. Weston, MA: M and S.

Brundage, W. Fitzhugh. 1993. *Lynching in the New South: Georgia and Virginia, 1880–1930*. Urbana: University of Illinois Press.

Buck, Pem Davidson. 2001. *Worked to the Bone: Race, Class and Privilege in Kentucky*. New York: Monthly Review.

Caldwell, Gail. 2003. "Southern Exposure." *Boston Sunday Globe*, February 2, D6.

Delgado, Richard, and Jean Stefancic, eds. 1997. *Critical White Studies*. Philadelphia: Temple University Press.

Domínguez, Virginia. 1994. *White by Definition: Social Classification in Creole Louisiana*. New Brunswick: Rutgers University Press.

Du Bois, W. E. B. 1910. "The Souls of White Folks." *Independent* (New York) 69 (August 18): 339–42.

Flagg, Barbara J. 1997. "'Was Blind, but Now I See': White Race Consciousness and the Requirement of Discriminatory Intent." In *Critical White Studies: Looking Behind the Mirror*, edited by Richard Delgado and Jean Stefancic, 629–31. Philadelphia: Temple University Press.

Frankenberg, Ruth. 1994. "Whiteness and Americanness: Examining Constructions of Race, Culture and Nation in White Women's Life Narratives." In *Race*, edited by Steven Gregory and Roger Sanjek, 64–77. New Brunswick, NJ: Rutgers University Press.

———. 2003. "White Women, Race Matters." In *Oppression, Privilege, and Resistance: Theoretical Perspectives on Racism, Sexism and Heterosexism*, edited by Lisa Heldke and Peg O'Conner, 333–48. New York: McGraw-Hill.

Gallagher, P. 1997. "White Racial Formation: Into the Twenty-first Century." In *Critical White Studies: Looking Behind the Mirror*, edited by Richard Delgado and Jean Stefancic, 6–11. Philadelphia: Temple University Press.

Hacker, Andrew. 1992. *Two Nations: Black, White; Separate, Hostile, and Unequal*. New York: Ballantine.

Hale, Elizabeth Grace. 1998. *Making Whiteness: The Culture of Segregation in the South, 1890–1940*. New York: Vintage.

hooks, bell. 1991. "Representing Whiteness in the Black Imagination." In *Cultural Studies*, edited by Larry Grossberg, Cary Nelson, and Paula Treichler, 338–46, New York: Routledge.

———. 2004. "Overcoming White Supremacy: A Comment." In *Oppression, Privilege and Resistance*, edited by Lisa Heldke and Peg O'Conner, 69–75. New York: McGraw Hill.

Ignatiev, Noel. 1996. *How the Irish Became White*. New York: Routledge.

———. 2004. "Treason to Whiteness Is Loyalty to Humanity." In *Oppression, Privilege and Resistance*, edited by Lisa Heldke and Peg O'Conner, 605–10. New York: McGraw Hill.

Kivel, Paul. 1996. *Uprooting Racism: How White People Can Work for Racial Justice*. Gabriola Island, Canada: New Society Publishers.

Lopez, Ian F. Haney. 2000. "White by Law." In *Critical Race Theory*, edited by Richard Delgado and Jean Stefancic, 626–34. Philadelphia: Temple University Press.

McIntosh, Peggy. 1988. "White Privilege: Unpacking the Invisible Knapsack." Abstracted from "White Privilege and Male Privilege: A Personal Account of Coming to See Correspondences through Work in Women's Studies," all rights reserved. Wellesley College Center for Research on Women, Wellesley, MA.

Myrdal, Gunnar. 1944. *An American Dilemma: The Negro Problem and Modern Democracy*. New York: Harper and Brothers.

Ogbu, John. 2003. *Black Disengagement in a Suburban, Affluent Community*. Mahwah, NJ: Lawrence Erlbaum Publishers.

Rhode Island Historical Society. 2003. *Rhode Island and the African Slave Trade: John Brown and the Colonial Economy of Slavery*. Providence: Rhode Island Historical Society and Rhode Island Black Heritage Society.

Roediger, David. 1992. *The Wages of Whiteness: Race and the Making of the American Working Class*. London: Verso.

Sacks, Karen Brodkin. 1994. "How the Jews Became White Folks." In *Race*, edited by Steven Gregory and Roger Sanjek, 78–102. New Brunswick, NJ: Rutgers University Press.

Smedley, Audrey. 1993. *The Idea of Race in North America: Origins and Evolution of a Worldview*. Boulder, CO: Westview.

Tate, Greg, ed. 2003. *Everything but the Burden: What White People Are Taking from Black Culture*. New York: Harlem Moon Broadway.

Wexler, Laura. 2003. *Fire in a Canebreak: The Last Mass Lynching in America*. Boston: Scribner.

Wildman, Stephanie M., and Adrienne D. Davis. 2000. "Language and Silence: Making Systems of Privilege Visible." In *Critical Race Theory*, edited by Richard Delgado and Jean Stefancic, 657–63. Philadelphia: Temple University Press.

# 7

# Comparative Perspectives on Race Relations

Examining selected international perspectives on race relations can help to shed light on the history of thought about race in the West. Cross-cultural perspectives can help to clarify the special case of racialism and racism in the United States while broadening conceptions of race and racism to the global arena. American provincialism can lead many to believe that the U.S. cultural system is generalized to the world, and thus many naively think that the American view of race is the universal one. Nothing could be further from the truth. In this chapter we explore some of the complex dynamics of race, racism, and color coding, as well as ethnicity and ethnocentrism, in other cultures. In this light, class and caste in India are examined for their important similarities and differences.

There are multiple places and cases in the United States in which a comparative perspective on race and racism is a useful exercise. Students and teachers using this book might construct their own studies. One interesting case is the newest state of Hawaii, which is 40 percent mixed race, mainly of Asian and white mixtures. Terms unfamiliar to mainland Americans, such as "Haole," meaning half-Asian (mainly people of Japanese, Chinese, and Korean ancestry) and half-white, carry racialized meaning. "Haole" originally meant foreigners, but later came to mean white; it can be a neutral or negative term depending on context. Haole, who are often economic elites, may be resented because their white ancestors took the island and became the businesspeople who control Hawaiian assets. The term "Hawaiian" is used for anyone with original (i.e., indigenous) blood, consisting of one ancestor, and this must be officially documented. "Good" blood is Hawaiian, Japanese, or Chinese, while white ancestry is not highly valued, in dramatic contrast to mainstream, mainland American culture. The presence of military bases has provided opportunities for acquaintance with blacks, who have historically not been a part of this unique equation. Other examples of the contemporary dynamics of race can be discussed by imaginative teachers and energetic students.

This chapter is informed by the fortunate opportunity of offering the course Anthropology of Race and Racism while sailing around the world with the Semester at Sea program. For four months the class was focused on observing where race is a significant feature of cultural and human relations and the many places where it is not. The class was also informed by my decades of teaching students in Anthropology of Race and Racism from racially diverse backgrounds; these students have shared their lives and emotions with me and their fellow students. Given their interest and the importance of a comparative perspective on race, I developed an advanced seminar, Comparative Race Relations, in which selected societies around the world are examined and discussed regarding race and race relations.

## RACE AND RACISM IN SELECTED
## EUROPEAN NATIONS

Except for in antiquity, the European countries were not slave societies that produced contemporary populations of national descendants of slave origin, like the nearly 20 percent African American population in the United States. However, the majority of European countries participated in the Great Atlantic Slave Trade—which lasted for over four centuries, from the early 1500s to the early twentieth century—and they were the colonizers of Africa after the end of the slave trade. The Portuguese and Spanish began the trade after the "discovery" of the New World, and the Dutch East India Company played a significant role, but it was the French and British who grew fabulously rich on the trade. This wealth positioned them well to become the dominant colonial powers after the trade was no longer useful to their economies. In 1884 the Berlin Congress divided the African continent into European parcels of interest—to Great Britain, the great Nile Valley, strategic coastal areas, and interior parts of west, southern, and east Africa, as well as Mount Kilimanjaro as a special gift for Queen Victoria. France received less strategic coastal parts of west and east Africa, with near total control of northwest Africa, the Maghrib, and Saharan west Africa. To the less powerful European power of Belgium, the Congo was allotted, and to Germany, Southwest Africa (Namibia) and Tanganyika. These colonies were lost by Germany after its defeat in World War I, but Germany recovered twice after defeats in both world wars, and its economic power has drawn immigrants from Asia as well as Africa, especially after the wave of African independence in the 1960s.

European powers, especially Britain and France, also dominated the Middle East, central and south Asia, and China during the great age of imperialism. This meant that Western languages, politics, and culture were exported wholesale to the non-Western world during colonialism. As a result England, France, Portugal, Spain, and Holland were the "motherland" countries that were the first choice of emigration for people from the former colonies, as places where levels of cultural and linguistic familiarity were the greatest.

## United Kingdom, France, Germany

A 2001 government report in Great Britain paints a picture of race relations that mirrors U.S. relations described in 1992 in the book *Two Nations Black and White, Separate, Hostile, Unequal* by Andrew Hacker. The British report says that whites and "ethnic minorities" in Britain—largely people of color from the major former colonies of India, Pakistan, Africa, and the Caribbean—lead separate lives with no social or cultural contact and that Britons "tiptoe" around the subject of discrimination. According to the Office of National Statistics, Britain is 7 percent nonwhite, with nearly 2 percent of its population classified as "black," 4 percent as Asian, and 1.2 percent as "other" (Hoge 2001).

Like the parallel American case, the report was commissioned after the worst race riots in twenty years took place in Bradford, Burnley, and Old-ham—three communities in northern England with large Asian populations—during the summer of 2001, costing an estimated fifteen million dollars in damages and injuring more than three hundred police. The report appeared to be surprised at its own finding, that racial divisions are deeper and more polarized than previously believed, and that questions of language (English only), and religion (a substantial minority of Britons are Muslim) complicate matters of race.

Prime Minister Tony Blair appointed Great Britain's first black cabinet member in May 2002. Paul Boeteng, born in London and raised in Ghana, was named deputy treasury secretary, making history twice, as Mr. Boeteng had been appointed, also by Blair, as Britain's first black minister to any post when he was appointed to a health department position in 1997 (Hoge 2001).

In France, North African immigrants from the former colonies of Morocco, Algeria, and Tunisia have challenged French liberalism, with its basis in the highly admired French Revolution, which provided the foundation of civil and political rights in the country—liberty, fraternity, and equality. The electoral success of avowedly racist and antiimmigrant politicians, such as Jean-Marie Le Pen, who had a runoff election with Jacques Chirac in 2002, reveal a persistent French chauvinism, despite the country's liberal traditions.

Germany, with its complicated history of racism and genocide during the era of the Second World War, retains broadly based social patterns that remain racist. Those who cherish notions that humans learn from their history are easily dislodged from such notions with the critical study of race and racism. Although Germany did a great deal to repair the damage done to Jewish populations during the Nazi era through aid and support to the state of Israel, overtly racist violence persists throughout the country, including the formerly communist east. These incidents attract headlines, perhaps more so because of Germany's past. Attacks by skinheads on immigrants from the "third world" as well as Eastern Europe occur often, and some of Germany's universities frankly admit that they are not able to house dark-skinned students in their dormitories because they are unable to guarantee their security (Perera 2002, A41). African American servicemen have been attacked as well, and the U.S. State Department does warn its citizens traveling to Germany that "looking foreign" might put them at risk of attacks by drunken skinheads.

## Russia

Immigrants from the formerly colonized third world face discrimination throughout Europe, including in the regions of the former Soviet Union, where antiracism was official government policy during the communist era. This sad lesson demonstrates that propaganda and education, while important in eradicating racism, are never sufficient. Official solidarity with the anti-imperialist struggles of the former European colonies in Africa, Asia, and Latin America was preached during communism, but internal subordination of dozens of ethnic minorities and the privileging of Belorussians or so-called white Russians made this a hypocritical policy at home. However, there is a more persistent and chronic issue of racism extended toward Russia's ethnic minorities. If the discrimination were purely ethnocentric, it would be displayed exclusively in terms of Russian cultural superiority, but there are clear indications that this discrimination is racial as well as ethnic. Ironically, among the minorities who experience discrimination are the "Caucasians" from the Caucasus mountains of Georgia—Chechnyans, Azerbaijanis. Armenians, Kurds, and Turks (Tavernise 2002, A8) are also victims of job, housing, and other forms of discrimination. Caucasians are often described as *chorniye*, for "blacks." The extremist violence in Russia can be directed against the "blacks," anyone who is not Slavic Russian or white skinned. Darker-skinned Russian citizens, especially from the Caucasus, Tajikistan, Kazakhstan, and other "eastern" regions, as well as Indians, Africans, East Asians, central and Southeast Asians, and Gypsies are all vulnerable to racist skinhead or ultranationalist attacks. African or Latino Americans serving in Russia have not been immunized from such attacks by their nationality, and one Latina congresswoman was harassed while shopping in Moscow (McDonald 2004, A20).

In the post–Cold War era of economic hardship, as Russia passed through the painful stages of early capitalist development, neofascist and racist groups openly vied for power, and the skinhead movement was borrowed from Western Europe. Africans resident in the major cities have been especially victimized, leading to an unprecedented appeal by the ambassadors of thirty-seven African countries to the Foreign Ministry for protection in the city of Moscow (Tavernise 2002). African American embassy personnel have also been targets of racist attacks, which the government has minimized, saying that they are just part of growing hooliganism—perhaps part of a denial rooted in the past contradiction between official antiracism and de facto racial and ethnic discrimination. There appears to be little popular sympathy for immigrants, as in other European contexts, where relatively poor whites seek to keep their slightly higher status above immigrants of color. The experience of Taddele Gebre, a refugee from Ethiopia, appears to be typical. He was confronted in the Moscow metro by about twenty youths, some with shaved heads—"You, black, go home or you'll be a corpse here!" This was the most recent of several similar attacks during his four years of residence; at times he was beaten with chains.

After the European Holocaust it may seem obvious to note that anti-Semitism has deep roots throughout the continent, including in Russia. However, it is important to point out that the end of the Second World War did not end anti-Semitism, which indeed expanded to include Arabs as well, who, although they are Semites, are often conceptually linked to other third world immigrants. Few Jews remained in Europe after World War II, and many who survived emigrated to the newly created state of Israel after 1948. European support for this new state in historic Palestine may be viewed as an effort to compensate for its failure to stop the genocidal efforts of the Nazis. Racial and sociopolitical relations between Israelis and Palestinians are discussed in the Middle East section below. However, in postwar Europe old fascist and neofascist groups continued decades after the end of the war and became reinvigorated with economic downturns and with the end of communism in the former Soviet Union. Anti-Semitism is often confused with hooliganism and class anger, and its denial mirrors denial of other forms of racial discrimination. Poor working-class Russians, like poor whites in the United States, can feel superior to the "non-Russians" like the Jews, the Caucasians, and the immigrants.

## RACE IN THE NEW WORLD HYBRID SOCIETIES: THE CARIBBEAN AND LATIN AMERICA

The first lesson that is learned upon encountering race outside the United States is that the rules regarding race are very different, even among relatively close neighbors, such as Puerto Ricans, Cubans, Dominicans, or Haitians. If the one-drop rule can be said to prevail, it is that one drop of European, "white blood" can "lighten" and can make you "white," in marked contrast to the one-drop of black blood in the United States that "darkens" and made you "black." There are Dominicans or Haitians or Brazilians whom the average American would classify as "black" or African American, but who would self-identify as "white," *blanco*, or *branco* in their home societies. In America they discover that they are "black" and quickly surmise that they must learn the American rules or risk embarrassment or more serious forms of racial discrimination in housing, police relations, and myriad other social contexts. A light-skinned Dominican woman shared in class that her family had been puzzled by American race relations, but that once they "learned the rules" her mother told her that she could date white boys but her darker-skinned sister should date only black boys. She thought this was wrong, unfair, and racist on the part of her mother, but perhaps the mother felt that she was protecting her daughters from being hurt. Confusion, mired in the black-white binary, reigns about the correct way to describe Latino skin color in the United States. In my Race and Racism class a Latino student mentioned the "brown bag test"—if your skin color is lighter than a brown bag, you can be white; darker than the brown bag and you are black. This diagnostic test caused students to laugh out loud when a Laotian American student reported that her culture describes Hispanics as orange in skin color.

A second important lesson about race in the New World societies outside of the United States is that in the absence of the one-drop rule making you black, the concept of race as a cultural category is much more fluid and can be thought of more as a continuum than as the black-white dichotomy that dominates American thinking about race. The question—"What are you, black or white?"—often asked of mixed-race or biracial persons reveals that dichotomy in the United States. Children of a white mother and black father describe themselves as "black" because of the continuing power of the one-drop rule. Racial fluidity in the Caribbean leads away from a black-white opposition and rather flows along a continuum from light to dark—from *blanco/blanca* to *"negro/negra"* with a significant middle position, "mestizo" or *criollo* (Creole), and lots of other stops along the way. These terms are heavily used as descriptive in the New World societies of the Caribbean and South America, which are highly race conscious; however the view of race in these countries is more flexible and contextual than in the United States. For example, class definitely whitens, and wealthy, powerful families can be thought of as "white" or "light" irrespective of color. True, some of the wealthier families are indeed light skinned, descending from the landed and aristocratic families originating in Europe during the days of colonialism, slavery, and the wealth generated from the great plantation crops of the New World—sugar cane, cotton, tobacco, and spices. However, new wealth can be made from entertainment or sports. For instance, the famous dark-skinned, superb soccer player Pele from Brazil became wealthy and "whiter" from his personal success. Other, more dark-skinned Brazilians, more African in appearance, are not so fortunate.

The third important lesson about race in the New World is that in South as well as North America, Indian populations were decimated in the encounter with Europeans, and the application of the term "genocide" is appropriate. Throughout the Caribbean and Latin America the indigenous or Indian peoples are endangered. However, admixture of indigenous people with Europeans is a Latin American phenomenon—much more so than a North American reality—and overall 58 percent of Central American people and 77 percent of South Americans are "mestizo" mixtures of European and Indian backgrounds.

In a 1998 pan–Latin American survey reported in *Los Medios y Mercados de Latinoamerica*, interviews were conducted in six South American countries in which the interviewers (not the interviewees) classified the respondents using one of seven racial categories judged by the researchers to be pan-American. These included: 1) white, 2) black, 3) indigenous, 4) mulatto (mixed white and African), 5) mestizo (mixed white and Indian), 6) Asian, 7) "don't know."

Race in the Caribbean is constructed along a continuum of phenotype and class, with greater activity and variation in the "middle" groupings of mixed-race populations, amounting to distinctive, recognized folk categories of race or physical type. The folk categories of race vary according to countries' particular historical experiences as slave or plantation economies under European colonialism. Black-white identities were imported during colonial times—whether *negro-blanco* in countries colonized by the Spanish, or *noir-blanc* in those colonized by the French, or *negro-branco* in Portuguese colonies, or of course black-white in English colonies. Terms for "black"—*prieto/prieta* or *prêto/prêta* in Spanish or Portuguese—can be used as words that can wound, connoting inferiority and unattractiveness. *Noir*, like "black" in American English, can be used negatively and it can be used as a source of black pride, as in the case of *noirism*, innovated by writers like Anténor Firmin, Aimé Césaire, and Leopold Senghor and also known as "Negritude."Anthropologists (Wade 1997; Harrison 2002) have acknowledged that three polar categories—black, white, Indian—have social meaning and integrity in Central and South America and that black and Indian are mainly marginal to the dominance of white privilege and power. Black and Indian phenotypic identity are mediated through culturally specific contexts. Blacks may be more or less permanently assigned to second-class national status, while Indian indigenous heritage may be treated differently through specific legal protections (Wade 1997). Of course, classifications reflect the respective histories of the various Central and South American countries: some have relatively large indigenous communities, such as the Aztec, Mayan, and Incan empires of Mexico, Guatemala, and Peru; some have significant imported slave populations from Africa, such as Brazil, Ecuador, Colombia, the Dominican Republic, and Venezuela; and some have mass immigration from Europe, such as Argentina, Brazil, Chile, Colombia, and Uruguay. In general Latin American elites have accepted the social fact of white domination, but they have strongly denied "the immutability and absoluteness of 'race' and have rejected the Euro-American doctrine derived from Gobineau that racial hybrids are degenerate and represent a danger to the 'purity' of the white race" (Yelvington 1997, quoted in Harrison 2002). An exception to the Latin American lightening is the case of Asians—especially Chinese and Indians in the Caribbean and South America—who are considered to be culturally and racially "saturated," possessing a civilized culture that, although not equivalent to white culture, is superior to the "primitive" African culture of the formerly enslaved (Harrison 2002, 158).

Mexico developed an elaborate caste-race system under the Spanish, whose legal categories of race included not only "mestizo" and "mulatto," but also "throwback," "Moor," "wolf," "coyote," and other derogatory terms whose legacy is still felt. Today, the overwhelming majority of Mexicans (77 percent) describe themselves as "mestizo" ("Racial Classification in Latin America" 2000). By contrast, in Argentina, the overwhelming majority self-identify as "white," with only 6 percent identifying as "mestizo," reflecting the strength of European immigration to this South American country, a decimated Indian population, and the lack of a historical slave economy.

None of the above is meant to deny the significance of race in the New World, whose economies were built on European conquest, the near genocide of American Indians, and the Great Atlantic slave trade. In the overall picture of the New World it is the American one-drop rule that

stands out as aberrant. As we have seen, where race is strongly constructed, there is also racism. The most racialized terms, the terms that
come closest to the racist sting of the American word "nig—r," is *prieto/
prieta* in Spanish and *prêto/prêta* in Portuguese. These are words that can
wound but also can be used as terms of address between close friends or
families, in the same way that the common American racist term has been
appropriated by African Americans in rap in daily conversation. But the
power of these terms to hurt also speaks to the negative connotation that
blackness carries. In anger *prêto* or *prieta* may be uttered; these words may
be fighting words and lead to violence, or a grandfather in the Dominican
Republic may refer to his sweet darker-skinned granddaughter as "my
little prieta." Many phenotypic mestizo people may self-identify as white
for the negative connotations that blackness carries.

Some of the most important social and political movements of the New
World have revolved around the race question. First and foremost is the
revolutionary struggle led by Haitians that resulted in the first black
republic in 1804 (and the second independent state in the hemisphere
after the American Revolution). After this historic event might be mentioned the beginnings of pan-Africanism, the early black pride Marcus
Garvey movement in Jamaica and the English-speaking Caribbean, the
American civil rights movement, the Rastafarian movement in Jamaica
(with Bob Marley becoming an important global contemporary symbol
of black pride), and the black pride civil rights movement among Afro-
Brazilians today. These movements speak volumes about the importance
of race in the New World societies of North and South America and the
Caribbean.

Those societies were shaped by European views brought by the European explorers, entrepreneurs, and colonists who settled the New World
and brought it under their control for five centuries preceding the present
era. Ideas that dominated European thought from the seventeenth to
nineteenth centuries (summarized and critiqued in chapters 2 and 3)
influenced the creation of New World institutions, economies, and governments. The great Atlantic slave trade brought tens of millions of
enslaved Africans to the plantations in the Caribbean and North and
South America. These societies of slaves and masters developed in Spanish, Portuguese, English, and French linguistic contexts, while racial attitudes reflected cultural differences among them. The Spanish had their
greatest encounter with the aboriginal peoples of the Americas, whom
they at first regarded as nonhuman. It was not until Indian advocate Bar-
tolomeo De Las Casas declared early in the seventeenth century that Indians had souls that Spanish theology and politics were forced to
acknowledge this fact. These were the Spaniards who in 1492—when
Columbus set sail for India and instead opened the New World to West-

ern commerce—had cleansed the Iberian Peninsula of "the Moors," darker-skinned Muslims from North Africa, and all Jews. The Portuguese by Vatican fiat divided their exploits between Africa and the New World, with their only major South American colony being Brazil. The Portuguese favored the "lightening" of the lower dark races through the positive admixture of white European blood. They accepted mixed-race persons in their colonies, affording to them *assimilado* status provided that they became Portuguese in language, dress, and manner. They used some of these mixed-race peoples, especially Cape Verdeans, as mid- or lower-level colonial functionaries in the African colonies—not as equals to the Portuguese but as superiors to the Africans.

The French developed the "Black Code" early in the slave colonies of the Caribbean, with Haiti as the archetypical example. These codes organized and controlled race relations in the French colonies and were imported to the United States courtesy of the Louisiana Purchase in 1803 by French exiles fleeing from the black revolution in Haiti. The English became the leading slave traders in the seventeenth and eighteenth centuries, and their colonies in North America and the Caribbean were established both as strategic ports in the triangle trade and as lucrative plantations. Ideas of ranked racial difference and European superiority justified this enterprise, and, in the nineteenth century, as slavery was gradually abolished in the colonies, the British came to see themselves as the only civilized nation, whose Manifest Destiny it was to rule the entire globe. Indeed for a time the sun never set on the British Empire. This and other empires required the concept of superior and inferior races to establish and maintain themselves.

Before 1492 only native peoples occupied the Americas. After 1492 and the European opening of the Americas, near genocide of Indians had occurred and a new racial diversity of peoples from Europe, Africa, and elsewhere became the norm.

## SELECTED CASES

### Haiti

Haiti was once St. Domingue, a colonial slave plantation under the French, until it freed itself from both slavery and colonialism in 1804, making it the second independent nation in the New World and the first black republic. The first independent nation was the United States, gaining its independence from the English. Both revolutions had tremendous repercussions in world history, although one is glorified and the other forgotten, and their racial constructions were vastly different. The American Revolution delivered democracy and freedom for a minority of propertied white males, leaving out of its democracy all minorities, including Indians, enslaved Africans, and women of all races. Haiti's black republic, coming into existence only twenty-eight years after the declaration of American independence, was configured as free and black, with all citizens being classified as "black" irrespective of skin color or phenotype. White was associated with the enemy, foreigners, and the French. An interesting case is that of Polish persons resident in the Haitian Republic at the time of independence, who were also classified as "black." For Haiti's first president, Jean Jacques Dessalines, there was only one cursed color, the color white, and thus the color white was stripped from the French tricolor, creating the red and blue flag of Haiti today.

Such racialized thinking may seem extreme today, but Haiti's history is relevant. The colony of St. Domingue had been founded in 1697 as a plantation-colony mainly for sugar and coffee production for the world market. About a century before the beginnings of the successful slave revolt, the French under Louis the Fourteenth in 1685 implemented the *Code Noir* or the "Black Code," which set down the rules enforced by law for the interpretation of slave status in the colonies and the proper treatment of slaves. Promulgated as a series of reforms, the Black Code was intended as a "humane" approach to the slave system, setting limits on the punishments that masters could lawfully inflict on enslaved persons. In fact, the *Code Noir* is a testament to the brutality of the plantation slave system. In sixty articles the Black Code established slaves as property, as "things," and "beings for others." Written as a protection for the planters' property, the code made lawful dismemberment as a punishment for rebellion. While calling for the conversion and baptism of slaves the code did not apply Christian principles to improving the conditions of enslaved humans. It is not surprising then that the code has been obscured and all but vanished from the French history books. It has never been translated into English, although essential features and practices from the code were put into practice by French settlers in Louisiana fleeing from the slave revolution in Haiti. For example:

Articles 18–21 established a distinction between "subject" and "slave," denying slaves access to earnings or savings, or any personal initiative. A slave was prohibited from selling sugar cane.

Article 19 provided for slaves to travel with produce providing they had been issued passes indicating they had permission from their masters to do so.

Article 22 provided for the minimum weekly ration of food for nourishment.

Article 25 provided for the amount of cloth to be provided to each slave per year (four bolts).

Article 26 allowed for the "thing" to complain by way of written testimony (*memoires*) in the case of inhumane treatment, but a slave could
never sue a white.
Articles 22–29 obliged the master to feed, clothe, and house the slave,
but excessive kindness reduced what was "human" about the slave.
Article 33 legalized corporal punishment, even death, for rebellion, and
death to the slave who struck his master or mistress.
Article 44 declared slaves to be "chattel," and as such they entered the
community having no consequence other than that of something
mortgaged. Slaves were declared to be the property of France for the
state production of sugar and coffee. (Dayan 1995, 202–12)

The Black Code was heralded as "progressive" for its time, for it prohibited excessive brutality toward slaves, but it imposed no limits on the
number of lashes a slave could receive, or the number of hours a slave
could work. The average lifespan of a slave in the French plantation colonies was less than forty, and a large number of slaves died within two
years of their export to the plantations.

When the slave rebellion began in 1791 the Black Code was still in
effect, meaning that all of the one hundred thousand slaves who participated were risking certain execution if captured for their act of revolt.
Their strategy was to burn the plantations, and for three weeks in August
1791 twenty sugar and twelve hundred coffee plantations burned. The
call to rebel was sounded through the conch shell that became the symbol
of the revolution. American plantation owners in the South took notice.
Touissant Louverture, the leader of the rebellion and father of Haitian
independence, was a plantation carriage driver who was nearly fifty years
old when the revolution began. Spain and England sought to take control
of Haiti from France, taking advantage of the successes of the slave revolt,
but Louverture was determined not to allow the whites the honor of freeing the slaves of Haiti. Despite his deep sentiments about freedom he was
a nonracialist who sought to integrate Haiti's white minority. Needless to
say Touissant Louverture was a thorn in the side of Napoleon, who was
emperor of France at the time and who resented Touissant being compared to him. Louverture would write to Napoleon, addressing him as
"the first among the whites," signing himself "the first among the
blacks." Touissant Louverture, whose threat to the French had to be eliminated, was tricked into meeting one of Napoleon's generals; he was
arrested and taken to France, where he died alone in prison in 1803. Haiti
rose again in arms against the French, this time led by Touissant's second
in command Jean Jacques Dessalines, and the defeated French surren-
dered on November 23, 1803. Dessalines ripped the white color from the

French flag and proclaimed the Haitian Republic. Haiti's flag today remains red and blue, minus the white.

The French lost Haiti and sixty thousand soldiers, and Napoleon was forced to give up his dream of an empire in the Western hemisphere. Thanks to the Haitian revolution France gave up its ambitions in North America as well and sold its Louisiana territory for four cents an acre; this included the states of Kansas, Nebraska, Iowa, Wyoming, Montana, and the Dakotas, as well as most of Colorado and Minnesota, at the time uncharted "Indian territory." Touissant Louverture and the success of the black republic were indirectly responsible for a vast extension of the American republic, while the slave revolution struck fear in the hearts of American slave owners and served as a beacon of black freedom throughout the New World. The United States would not recognize the Haitian Republic until fifty-eight years later, in the middle of its Civil War in 1862. After the war Frederick Douglass was named American ambassador to Haiti. This history is offered here in some detail because it is poorly known and little appreciated outside of Haiti. Also, this history provides the necessary context for the major work of anthropology and antiracism *The Equality of the Human Races*, which was written by Haitian scholar Anténor Firmin in 1885, eighty-one years after Haiti proved to the world that Africans were not natural-born slaves, and that freedom and equality are the rightful conditions of the human race.

### Complexities of Race in Contemporary Haiti

With this extraordinary history and the emancipation and regeneration of blackness that Haiti represents, a positive outcome might be expected. However, Haiti was divided politically between its lighter-skinned *mulatres*, who dominated the capital, Port-au-Prince, and the "blacks" of the north, based in Cap Haitien; at one point the country actually split into two. The lighter-skinned Haitians migrated to the cities, where they developed into an elite merchant class. Rural Haiti became phenotypically blacker as the economic divide widened. The black republic remained isolated from France and Europe, which feared it, and also from the United States, from which it feared domination, so that its economy

−HAITI FOR LIFE−

**Figure 7.1. Conch call to rebellion and freedom, Haiti, 1804.**

stagnated and the state became undemocratic. Economic impoverishment fuels racial divisions, and Haiti's folk categories of race are complex in spite of the official state position that there is only one black race, *nèg*, which has also come to mean "Haitian" or "person."

Not surprisingly, *blan* translates in Haitian Kreyol as both "white" and "foreigner."

Many complex categories of phenotype operate in Haiti today that are best negotiated and understood by Haitians themselves. They inlcude: *nèg/négés*, *nwa* (all meaning black); *marabout*, *brin*, *grimo/grimèl*, *grifonn*, *wouj* (red); *jonn* (yellow); *milat/milatrès* (mulatto); and *blan* (white) (Avril 1997, 5). In everyday usage these terms are used descriptively and not pejoratively, but they do connote class, status, and position that privilege light skin, straight hair, and fine features, especially among the upper classes, who control access to jobs and resources. There is a popular saying that "a rich black is a mulatto, a poor mulatto is a black" (Avril 1997, 5). Although rural, poor Haitians might acknowledge the class superiority of lighter-skinned Haitians who dominate the economy in Port-au-Prince, there is little evidence to suggest that they ever accepted their racial superiority (Avril 1997, 7). Although race has always been part of the Haitian story, it is possible that class considerations could eventually overwhelm race, given the remarkable history of the country. Class can be "heard" in Haiti by a person's use of French, for the elites, or Kreyol, for the predominantly poor, rural, and illiterate; class can also be observed in the practice of religion. The Kreyol-speaking majority are more likely to serve the Afro-Haitian *lwa* deities in a complex referred to as Voudou, a religion that has much in common with other syncretistic religions of the Caribbean, such as Santeria, practiced in Cuba, the Dominican Republic, and elsewhere. Voudou has been stereotyped as a primitive African religion whose Haitian practitioners are a backward people; however, Haitian patriots bear witness that Voudou was an important part of their struggle for freedom.

Haitians in the United States, like other immigrants of color, must learn to cope with the realities of the one-drop rule. This means that Haitians who might have self-identified as white find that they are classified and treated as black. In the United States they must also face their "othering" as French-speaking blacks from the Caribbean, adding ethnic and linguistic markers to the racial ones.

## Brazil

Brazil is an important case because it has often been referred to as a democratic "racial paradise" for all of the race mixing that has seemingly occurred without conflict or a one-drop rule. As a Portuguese colony from 1500 and as the last country to officially abolish the slave trade, in

**Figure 7.2.**   Diversity of phenotype, Capoeira in Salvador, state of Bahia, Brazil, 1996. Courtesy of the author.

1888, Brazil has some important features and lessons about race and race relations.

Brazilian Indians experienced the near genocide of other indigenous peoples in the Americas; it is estimated that they numbered 2.8 million before European contact, and their numbers were reduced to two hundred thousand by the twentieth century. Until recently Amazonian Indians were hunted like animals in the provinces of Mato Grosso and Bahia, eliminated as barriers to progress and civilization by developers interested in clearing the forests for lumber and cattle raising. As a result of this historical ethnic cleansing the number of Indians who survived to contribute to the overall genetic mix of Brazilians is very small. Others of the surviving Indians live in isolated and remote areas, making intermixture unlikely.

According to Brazilian scholars the difference between the Portuguese and other models of colonization comes down to a difference between the social separation the British and French practiced and assimilation practiced by the Portuguese (Freyre 1933). The Portuguese view that slavery was a necessary human evil was different from the Anglo-Saxon view of slaves as less than fully human property. In marked contrast to the Anglo-American model slaves had protections under Portuguese law, such as an entitlement to own property, to marry freely, and to seek another master if treated too harshly. Manumission (freeing a slave) was common and expected. Race mixing between enslaved Africans and Europeans was also common due to the small number of Portuguese women in the colony, but not stigmatized or viewed as polluting, and *assimilado* status was readily afforded to emancipated slaves who adopted Portuguese language and culture. At the time of abolition there were more than three times the number of freed slaves as enslaved persons.

This is not meant to apologize for Brazilian slavery. Critics have justly pointed out that slavery is slavery, and this seemingly more humane system produced many slave rebellions and a large number of fugitive slave communities, known as *quilombos*. While emancipated blacks might have been a potential economic threat in the labor market, European immigration was strongly encouraged to "whiten" Brazil, and this quickly overwhelmed the numbers of blacks and their social mobility.

Brazil has received a great deal of attention for its flexible way of looking at and classifying races. Following the Caribbean and South American pattern there is no black-white binary, but a continuum of color and phenotype with most of the action in the middle. Most Brazilians self-identify as "white," although many of these whites would not pass the American one-drop test, while a minority self-identify as "black." The continuum of Brazilian skin color coding is profoundly affected by class, softening the lines between black and white. In terms of power and wealth lighter-skinned elites dominate even in the most African of provinces, Bahia. The "mulatto" woman, however, is often held as the epitome of Brazilian feminine beauty, especially in a sensual way. However, when it comes to marriage in Brazil the preference is to marry a person of lighter skin color. This is in line with the whitening ideal, and there are more marriages between blacks and "mulattoes" than between blacks and whites, who are more racially endogamous.

Although racial categories were formally abolished in the 1930s as part of the myth of Brazil's racial democracy, and racism has been made unconstitutional and criminalized by recent legal reforms, race remains a powerful way to stratify human relations. Race in Brazil can be presented very simply, as in the following general racial categories by which Brazilians self-identify. White skin preference is evident both in the majority who identify as *branco* as well as in the small percentage (7%) identifying as *prêto*, or black.

Brazilians self-identifying as *branco* (white) = 55%
Brazilians self-identifying as *pardo* (mestizo/mulatto) = 38%

Brazilians self-identifying as *negro/prêto* (black) = 7%
("Racial Classification in Latin America" 2000)

Race becomes remarkably complex as the subtleties and nuances of Brazilian racial folk categories are included. Literally hundreds of different racial descriptions (Freyre 1933, 492, in Harris 1964) have been recorded by anthropologists, producing a view of race that is not a rigid taxonomy, like those to which we are accustomed. Folk terms such as *alva* for pure white are modified to *alva-escuro* (dark or off-white) or *alva-rosada* (white with pink highlights)—shading to *branca* (white) or *clara* (light) and *branca morena* (darkish white) or *branca suja* (dirty white)—shading to *café* (coffee colored), *café com leite* (coffee with milk), *canela* (cinnamon)—shading to Cabo Verde (black, Cape Verdean), Crioula (African, meaning also "slave") to *prêta* (black) or *prêtinha* (black of a lighter hue). According to DNA studies by Brazilian scientists as many as 80 percent of Brazilians have some African ancestry (Rohter 2001, A3).

The negativity of *negro* or *prêto* can be softened with the description "a little *prêto*." There are many lightening terms to soften the perception of the harshness of dark skin color, often as a matter of social etiquette. "Mestizo" is the most commonly used term to ameliorate dark skin color and to avoid the offense of the *negro* reference. The lack of discourse around "blackness" has retarded an effective black pride or black consciousness movement in Brazil comparable to that in the United States or South Africa, although many dark-skinned Brazilians complain of racial discrimination against them. Although discrimination on the basis of race was made a criminal offence in 1951, "my color" or "my race" was reported by anthropologists conducting research in the early 1990s to explain the failure to get a job, and Afro-Brazilian men report more incidents of overt racism. Afro-Brazilian men are more likely to report outright rejection by Euro-Brazilian men than Afro-Brazilian women, reflecting perhaps the sensual attraction of the darker Brazilian woman. White debutante balls reminiscent of the American old South are held throughout Brazil, allegedly to promote both class and racial endogamy, or marriage within class and race.

These categories and their negative associations with blackness are reinforced by ethnographic study of the everyday lives of Euro-Brazilians and Afro-Brazilians. Such studies show that the latter experience social ostracism, experience a lack of educational and leadership opportunities, are represented pejoratively in the media, and are considered undesirable for marriage with whites. Nonetheless Twine (1998) reports that whites readily enter into sexual liaisons with blacks and mulattoes, the latter hopeful that their offspring may be "lightened" in the process, providing the desired social mobility accorded those approximating Eurocentric standards of beauty. Often such children are registered at birth as "white," thus contributing to the grossly inflated number of whites in the official statistics. The widespread practice of adoption of darker, less advantaged children by white households for employment as domestic help is regarded as benign and evidence of the country's lack of racism. The resulting racial mixing within households, combined with the acceptability of erotic desire and relations across racial lines, permits a national denial of racism; interpretations of racism are replaced with an ideology of official racial egalitarianism (Harrison 2002, 160).

Racial discrimination in Brazil's universities is currently being addressed through a method born in the United States, that of affirmative action. The composition of Brazil's universities is less than 2 percent black, a number vastly disproportionate to their numbers in the general population. A Bahian woman PhD recounted to me that university students left her class because, she believed, they did not want to have a black professor, and other black professors have reported similar disbelief from students when they begin their classes. Some states, such as Rio de Janeiro, have required a 40 percent quota of black students, setting aside this number of seats in the university for incoming freshmen. The Brazilian congress is considering making race-based quotas a requirement at all fifty-three federal universities (Rohter 2001). Quotas of 20 to 40 percent black representation set aside for government employment and elections are actively being considered for 2003 and 2004. The dominant cultural aesthetic of whitening results in few blacks in television, films, or commercials, although quotas requiring the inclusion of 25 percent black and mixed-race actors have also been proposed.

Ironically, given Brazil's history of an aversion to racial labeling—despite hundreds of living folk categories such as those mentioned above—it is now faced with constructing racial categories for official use. The census designations that rely on the old skin color criteria are: "white," "black," and "brown." The Brazilian racial morass may continue, as the vast majority that formerly self-identified as "white" may now begin to label themselves as "black" or "brown" in order to take advantage of the new quotas.

With the near extermination of native peoples in Brazil, an assault that continued well into the late twentieth century, the racial consciousness of "Indianness" is limited to relatively few activists. There is little pro-Indian national discourse. Indians who are part of Indian pride movements have perhaps had more success on the international front, with human rights activists, because of the recent controversy involving the Yanamami, an indigenous people of Brazil and Venezuela. They are more likely to speak frankly about race and to challenge racism. Indians take justified pride in their history without the shame of slavery. *Pardo* is most often used to describe mixed-race persons with Indian blood, but the term "Indio" is not much used in racial discourse.

Gilberto Freyre's 1930s model of racial democracy, with peoples of different skin tones mixing freely and enjoying themselves at the beaches and at carnival time, has now been widely challenged as mythology (Twine 1998). Freyre's classic work *Masters and Slaves* was written in 1933 largely as a counter to the racist ideas of Gobineau and the rising ideology of Nazism that warned against the social harm of race mixing. Freyre then noted 150 different skin tones in Brazil, from "dawn white" to "navy blue," with a decided romanticizing of the exotic and erotic "mulatto." His work led to the abolition of racial categories, so there is no official acknowledgment of race to this day in Brazil or therefore of race discrimination. The legacy of Freyre's work, many argue, is one of major social and political denial about race and racial discrimination. One turning point came with a 1991 visit of Nelson Mandela, just released from twenty-seven years in South African prisons and ready to reconstruct his country. Still influenced by the legacy of Freyre's work, he said, "You are far more advanced than we are in building a multiracial society. We will use Brazil as our guide" (Margolis 1992, 4). These comments sparked immediate protest from Afro-Brazilians, who complained so bitterly of their unequal treatment that Mandela upon his departure amended his remarks: he called on Brazil to respond to the petitions of its black citizens for equality. In the 1990s a nascent black pride movement sprang up in Bahia, Brazil's most African-influenced province, with numerous cultural symbols such as Afro or dreadlock hairstyles and a celebration of the vibrancy and syncretism of Afro-Brazilian music. I personally witnessed a revived traditional black carnival celebration in Salvador in 1996, with small bands and drummers parading through the streets of the old city by night and the sale of Bob Marley music, Rastafarian items, and buttons sporting the logo "Negro è Lindo"—"Black is Beautiful." Oludum drumming is especially associated with Afro-Brazilian music and was brought to the attention of North Americans with Paul Simon's popular release in the early 1990s "Rhythm of the Saints." The complaints of Afro-Brazilians appear to be borne out by statistics of their representation in public political life. The surface appearance of racial harmony led many African Americans to visit the country. Their multiple and complex reactions have been summarized in the book *African-American Reflections on Brazil's Racial Paradise* (Hellwig 1992).

## RACE IN AFRICA: SELECTED CASES

### Cape Verde Islands

The Cape Verde Islands lie about 250 miles off the coast of Senegal in West Africa and were colonized by the Portuguese in the fifteenth century. A Creole population—a mixture of indigenous Africans from the west coast, Portuguese colonials, and Moors and Jews expelled from Spain after the Inquisition in 1492—was born over the next several centuries. Power rested in Portuguese hands until independence was won in 1975. Of the European colonizers the Portuguese were the first in and the last out of the African continent and relinquished power only after wars of liberation in each of their African colonies, Mozambique, Angola, Guinea Bissau, and Cape Verde. We have already become familiar in the discussion of race in Brazil with Portuguese ideas about race and the ideal of becoming *assimilado*. What is interesting about Cape Verde is the intermediate racial position that Cape Verdeans held between "inferior" black Africans and "superior" white Europeans. Originally, during the fifteenth-century settlement of the colony, there were only two racial groups: *brancos*, white rulers, merchants, and administrators, primarily but not exclusively Portuguese; and *prêtos*, "blacks" who initially were all slaves or those Africans armed to enforce the slave system. (Recall the discussion of the term *prêto* in Brazil, with its strong connotations of blackness, slavery, and inferiority.) This system quickly developed a majority *mestiço* appendage, with the two "separate" populations readily mixing in the slave, shipping, and agricultural colony of the Cape Verde Islands. Between 1550 and 1950 a consistent 69 percent of the population was identified as mixed or *mestiço*, with between 1 and 2 percent "white" and between 28 and 34 percent "black" (Lobban 1995, 55). For example, toward the end of Portuguese colonialism in Guinea Bissau in 1963, 75 percent of colonial officials were of Cape Verdean origin (Mendy 2002).

*Mestiços* were Africans of Balanta, Mandinka, Manjak, or other ethnic and linguistic origins who had assimilated or partly assimilated to Portuguese language and culture through forced or voluntary race mixing. The term "Moreno"—having a "Moorish" or North African appearance— might be used for a light-skinned Cape Verdean, or an "Oriental" Jewish or Muslim person, or one having these origins. In the Criolo language of Cape Verdeans *nyambob* was used to refer to whites, coming from the Mandinka word, *tubob*, for whites. As *mestiços* became the norm for Cape Verdean society and the ideal of whitening and lightening was fixed in Portuguese-derived racial hierarchies, an intense interest in hair form occurred, resulting in a typology as complex as that related to skin color. *Cabeca seca* for dry or wiry hair, *cabo crespo* for "frizzy" hair, and *cabo encrespado* for curly hair described a range of hair type from "bad" to "good," with "good" matching closeness to a white ideal. As in patterns already noted in the Caribbean, wealth and status tend to lighten a person's racial classification, while low status darkens a person's classification.

## Victims and Victimizers

Cape Verdeans were commonly used as strategic intermediaries in the colonial system in other Portuguese colonies where the mechanism of divide and rule neatly fit a racial caste system. Cape Verdeans were both enslaved and enslavers, both victims and victimizers, in the colonial structure. As Portuguese colonialism matured Cape Verdeans were placed in multiple positions of lower-level authority and were able to observe the relative position that Portuguese administrators placed them in. They were better off in relative terms than Africans in the other colonies. Moreover, five centuries of Portuguese rule led many justifiably to the conclusion that white colonial rule was a permanent condition and what small benefit they might derive would be worthwhile. This may be why Cape Verde was the only Portuguese African colony not to fight its own war of independence. The Party for the Independence of Guinea Bissau and Cape Verde, led by Amilcar Cabral, who himself was of Cape Verdean origin, fought its major battles in Guinea.

The intermediate racial position that Cape Verdeans held left a legacy of mixed racial consciousness. Moreover, since the nineteenth century

**Figure 7.3.   Cape Verdean immigrants aboard the *Savoia*. They arrived in New Bedford on October 4, 1914.**

chronic poverty, drought, famine, disease, and limited opportunities have turned the country into a nation of emigrants. Historically Cape Verdeans are the only people to emigrate voluntarily to the United States from Africa before the end of European colonialism in the continent. Most came to New England, where they worked in the whaling, cranberry, and maritime industries.

Because Portuguese colonialism ended decades after the great wave of African independence, Cape Verdeans came to the United States with Portuguese passports or identity cards. Immediately they became known in the United States as "black Portuguese," and many Cape Verdeans insisted that they were indeed Portuguese, despite American racial stereotypes. Other Cape Verdeans identified closely with the American black power movement of the 1960s and easily translated its message into an assertion of African identity as the liberation movement leading to independence gained momentum.

Young Cape Verdeans learn early that their racial and ethnic identity will be the subject of curiosity and questioning. The mixed ancestry of Cape Verdeans has created a typical Creole, diverse population common to Caribbean nations, with skin tones from light to dark and hair form from straight to tightly curled in the same family. Cape Verdeans do not easily fit into—nor will they readily succumb to—the American black-white dichotomy. Historical populations of Cape Verdeans in southeastern New England have avoided settling or mixing with African American populations, preferring segregated communities closer to Portuguese immigrants. The question of racial identity is still actively discussed (Wahnon 2002). Phenotypically Cape Verdeans may pass for African American. Or they may be asked, "What are you? Black, white, some funny kind of 'Puerto Rican'?" On American census forms they have often checked "other" because they do not fit the racial or ethnic categories described on the forms. If a Cape Verdean self-identifies as Portuguese, he or she may be told, "Well, then you're not black." "Well, I may be, look at my color" (De Andrade 1997, 24). In Cape Verde to be black means to be a slave, so "black" is often not used except to hurt and offend. Cape Verdeans often insist on having multiple racial identities, an idea in America that is ahead of its time.

Cape Verdeans are multiracial people with a single ethnic identity; they speak a common language, Criolo, and trace their heritage to the islands of the Cape Verdean archipelago. The Cape Verdean experience is one of many from the post-1492 world that teaches us that race has been socially constructed mainly under European-based economic structures, from the Atlantic slave trade through colonialism to various New World configurations of race handed down to us as a powerful legacy from the preceding centuries.

## South Africa

Apartheid in South Africa and Jim Crow segregation in the United States shared a great deal in common, except that American apartheid was built on slavery and South African apartheid was built on white settler colonialism. In terms of settler colonialism South African apartheid resembles the European settlement of North America, which ultimately expanded to include the fifty United States, in that whites came, settled, and systematically took the land away from the indigenous peoples. The historical outcome for American Indians was their near extermination, with the remnants placed on reservations. In South Africa the African majority survived but were restricted to reserves the South African apartheid government called "homelands" or *bantustans*. They were also confined to segregated townships on the outskirts of the newly created colonial cities of Cape Town, Johannesburg, and Pretoria. "Settler colonialism" means that foreign colonials come to stay, and they come to believe that the land they stole is theirs; it means that force must be used to enter, to dominate, and to maintain economic and political control of the new land. This is what the European settlers did in North America in the seventeenth and eighteenth centuries, and this is what the Dutch settlers (called Boers and later Afrikaners) did in South Africa in the 1830s, followed by the English in the nineteenth century, who vied with the Boers for control of the valuable and strategic Cape colony and the whole of South Africa. Whites retained control of South Africa until Nelson Mandela was freed in 1990, after twenty-seven years in prison, and was then elected president of the new South Africa in 1994.

White rule reached its aggressive and brutal climax with the establishment of the apartheid state in 1948, when the Afrikaners took over from the British, whose colonial holdings had been weakened by the Second World War. "Apartheid" means "separateness" in the Afrikaans language, and its speakers, the Afrikaners, erected a state that legalized segregation in every basic social and political institution. Strict separation of all nonwhites from whites was the primary racial barrier erected; however, apartheid laws also kept Africans and colored separated, and colored separated from Asian minorities. Although the apartheid laws were passed only in the 1950s, they legalized racial exclusion that had been practiced since early colonial times. Apartheid was comparable to Jim Crow practices of segregation in the United States. For example, all facilities were racially separated—all residential communities, all schools and universities, all places of worship, all public facilities from buses and trains to restrooms. Interracial blood transfusions were prohibited, although it is widely believed that medical personnel ignored this absurd and unscientific law. All ambulance services were segregated, resulting in tragic occasions when injured persons of color were refused service by white ambulance drivers, or when whites were in a life-or-death situation on a highway near a township.

Special reforms to apartheid were instituted, for instance allowing colored women to wash the hair of white women in beauty parlors. One noble experiment in interracial living whereby progressive whites lived with Africans, colored, and Asians—District 6 in Cape Town—was bulldozed by the apartheid government as an intolerable example of "race mixing." Since the dismantling of apartheid in 1994 District 6 has been turned into a Museum of Racial Healing. I visited this museum in 1996 and was moved by the many items of everyday life—from street signs to family pictures—that had been retrieved from bulldozed rubble as sacred relics of this courageous act of resistance to apartheid.

Despite the many similarities with the United States, race is configured differently in South Africa. The white minority—predominantly Boer and to a lesser extent English settlers who came to South Africa from the seventeenth to the nineteenth centuries—constitutes only about 20 percent of South Africa's population. Nonetheless whites controlled all of the basic economic, political, social, and judicial institutions and all of the best lands. The 65 to 70 percent African majority, racially classified as "Bantu," or by the racist referent "Kaffir," were segregated into townships on the outskirts of South Africa's major cities. They provided cheap, unskilled labor to the whites of Johannesburg (Southwest township and Soweto), Cape Town (Crossroads and Guguleta townships), and other cities, allowing the whites to enjoy one of the highest standards of living in Africa or the West. Reserves, or *bantustans* (comparable to American Indian reservations), were legalized under apartheid, making South Africans effectively strangers in their own land. The African "homelands" were created on 13 percent of South Africa—its worst, least arable lands. Each African person was assigned to a *bantustan* by "tribe" or region of origin and made to carry a "passbook" at all times indicating his or her "homeland." Pass control permitted Africans to travel and work only in areas designated by the apartheid government, meaning that people living in the townships had to travel in and out of the white cities daily as laborers and domestics. Nannies might be permitted to stay overnight to look after their white charges, which meant that they could not look after their own children. Families were frequently broken apart by this system, with the elderly and some women and children living in the *bantustans*, the adult males working in the gold and diamond mines, and adult women working in the cities and living in townships. Resistance to the "pass laws" was the spark that lit the fires of the antiapartheid movement, led primarily by the African National Congress (ANC).

The mixed-race colored, whose racial origins were mainly in the coastal cities, especially Cape Town and Durban, were and are racially segregated in South African cities. Their fate under apartheid was slightly better than that of the Africans (indigenous people), and as people often carrying Afrikaner (Boer settlers) names and speaking the Dutch-derived language Afrikaans, their identity was racially tied to white South Africa. The colored, about 10 percent of South Africans, range in phenotype from light to dark skin tones; however, their language and heritage as partly white conveyed some slight privileges during apartheid whereby they were permitted to live in cities and could obtain some education to become professionals and bureaucrats; in the waning years of apartheid they were granted a separate parliament and elected officials, privileges always denied to the "inferior" Africans. In the nineteenth century an American ship, the *Alabama*, made annual stops in Cape Town, where the minstrel tradition was introduced from the United States and was reinterpreted and incorporated as an annual celebration of colored pride.

South Africa did not employ the one-drop rule in its system of racial classification; however, it made practical use of phenotype through race classification boards. A light-skinned colored, for example, might appeal to one of these boards, requesting reclassification as "white" based on phenotypic appearance. If the person could "pass" as white, the board would make the legal adjustment, allowing the person to attend white schools, live in white areas, and enjoy a higher standard of living. The only requirement for racial reclassification was that the person sever all ties with his or her colored family, because affiliation and association was what defined a colored person. After the end of apartheid the colored population is undergoing a process of self-examination in regard to their identity as Africans of mixed-race ancestry.

South Africa is credited with providing the world with a model of racial discourse and potential healing in its Truth and Reconciliation Commission, headed by bishop Desmond Tutu, which held hearings for several years after apartheid's end. Amnesty was provided for all who came before the commission; it was a mechanism that allowed both victims and victimizers to tell their stories, confess their wrongs, make apologies, or request at least some social compensation for loss of life, torture, or imprisonment. While the commission had its critics, especially those who complained about apartheid government officials exchanging amnesty for their testimony, nonetheless the Truth and Reconciliation Commission is widely acknowledged as having played a vital role in keeping postapartheid racial tensions from erupting into the violence that many predicted would occur.

The necessary recasting of historical truth is now underway. The Afrikaner version of South African history had the Boer Trekkers fighting "savages"—such as King Shaka of the Zulu and the fierce Xhosa—while

Figure 7.4.   South African colored pride parade, Cape Town, 1996. Courtesy of the author.

they made their way to the interior and established settlements in the "dark continent." Replacing this Eurocentric version of the country's history with an Afrocentric narrative of African resistance and liberation has not been easy, as the bloodless transition to a postapartheid country has left many former supporters of apartheid wanting to keep their privileged position in life as well as in history. The ANC, which led the antiapartheid struggle, has a justifiable interest in telling its story. And the women of the African National Congress do not want to be forgotten either. While men were jailed, exiled, or working outside of the cities, ANC women kept the resistance in the townships going and are the unsung heroines of the struggle.

In 2004, ten years after the end of apartheid and the birth of multiracial democracy, the ANC was overwhelmingly supported in national elections. However, the entrenched racism that characterized the apartheid era continues, and the nation's thirty-four million blacks and citizens of color are still estranged—economically, politically, and socially—from the six million whites. The younger generation of whites have a special responsibility to renounce their historical supremacy and embrace with optimism the equitable multiracial future for South Africa that the ANC and Nelson Mandela envisioned.

### Egypt and Sudan

It may be easier to understand racism within the African continent when it is so clearly a matter of white over black, as in the previous, South African case. But when the issue of racism between African peoples is raised, such as between Egyptians and Sudanese, or between northern "Arab" Sudanese and southern or western (from Darfur) "African" Sudanese, the matter becomes more complex and sensitive. Ancient rivalries along the Nile between the Pharaonic Egyptians and their Nubian neighbors to the south established a pattern of conquest, dominance, resistance, and rebellion that set the tone for the racially tense relations that were to follow. At times during the three thousand years of Pharaonic rule in the Nile Valley, Egypt ruled rebellious Nubia with an iron hand to keep the gold, slaves, and other precious commodities flowing. At other times relations were relatively peaceful, and political autonomy and mutual respect prevailed. And there were times when Nubia ruled Egypt, such as during the twenty-fifth so-called Ethiopian Dynasty. Nubians were portrayed in Egyptian iconography as "perfectly handsome" when they were allies, or as caricature enemies when the two peoples were at war (Firmin 1885, 231). Nubians were enslaved along with Libyans to the west of the Nile Valley and Assyrians or Hittites to the east, and all were portrayed as subjugated slaves, as non-Egyptian "others." The ancient Egyptians noticed and recorded phentoypic and ethnic differences between themselves and the peoples whom they contacted and conquered, or by whom they were vanquished. However, they did not develop a hierarchical system of racial phenotyping and stereotyping, nor did they equate skin color or any other form of outward appearance with slavery or innate lower status.

As one of the two oldest world civilizations, the Nile Valley has a vast history that must be examined closely to reveal the dynamic nature of human interactions over millennia. Skin color and other phenotypic features vary greatly in the region, following the course of the Nile: from southern, tall, ebony Nilotics to the rich brown color of the people of central riverine Sudan, imbued with West African traits through centuries of pilgrims making their way to Mecca. Continuing north one encounters the northern Sudanese and southern Egyptian Nubians with their dark skin and wavy to curly hair; the red brown color of the central Egyptians;

**Figure 7.5.** Ancient Egyptian depiction of physical diversity known to them: left to right, Nuba or south Sudanese; Asiatics from Syria-Palestine; Nubians; Libyans, sketch from tomb of King Seti I, Thebes, nineteenth dynasty, c. 1300 BCE.

the light brown skin of the Egyptians of the delta; and the occasionally fair-skinned people of Cairo and Alexandria, whose roots may be traced to southern Europe, Turkey, or to Syria-Palestine. This multiracial mix reflects thousands of years of contact and physical and cultural exchange. The study of race in the Nile Valley is relatively new, except for the literature that might be characterized as "vindicationist" in the nineteenth century and Afrocentric in the late twentieth century, whereby the achievements of Egypt as one of humanity's great civilizations are viewed as black African accomplishments (Firmin 1885; Delany 1879). The study of modern race relations in the Nile Valley from these ancient times through the spread of the Arabs and Islam to the advent of European colonialism is more recent (Fluehr-Lobban and Rhodes 2004) and requires a layered, multiple sensitivity not only to race but to power relations mediated through colonial and neocolonial structures and their legacies. During the Islamic era, from the sixteenth century to the nineteenth, the Turkish and "Arab" slave trade reflected some ancient routes of exploitation of the south by the north. In the nineteenth and twentieth centuries the British colonized Egypt but turned Egyptians into colonial agents in the Sudan, and northern "Arab" Sudanese were favored over southern Africans. This created a "double consciousness" among Egyptians (Powell 2000), as they were constructed as subordinate to the English but were "rewarded" by a proscription of superiority over the Nubians and northern Sudanese "Arabs." These, in turn, were racially constructed as superior culturally and physically to the African southerners (Fluehr-Lobban 2004). Anthropologists aided British colonialism in constructing a racial hierarchy in the Nile Valley from north to south that was linked directly to colonial policies and administration.

Jok Madut Jok, one a new generation of southern Sudanese scholars, has explored the legacy of race from colonial times to the turbulent post-independence period (2001). He shows that British colonialism was built on existing relations of race and slavery before the British arrival in the nineteenth century. Northern "Arab" administrators who seized power at the time of Sudanese independence in 1956 left unresolved contradictions of race. These have fueled chronic civil war and left undone the business of nation building. Protracted civil war has resulted in massive death and displacement of southern Sudanese, perhaps as many as two million souls. It has also compelled northerners who oppose regimes that have waged this war—whether in a revival of the old colonial "civilizing" mission or more recent Islamist expansion—to expatriate as political refugees. Some of these refugees have engaged in self-critical assessment of their historical role as exploiters of southern cocitizens.

Others (Poole 2004; Jennings 2004) have examined contemporary attitudes about race and aesthetic prejudices in Cairo, and in Aswan in

Nubia. A preference for lighter skin, comparable to that expressed by black and white Americans, is revealed, showing that race is a significant marker of social status. Anne Jennings explores her experience as an African American anthropologist working in Egypt, in Aswan, the unofficial capital of Nubia. "We like you Ani, because you are the same color as us," her Nubian hosts told her. Jennings had some of her most significant experiences regarding race in Cairo, where she was often taken as "African," with the corollary attitude that Africa was a place far away from Egypt. Moving south, where the skin color of Egyptians darkens, Jennings reported greater ease of acceptance and the insignificance of her color.

## RACE IN THE MIDDLE EAST

### Arabs and Jews

The term "Arab" is an elusive ethnic, cultural, and linguistic term—and has been used as a racial designation. Ethnologically, an Arab is one who traces descent to the Arab tribes (lineages) of the Arabian Peninsula. This would be simple enough were it not for the explosive spread of Islam by the Arabs during the eighth century of the common era, Islam having been introduced in Arabia in the seventh century. Given that great historical expansion and migration of people through the first jihads—in southwest Asia (contemporary Iraq, Iran, and Syria-Palestine) and North Africa from Egypt to Morocco, as well as southern Europe—Arabs settled and mingled with local populations and forged a new Arab-Muslim identity in these areas over the succeeding centuries. The tracing of descent through Arab lineages, especially through the line of the Prophet, the Quraysh, has always been favored with the honorific term *sayyid*, and, perhaps, amplified beyond actual genealogy and therefore more fictive than real.

This blending of people and cultures through the spread of Islam fostered indigenous concepts, such as "Afro-Arab" identity, which arose in the context of the Sudanese nationalist movement, as well as in Muslim East Africa, in Kenya and Tanzania. This was intended to solve the problem of having to identify exclusively with either African or Arab nations and cultures at the time of independence, and it flourished more as a political than as a cultural concept.

While the precise definition of "Arab" is elusive, the sociological definition is more easily derived—by simply asking people if they identify themselves as Arabs. The question is simple but the answer is not. People who speak Arabic as a first language may identify themselves as Arabs in a generic sense, but they are as likely to identify themselves as Egyptian, or Palestinian, or Lebanese. The term "Arab" in the Arabic language has multiple meanings and derivations, and depending on one's social background and place in society may evoke different responses.

In its purest sense, the term "Arab" refers to nomads, or Bedouin, meaning people who move about and use animal husbandry as their major economic adaptation. The colloquial Arabic term for automobile is "arabiyya," or literally a thing that moves about.

### Racial Identity: A Semitic Race?

The designations "Semite" and "Semitic" have been used to describe the Arab and Jewish peoples. In Euro-American history and culture, "Semite" has been applied to the Jewish presence in Western society, so that the negative referent "anti-Semitic" has been used almost exclusively to mean bigotry or racism as applied to Jewish people. Anti-Arab prejudice has witnessed an alarming increase in the West in the past several decades and especially after the events of September 11, 2001, and can justifiably be included as another unfortunate form of anti-Semitism.

The Semites are an ancient people tracing their common linguistic heritage to Mesopotamia about 2500 BCE. The "sons of Shem," Semites diverged into distinctive language and cultural groups that included the Arabs and Hebrews—the legendary descendants of the sons of Abraham, Ishmael, and Isaac—and also people speaking related Semitic languages, such as Aramaic and Amharic. The Hebrews originated the idea of a single, unchallenged deity through the prophet Abraham, who is revered as progenitor to all of the Abrahamic faiths—Judaism, Christianity, and Islam.

The Hebrews were already a distinctive people at the time of Babylonian captivity and in the tenth century BCE, when the Hebrew territories of Judea and Samaria were united into the kingdom of Israel under King David. This kingdom existed for only a century, after which the Hebrew peoples dispersed into parts of southwest Asia, North Africa, the Iberian Peninsula, and other parts of Europe.

The Arabs settled and flourished in "al-Jazira al-Arabiyya," literally the "island of the Arabs," the Arabian Peninsula. The northern Arabs were nomadic camel herders or oasis dwellers, and the southern Arabs engaged in commercial trading regionally and internationally. It was into this context that the faith of Islam was introduced by the last of the prophets, Muhammad.

The experience of European Jews (Ashkenazi Jews) was dramatically different from that of the Middle Eastern and North African Jews (Sephardic Jews), who lived in relative peace with their Muslim and Christian neighbors in the cities and towns of Arab and Ottoman Turkish empires.

In Europe, Christian theologians blamed the Jews for the killing of Christ, and their isolation made them an easy target for religious and racial harassment, documented in histories of the Jewish ghettos of major European cities and the systematic pogroms of rural and urban Jews in czarist Russia. This historical context gave rise in Europe to the nineteenth-century Jewish nationalist movement, called Zionism, which called for an exclusively Jewish state. The fulfillment of Zionist aspirations after the end of World War II, with the creation of the state of Israel and the displacement of Palestinian Arab people, has altered the preexisting relationship between Arab-Muslim and Jewish peoples.

An enmity engendered by politics has replaced the traditional tolerance between the religious-cultural groups. But whether or not this is racial intolerance is subject to debate. Arab anger over Israeli politics is not the same as anti-Semitism; one has to do with politics and the other with race. There is reason for optimism that a negotiated, just peace between Israel and its Arab neighbors will bring about a restoration of Arab-Muslim and Jewish relations as they once were, the essentials of this being tolerance, mutual respect, and peaceful coexistence.

Is there a Semitic race? Many Arab and Muslim peoples from the Middle East and North Africa have been confounded by the racial categories on U.S. Census forms, and when asked to fill out these forms, they have not known with which race they should identify. Some would say they are African but not black; others report that they are frequently taken for Hispanic and have been addressed in Spanish in American cities with large Hispanic populations; others, in frustration, might check "other" on the census form, since nothing else seems to fit. Some affirmative action guidelines have sought to clarify the question of race for North Africans and Middle Eastern persons by including these groups in the category "white/Caucasian."

## RACE IN MAJOR CULTURES OF ASIA

### The Indian Caste System: Contrasts and Parallels to Race Relations in America

Racism in America, especially affecting African Americans, has often been referred to as a "caste" system. This is because the status of race is conveyed at birth and cannot be changed by class mobility, for example. In the Indian caste system if you are born a Brahmin you are a Brahmin for life; if you are born an "untouchable," you will never rise above untouchable status.

An understanding of caste relations in India may make the parallel between American race relations and caste more or less compelling. *Jati,* the Indian term for caste, connotes human difference analogous to that of species. The caste system (Jajmani) can be traced to Indian feudalism and the formalization of basic client-servant relationships that over time became in-marrying, or endogamous, kin groups. The servants or laborers who worked for the wealthy landowning class/caste developed into endogamous kin groups dependent on their overlords in a common pattern of feudal paternalism. The type of work carried out by the higher castes came to be viewed as culturally "clean," while that of the lower castes was "polluted." Economic caste positions were reinforced with notions of purity and pollution so that the most "impure" workers—for example, those who tilled the soil or made leather—were considered so polluted that they came to be known as "untouchables."

Contact, especially any physical contact, with untouchables contaminated higher-caste individuals. Mahatma Gandhi combined the struggle for Indian independence with a commitment to the elimination of untouchable status, and indeed it was abolished in the newly independent Indian nation in 1951. Further, India placed untouchables under "protective discrimination," an early form of affirmative action in which castes that were "scheduled" or discriminated against would be offered set asides in government institutions. Despite such programs and Gandhi's powerful legacy the *harijan* (meaning "chosen of God" and Gandhi's referent for the untouchables) remained at the bottom of Indian society long after independence.

The principle of purity versus impurity continues to pervade Indian society and partly explains caste. Hindu ritual demands that sacrifices be made to the gods in a state of purity. Brahmins have traditionally carried out these rituals. Another basic principle is that any waste product from a human, animal, or deity is impure, and those having contact with waste are likewise impure. Even a Brahmin priest, or *tantri*, becomes polluted by eating and eliminating his own waste, or by birth and death in the family, but these states of impurity are temporary, whereas impure castes are born impure and remain impure throughout their lives. Anything touched by a polluted person contaminates the person contacted. For example, food or water may not be offered or accepted from lower caste to upper caste except under highly specified conditions. The receiver is always superior to the giver, and the served is always higher than the server. Caste groups live separately from one another, with the impure untouchables living in the most isolated locales. Marriage across caste lines are strictly forbidden.

The number of caste rankings in India can vary. One village studied by Pauline Kolenda (1985) numbered fifteen castes, determined by occupation and by birth: from Brahmin, merchant, goldsmith, and genealogist at the top or near top, known collectively as "Brahmins"; to "Kshatriyasto"—barber, water carrier, grain parcher, and shepherd—in or near the middle ranking; to beggar, shoemaker, leatherworker, and sweeper in the lowest caste, untouchable. As a system of occupational rankings the caste system is relational and interdependent but not egalitarian. Some limited caste mobility is possible through territorial acquisition by purchase or conquest, or through service to a ruler—for example, the British colonial authorities, who did little to undermine the caste system. Likewise, losing land meant downward caste positioning. The Hindu belief system reinforces the caste system and has hampered efforts to reform it.

Untouchables refer to themselves as *dalit*. Normally I would defer to this preference, but for the purposes of comparing them to populations that have experienced racial discrimination in the West, I will use "untouchable" to underscore the point of their historical discrimination. In the early decades of the twentieth century activists agitated to permit untouchables to have access to temples and to have representation in local and national government. This move was successful, and as a result one of seven sets in central government and state legislatures are reserved for untouchables. This ratio is proportional to their numbers in the general population, at about 12 percent of Indian society. This system continues to this day. Most recently demands have been for an affirmative action system whereby university seats are also reserved for untouchables, but this has created a widespread backlash among dominant Hindus, who also seek a desirable university education. Untouchable resistance over the centuries has included defection from the Hindu religion and conversion to Christianity. Meeting a Christian in India implies that the person is of low caste or untouchable origin. Untouchables have also converted to Islam, Sikhism, and Buddhism, although such conversions have usually not changed Hindus' views of their social position.

Despite heroic, noble, and repeated efforts to eliminate the caste system in India, it has remained essentially intact. Marriage within caste is the norm, and those outside of caste are referred to as "mixed marriages." The basic social unit is the endogamous descent group along patrilineal lines. Kolenda (1985) believes that these will ultimately compete and replace the caste system. There is an assumption that employers give preference to members of their caste in hiring and promotion. Prominent and influential positions in industry, finance, and government are dominated by high-caste individuals. Education appears to be a caste equalizer, with great potential to break down the old division between manual and nonmanual labor. In Kolenda's analysis, few, if any, castes have modernized (a loaded term) or adapted entirely to contemporary life, although the maturation of Indian democracy is undermining the caste system.

There are many parallels between the caste system's treatment of untouchables and the American Jim Crow system of segregation of blacks from whites. It is easy to see why the comparison, indeed the equation, of caste with race in America has taken place. Similar notions of pollution through contact with an undesirable race/caste—in bathrooms, in waiting rooms, and at water fountains—as well as residential segregation and bans on intermarriage are shared by the two systems. However strong the comparisons, the idea of equating caste with race may also be questioned.

First, there is an important difference between the historical background of an occupation-based caste system and that of a slave system. The idea of human beings as property in the slave system, the fundamental denial of personhood, and the designation of that status by race (i.e., phenotype) constitute a major difference. Untouchables, while of the lowest socioeconomic status, were not denied personhood in Hindu beliefs. To the Indian outsider a high-caste and low-caste or untouchable person may be indistinguishable from a Brahmin, except by street address and dress. American efforts to racialize the caste system, that is, to project lighter skin onto the superior castes and darker skin onto the lower castes, fail. Indians vary by skin color from light to dark, and while there is an aesthetic preference for light-skinned actors to appear in films and advertisements, Indian society does not appear to be a racially divided one in which phenotype is the major indicator of status. Racial profiling in the

Figure 7.6.    "Dalit" Indian women in Madras; "harijan" ('chosen of God'), 1996. Courtesy of the author.

American sense would be ridiculous, but caste preference is normal and expected.

Secondly, despite legal and social bans on interracial relationships and marriage in America, such relations have been frequent and continuous, whether involuntary or voluntary, such that American society is already very racially hybridized, although it fails to acknowledge this fact. Strong norms and sanctions against intercaste marriages, always formalized, have resulted in little real caste mixing in India despite the high degree of caste familiarity and interdependence.

The notions of pollution and segregation of low caste/inferior race do offer a favorable comparison, although for different reasons. Hindu religious beliefs regarding purity and impurity lie at the base of caste segregation, while the American system of segregation was erected as a means of stemming the tide of "Negro advancement" after the end of slavery, as a way of keeping the Negro "in his place." If I ask my students, "Who are the American untouchables today?" they respond that people with AIDS and the homeless are the modern American untouchables.

### China

The ancient Chinese thought heaven was circular and projected its shadow onto the center of the earth; the area where the shadow fell, Tian Xia (zone beneath heaven), was China. The rest of the world was home to "barbarians," and the one place where trade with them was possible was in Canton. Only the "Gong Hong" merchants were authorized to deal with the foreigners. The Chinese view of "others" constitutes a racialized system that did not become a global racist system like that of Europe, since it was never an ideology that was put into practice. However, it is an extremely interesting racial worldview, as the Chinese made racialized barbarians of virtually all non-Chinese with whom they came in contact (Dikötter 1992).

In Chinese thought there is no viable distinction made between culture and race. While Chinese history has been predominantly one of isolation, trade and empire brought the Chinese into contact with the outside world, although without the global empires the Europeans established in the non-European world. The Chinese tendency toward isolation evoked a highly Chinese-centered view of others beyond their mental border—the Kunlun Mountains, a chain of mountains north of the Himalayas, running east and west from central China to the modern borders with India and central Asia. The Chinese concept of world geography was divided into the familiar Chinese territories and the lands beyond the Kunlun Mountains.

In the world beyond these mountains there was a blurring of the line between human and animal in the way that Europeans, when they first encountered aboriginal Americans after 1492, wondered scientifically and philosophically if they were human or not. Non-Chinese "others" may have been indicated in writing with the animal radical, with some peoples to the north associated with the dog, while others were associated with reptiles. This convention in writing persisted until the 1930s. The colors associated with people were more often those of their clothing or a particular color designation in Chinese of the direction the foreigner came from—black for north, red for east, with yellow at the center. A mythical country to the west existed where white people lived with hair that covered their shoulders. Only the Chinese were described as *ren*, or true men. Some outsiders, for example from Malacca in Southeast Asia, were described as black, while slaves of Chinese descent were referred to as "black men" (*renli*), with the "li" referring to a scorched cooking pot, not black skin color (Dikötter 1992, 11).

Barbarians at the edge of the empire were feared and referred to as *kunlun*; for example this term was used to describe Vietnamese, Cambodian Khmer, and Malaysians. When Chinese seafarers contacted East Africa they combined *kunlun* and the Arabic word for blacks, *zanj* to make the term *kunlunzanji*, in other words black people at the edge of the empire. A white-black polarization juxtaposed the white, civilized center of China and the black edges of the empire, where uncivilized savages and barbarians dwelled. Africa was described as a chaotic continent inhabited by the most backward peoples and with the worst climate.

The difference between Chinese and others was reinforced with the cultural belief that the natures of the Chinese and the barbarian were fundamentally incompatible. The Chinese nature was thought to be impenetrable by the barbarian, and only foreigners could be influenced by the Chinese, not the other way around. *Kunlun* slaves were brought to Asia from Africa by Arab and Persian merchants as early as the eighth century CE. When the Portuguese settled in Macao in the sixteenth century they brought African slaves with them. Many of these slaves ran away and established a separate community in Canton (now Guangjou), where they often acted as Portuguese interpreters for Chinese merchants.

Barbarian "others" included westerners, whose white skin was as curious to Chinese as the color of Africans. As early as the eighth century CE one commentator noted that the Europeans had "blue eyes, red beards and looked like macaques" (a type of monkey). I recall on my voyage around the world in 1996 that a blond, long-haired, and bearded American student from the Semester at Sea program was greeted by a tourist at the Great Wall, "Look a monkey!" Western skin was described as "ashen white," resembling the dead, and westerners often were referred to as "ghosts" or "goblins." By the eighteenth and nineteenth centuries ethnic stereotyping and the classification of races according to color began to appear in China. Many texts of the period refer to the invading English enemy as "foreign, barbarian devils," "blue-eyed barbarian slaves"; the English were not even considered human beings. Other terms used were "white devils" for invading Europeans and "black devils" for their slaves—presumably Indian Sepoy troops in service of the British. In a marvelous reversal of the outlandish racist ideas that Europeans held about people of African descent, the Chinese stereotyped the English, whom they fought in the Opium War (1775–1855), in the following ways:

1) The white ones are really ghosts whose speech sounds like that of birds and whose green eyes suffer when they look at a distance; their white skin a result of daily baths in cold water or consumption of milk. (White was strongly associated with the West and death.)
2) They are hairy, bearded, with hairy bodies resembling monkeys; they have conch-like noses and squinting eyes. Even the females were thought to have beards and mustaches. The foreign barbarian has four testicles driving them to sexual excess.
3) Their bandaged legs cannot bend, and when they fall down they cannot get up. (This idea held well into the twentieth century, when Anglo-Chinese returning to China were asked if whites have only one straight bone in the leg, which cannot bend.)
4) The digestive system of the white barbarian is dependent on tea and rhubarb, without which they fall victim to disease.
5) The westerners have a peculiar odor; those arriving on ships smelled of rotten fish and a Chinese lady may hold a handkerchief to her nose when they pass. (adapted from Dikötter 1992, 43–45)

The stereotypic reversals found in these Chinese descriptions of whites offer a great lesson in racial othering undertaken by humans. These ideas are particularly telling because they are so similar to European ideas about their own racialized others, whom they not only contacted, as with the Chinese, but fought against, enslaved, subdued, conquered, and colonized. While the Chinese expanded their political and cultural influence in central Asia, Southeast Asia, Korea, and Japan, Han Chinese ethnocentrism followed. However, the Chinese did not develop a global colonial empire comparable to those of the European powers, and were colonized themselves. These basic facts make the Chinese racial worldview in a sense relatively innocent and not globally significant.

## Japan

Japanese attitudes regarding race have attracted some international attention because of the economic success of the country in the past several decades and the occasional jealousy that this has engendered in the West—especially in America, where a racialized Asian has often surpassed the United States in international sales of cars. The Japanese-American racial landscape is further complicated by the gnawing question of whether the atomic bomb was dropped on Hiroshima and Nagasaki and not on Germany because Germans are closer to the American racial norm than the Japanese. The internment of Japanese Americans during the Second World War is widely recognized as an example of American racial xenophobia. The U.S. government made a general judgment that phenotypic Japanese, irrespective of their being American citizens and culture bearers, were its potential enemies because the United States was at war with Japan. No comparable internment of German Americans took place during either the First or the Second World War, when the United States was twice at war with Germany. Japanese visiting the United States or resident in the United States have been subjected to homogenized racial stereotyping, being taken for Vietnamese and harassed as "gooks," or being recognized as Japanese and harassed by war veterans or for their economic success. Racial sensitivities were further complicated by remarks made by a former Japanese prime minister in regard to the lack, at one point, of American competitiveness in the auto industry. He is reported to have said that America's falling behind Japan was due to the amount of race mixing that has taken place in the United States.

Given such complexities it is worth exploring the historical origins of Japanese-American relations and the racial othering that took place on both sides. The opening of United States trade with Japan was recent, traceable only to the middle of the nineteenth century. The Commodore Perry expeditions initiated contact, which was sought by the United States and treated with caution by the Japanese. The Japanese had successfully asserted the right to isolation for two hundred years prior to the entry of the "black ships" (a Japanese reference to the black hulls of the steamships and the black smoke coming from them) into Japanese waters at Shimoda. Western naval powers, including British, Russian, and American ships, had sought to take advantage of trade with this "Far Eastern" jewel, but the Japanese had observed the conquest of India and the humiliation of China and worried about their own fate. In 1852 Matthew Perry was given command of the East India Squadron to make a decisive attempt at entering Japanese waters. Four ships were sent in 1853 and more in 1854, when negotiations (under threat of attack by Perry) were undertaken; a fascinating visual and textual chronicle of these negotiations was produced by the Japanese: *The Black Ship Scroll* (Statler 1963). Few documents provide such a strong impression of an initial encounter between cultures and races, especially from a non-Western point of view.

The Americans were permitted ashore once a treaty had been signed, and the scrolls are full of descriptions of everyday life in Japan and of the Japanese trying to fathom these strange barbarians. Although relations were somewhat forced and cautious, overall the impression left by the Americans was favorable, and trade relations were in fact opened. The portraits of the American commanding officers are all the more interesting because they are of "others" who are not enemies but are nonetheless portrayed as fierce, Nipponized foreigners. Portraits of Perry, Adams, and the son of Adams show the exaggerated hairiness of Perry (as a "Western Mikado") and Adams (who was bearded), and seem to continue the emphasis that the Chinese held as the most prominent physical feature of the Western barbarian. Adams's son, at age sixteen, is portrayed without facial hair and with combined Japanese and American features. (See figure 3.1 on p. 78.)

The crews of the American ships were, of course, dominated by Euro-Americans, but there were also a number of Chinese servants, and several "Negroes" who were brought for the effect that their presence in the entourage would have on the Japanese. The first formal reception of the Americans was preceded by a parade orchestrated by Perry, which included the crew dressed in their military finery. Letters of introduction from President Fillmore and from Perry himself were handed to the shogun's envoy by two blacks described in the narrative as "two of the best-looking fellows of their color that the squadron could furnish" (Statler 1963, 41).

## TREATMENT OF INDIGENOUS PEOPLES AROUND THE WORLD

Irrespective of nation or type of government countries around the world have treated native peoples not only as racial others, but at times as barely human, or as conquered "tribes" at a low level of civilization with few or no rights. Indians from North and South America faced near genocide, and have only recently rebounded as viable populations. Besides the biological reduction of populations, all indigenous peoples have faced near cultural extinction and have had to struggle to rebound culturally as well. Cultural revival among North American Indians has gained momentum in recent decades and has been aided by the existence of economic enterprises, such as casinos and bingo halls, on tribal lands that provide financial backing.

In South America the cultural survival of Indian groups is more the norm, and advocacy anthropologists from North and South America— notably the group Cultural Survival, led by David Maybury-Lewis—have addressed the basic issue of survival before confronting issues of appropriate development.

The histories and policies of national governments regarding indigenous peoples—from the United States to Canada to Australia—have been remarkably similar. In the initial encounter the emphasis is laid on removal of aboriginal peoples from lands desired by Europeans for settlement. Aboriginals who resisted were victims of wars of "pacification." "Nations" of people who may have negotiated worthless "peace" treaties were relegated to subjugated "tribes" and were removed to relatively undesirable lands known as "reserves" or "reservations." Colonial and quasi-colonial units were set up to administer aboriginals—the Bureau of Indian Affairs in the United States, the Canada Board of Indian Affairs, and the Australian Office of Aboriginal Affairs—and assimilation programs for the remnant populations established. Cultural assimilation efforts included establishing Western-style police and courts, Christian churches run by missionaries, English-language schools that forbade the use of local languages, and an economic dependency relationship with the government. In all of these cases governments removed children from their homes and placed them in missionary or government-run boarding schools, where they were forbidden to speak their native language, had their braids cut, were dressed in Western-style uniforms, and were taught a vocational curriculum. The Australian and Canadian governments have begun to confront their histories with indigenous peoples, with the latter offering an official "Statement of Reconciliation" that acknowledges the damage done to native peoples beginning in the fifteenth century with the arrival of Europeans. Canada officially decolonized a vast territory known as Nunavit and returned it to first nation peoples in 1999. Canada also pledged $250 million in a "healing fund" to help Indians who suffered physical and mental abuse in the government-run schools.

It was not until a national Indian movement in the United States began to address U.S. policies politically that cultural survival and revival were able to occur. The American Indian Movement (AIM) was influenced by the civil rights movement and was spurred on by AIM's occupation of both the Bureau of Indian Affairs in 1973 and the historic site of Wounded Knee in the same year. These events galvanized the movement and made it national.

The Australian Aboriginal movement developed in the context of a global effort to organize indigenous groups from around the world—embracing groups from the Ainu of Japan to the Yanomami of Amazonian Venezuela and Brazil. The United Nations has drafted a new Declaration of the Rights of Indigenous Peoples, which is still in preparation for final approval by the international body.

## Global Efforts to Eradicate/Ameliorate Racism

The United Nations, since its inception in 1947, has addressed racism as a global problem. The United Nations and the United Nations Educational and Scientific Cooperative Organization (UNESCO). Statements on Race in 1964 and 1998 have provided an international framework for objective, scientific accuracy about race and for demythologizing racist ideas that have permeated societies in the colonizing and colonized worlds, and in nations torn by racism. It was fitting that South Africa hosted the World Conference against Racism in September 2001 that ended divisively only days before the attacks on the World Trade Center and the Pentagon. The conference participants managed to agree on common language on the subject of slavery and colonialism, but negotiations broke down over Middle East racial politics and disagreements over whether to criticize Israel's treatment of the Palestinians. The language on slavery and colonialism developed at the conference is as follows:

- We acknowledge that slavery and the slave trade, including the Trans-Atlantic slave trade, were appalling tragedies in the history of humanity not only because of their abhorrent barbarism but also in terms of their magnitude, organized nature and especially their negation of the essence of victims, and further acknowledge that slavery and the slave trade are a crime against humanity and should have always been so, especially the Trans-Atlantic slave trade, and are among the major sources and manifestations of racism, racial discrimination, xenophobia and related intolerance, and that Africans and people of African descent, Asians and people of Asian descent and indigenous peoples were victims of these and continue to be victims of their consequences.
- The World Conference recognizes that colonialism has led to racism, racial discrimination, xenophobia and related intolerance and that Africans and people of African descent and people of Asian descent and indigenous peoples were victims of colonialism and continue to be victims of their consequences.
- The World Conference, aware of the moral obligation on the part of all concerned States, calls on these states to take appropriate and effective measures to halt and reverse the lasting consequences of these practices.
- The World Conference recognizes that these historical injustices have undeniably contributed to poverty, underdevelopment, marginalization, social exclusion, economic disparities, instability, and insecurity that affect many people in different parts of the world, in particular developing countries. The World Conference recognizes the need to

develop programs for the social and economic development in these societies and the Diaspora within the framework of a new partnership based on the spirit of solidarity and mutual respect. (Swarns 2001)

## SUMMARY

This chapter reveals not only the diversity and complexity of race around the world but its utter malleability and flexibility. There are few places in the world where race is not a factor in society and politics, although the rules by which race is socially constructed are very much shaped by the individual histories and struggles of peoples whose position is shaped by race. The contrasting visions of the one-drop rule—making one either "black" or "white"—in the United States and in other New World societies are instructive. Logic does not matter, and biology does not matter—the social construction of race is what makes all of the difference.

Advocating the use of specific numerical quotas is an interesting point of comparison, revealing a commitment to more rapid social change in countries such as Brazil, South Africa, and India. Known popularly as "affirmative action," the technique is openly being advocated outside of the United States, where it remains a contentious and divisive racial issue. The landmark University of Michigan case decided by the United States Supreme Court in 2003 permitted the continued use of race as *one* criterion in college admissions, but was allowed only as a temporary measure. This reflects a basic negative American attitude toward preference extended to racial minorities, while the country remains in fundamental denial about the importance of race in everyday life and the significance of pervasive, unconscious white privilege.

The Asian case of India provokes analytical consideration of caste and pollution for its analogies to American historical Jim Crow segregation. The cases of China and Japan offer dramatic and interesting inversions of Western racial stereotyping, and are entertaining as well as enlightening.

Awareness of the global reach and impact of racial formations, historically and contemporarily, need not produce in the reader a fatalistic response that racism is a fundamental feature of human life. On the contrary, it should be abundantly clear that race and its corollary, racism, are pliable and are historically and contextually based. Little of what has been described is permanent; indeed the dynamics of racial formation are the most notable aspect of this chapter. Race construction and racism have been in the hands of the powerful and the rulers; antiracism and resistance have been in the hands of the racially oppressed and their supporters. The overturning of the slave system in Haiti and the end of the apartheid system in South Africa have much in common with the American popular civil rights movement, which brought an end to segregation.

## REFERENCES

Avril, Gage. 1997. *A Day for the Hunter, a Day for the Prey: Popular Music and Power in Haiti*. Chicago: University of Chicago Press.

Dayan, Joan. 1995. *Haiti, History, and the Gods*. Berkeley: University of California Press.

De Andrade, Leila Lomba. 1997. "The Question of Race: Cape Verdeans Talk about Their Race and Identity." In *Revista Cabo-verdiana de Letras, Artes e Estudos*, Autumn/Winter, 23–27.

Delany, Martin. 1879. *Principia of Ethnology: The Origin of Races and of Color*. Philadelphia: Harper and Brothers.

Dikötter, Frank. 1992. *The Discourse of Race in Modern China*. Stanford: Stanford University Press.

Easterbrook, Michael. 2002. "Brazil Considers Quotas to Bridge Racial Divide in Higher Education." *Chronicle of Higher Education*, March 1, A38–39.

Firmin, Anténor. 1885. *The Equality of the Human Races: Positivist Anthropology*. Translated by Asselin Charles and introduced by Carolyn Fluehr-Lobban. Repr., New York: Garland, 2000.

Fluehr-Lobban, Carolyn. 2004. "A Critical Anthropological Analysis of the Race Concept in the Nile Valley." In *Race and Identity in the Nile Valley: Ancient and Contemporary Perspectives*, edited by Carolyn Fluehr-Lobban and Kharyssa Rhodes, 133–157. Trenton, NJ: Africa World.

Fluehr-Lobban, Carolyn, and Kharyssa Rhodes. 2004. *Race and Identity in the Nile Valley: Ancient and Contemporary Perspectives*. Trenton, NJ: Africa World.

Freyre, Gilberto. 1933. *Masters and Slaves: A Study in the Development of Brazilian Civilization*. Repr., New York: Knopf, 1944.

Hacker, Andrew. 1992. *Two Nations Black and White, Separate, Hostile, Unequal*. New York: Ballatine.

Harris, Marvin. 1964. *Patterns of Race in the Americas*. New York: Walker.

Harrison, Faye V. 2002. "Unraveling 'Race' for the Twenty-first Century." In *Exotic No More: Anthropology on the Front Lines*, edited by Jeremy MacClancy, 145–66. Chicago: University of Chicago Press.

Hellwig, David J., ed. 1992. *African-American Reflections on Brazil's Racial Paradise*. Philadelphia: Temple University Press.

Hoge, Warren. 2001. "British Life Is Fractured along Racial Lines, a Study Finds." *New York Times International*, December 12.

Jennings, Anne. 2004. "Reflections of an African-American Anthropologist in Egypt." In *Race and Identity in the Nile Valley: Ancient and Contemporary Perspectives*, edited by Carolyn Fluehr-Lobban and Kharyssa Rhodes, 275–88. Trenton, NJ: Africa World.

Jok, Jok Madut. 2001. *War and Slavery in the Sudan*. Philadelphia: University of Pennsylvania Press.

Kolenda, Pauline. 1985. *Caste in Contemporary India: Beyond Organic Solidarity.* Prospect Heights, IL: Waveland.

Lobban, Richard A., Jr. 1995. *Cape Verde: Criolo Colony to Independent Nation.* Boulder, CO: Westview.

Margolis, Mac. 1992. "The Invisible Issue: Race in Brazil." *Ford Foundation Report,* Summer, 3–7.

McDonald, Mark. 2004. "In Russia Nationalism Breeds Ethnic Violence." *Philadelphia Inquirer,* March 29, A1, A20.

Mendy, Peter Karibe. 2002. "Portugal's Civilizing Mission in Colonial Guinea-Bissau: Rhetoric and Reality." *International Journal of African Historical Studies* 36, no 1:35–58.

Perera, Rick. 2002. "Germany Tries to Make Itself Foreigner-Friendly." *Chronicle of Higher Education,* July 5, A39–41.

Poole, Maurita. 2004. "Distinctive Tastes: Aesthetic Prejudice in Contemporary Egypt." In *Race and Identity in the Nile Valley: Ancient and Contemporary Perspectives,* edited by Carolyn Fluehr-Lobban and Kharyssa Rhodes, 261–74. Trenton, NJ: Africa World.

Powell, Eve Troutt. 2000. "Brothers along the Nile: Egyptian Concepts of Race and Ethnicity, 1895–1910." In *The Nile, Histories, Cultures, Myths,* edited by Haggai Erlich and Israel Gershoni, 171–81. Boulder, CO: Lynne Reiner.

"Racial Classification in Latin America." December 24, 2000. At www.zonalatina .com/Zldata55.htm.

Rohter, Larry. 2001. "Multiracial Brazil Planning Quotas for Blacks." *New York Times,* October 2, A3.

Statler, Oliver. 1963. *The Black Ship Scroll: An Account of the Perry Expedition at Shimoda in 1854.* Tokyo: John Weatherhill.

Swarns, Rachel L. 2001. "U.N. Delegates Reach Compromise on Slavery, Israel" and text of adopted positions and disputed words. *Providence Journal,* September 9, A3.

Tavernise, Sabrina. 2002. "Bomb Attack Shows that Russia Hasn't Rooted Out Anti-Semitism." *New York Times,* June 1, A1, A8.

Twine, France Widdance. 1998. *Racism in Racial Democracy: The Maintenance of White Supremacy in Brazil.* New Brunswick, NJ: Rutgers University Press.

Wade, Peter. 1997. *Race and Ethnicity in Latin America.* London: Pluto.

Wahnon, Donald. 2002. "The Question of Cape Verdean Racial and National Identity." *Visao International* (Cape Verdean weekly in Portuguese and English), at http://groups.yahoo.com/group/capeverdeforum.

Yelvington, Kevin. 1997. "Patterns of Class, Ethnicity, and Nationalism." In *Understanding Contemporary Latin America,* edited by Richard Hillman, 209–36. Boulder, CO: Lynne Rienner.

# 8

# Racial Reconstruction and Transformation in America

At the dawn of the twenty-first century, America is ripe for racial reconstruction. The demographics are shifting decisively toward a "browning" of the country. This is occurring through dramatic immigration rates of Latino people and through people of color arriving from African and Asia as well, as evidenced in the 2000 U.S. Census. This fact, the growth of nonimmigrant Americans who identity as "biracial" or "multiracial," and low fertility rates among whites all point to "whites" becoming a minority, perhaps by the 2020 Census, with a decisive shift after 2050. The recent wave of immigrants mirrors the great wave of immigration from Europe in the late nineteenth and early twentieth centuries and will have a similar effect in transforming the American demographic picture.

White ethnicity and, increasingly, black ethnicity (Jamaican American, Haitian American, Nigerian American) have been obscured through cultural assimilation, while the particular ethnicities of diverse Asian groups has been officially noted in the latest census, even as Latinos/Hispanics are lumped into a single category. Race in America is a moving target that one must follow with persistence and vigilance. Some of the major questions regarding racial transformation in the twenty-first century include the following:

1) Will class distinctions among "blacks" who came to America's shores as involuntary immigrants (through enslavement) and whites who came as voluntary immigrants (through a process of immigration) become a gap amounting to recognizable socioeconomic differences, *or* will race (i.e., phenotype) continue to trump economic class?

2) Will certain Latinos "become white" by passing over the "Hispanic" racial line created for them in America?' Some of the candidates for this crossover are light-skinned Cuban Americans in Florida and the South, Mexican Americans in Texas, California, and other southwestern states, and Puerto-Ricans in New York and New England.
3) Will biracial and multiracial persons in the United States begin to form a mixed-race, "Creole" middle ground comparable to racial construction in the Caribbean and South America?
4) Will persons of European extraction become more conscious of their "whiteness" and resulting historic privilege, and what incentives might be developed to encourage them to do so?

## THE FUTURE OF RACE

While it is probable that race has little future as a biological concept, it is a great error to dismiss its ever-changing sociological significance. Eugenia Shanklin (1998) is critical of anthropology's "color-blindness"—dismissing the scientific importance of race while ignoring its continuing social relevance. Faye Harrison (1995) has reminded anthropologists and humanists of "the persistence of race" in scientific and popular discourse. Anthropology has often been left at the periphery of sociological dialogues on racism, its role relegated to serial statements about the unscientific nature of and irrelevance of race. The exclusive concern with the biological aspects of and myths about race has limited its ability to comment on the effects of racism in society, such as the legacy of racism for anthropology's primary laboratory of study, the American Indian, but also for other important cases, such as South Africa.

Will the United States move beyond the black-white binary? Will it accommodate itself to the "Creole" hybrid populations emigrating to the United States as their numbers necessarily increase? Will class emerge as a significant modifier of race in the early decades of the twenty-first century? Already class is being offered as an alternative to affirmative action, with merit and financial need replacing race or racial entitlement.

Anthropology's origins were not color-blind, as chapter 3 details, and an important part of its regeneration lies in reconnecting with the historical twins of race and racism. Biologizing race meant conceiving of racial groups and characteristics as fixed and immutable. Biological races are pure and they do not change, or social policy should see that they do not change, hence the popularity of antimiscegenation laws in the United States.

However, sociological analysis reveals that racial categories and racial groups are dynamic and ever changing. Terms change—such as "Negro," "colored," "black," "African American," or "Oriental," "Asian," "Korean American," "Chinese American." Other archaic terms have great staying power, such as "Caucasian," possessing little or no relationship to Europeans or their descendants, but only historical reference to nineteenth-century craniometry. The discovery of "whiteness" by contemporary scholars in history, anthropology, and cultural studies has shown that formerly racialized groups from Europe who were victimized by racism within Europe and by similar attitudes in America became "white" through a process of cultural and economic assimilation. "How the Jews Became White Folk" (Sacks 1994, 78–102) and *How the Irish Became White* (Ignatiev 1997) tell basically the same story—that in the New World lands of opportunity, being phenotypically white conveyed an advantage, a certain privilege, from which persons of African and Asian descent could not and did not benefit. Thus, the racialized and ethnically oppressed Irish and Jews of Europe constitute in America important cases of racial and ethnic transformation. Misunderstanding the fundamental issue of race and the persistence of racism, as compared with ethnic prejudice, leads many Americans to ask, If the Irish and the Jews "made it" in America, why can't the blacks? The advantage of white skin—unachieved and acquired as a matter of one's birth—conveys enormous advantages that many Americans ignore or do not wish to confront.

Another example of the dynamic nature of race classification is the growing acceptance of the racial myth of Asians as the "model minority" or the "smart minority." This new racial mythology is probably traceable to a combination of the economic success of Japan on a global scale and the hard work ethic of more recent Asian immigrants who have succeeded economically and academically within relatively short periods of time.

The fate of Latinos in America is already becoming differentiated between Cuban immigrants, favored for their anti-Castro politics and often lighter skin color, and darker-skinned Dominicans or Mexicans. Certain upwardly mobile Latinos, favored by lighter skin tones and relative social and economic position, will likely be the next candidates to become "white"; this is the probable next racial horizon in the United States, especially as this numerically huge population seeks to be better represented in the society at all levels.

Advancement in race relations in America requires acknowledgment and assessment of the fundamental contradictions built into the founding of the United States, in the constitution, among the "founding fathers." Thomas Jefferson and other slave-owning presidents are cases in point; many conflicting ideas about democracy and race can be found in their biographies. These presidents were progressive men of the Enlightenment who accepted the inequality of races; they were "democrats" who could not see full personhood in Negroes and Indians. Jefferson's conflicted "Enlightenment" ideas can be summarized in his own words: "I advance it therefore as a suspicion only, that blacks, whether originally a distant race or made distinct by time and circumstance, are inferior to whites in the endowments of body and mind" (1787).

To illustrate further this contradiction, the following language about the evils of the slave trade and the British plan to induce slaves to support them and rise against their masters was eliminated from the Declaration of Independence:

> Determined to keep open a market where men should be bought and sold, he has prostituted his negative for suppressing every legislative attempt to prohibit or to restrain this execrable commerce. And this assemblage of horrors might want no fact of distinguished die, he is so exciting those very people to rise in arms among us, and to purchase that liberty of which he has deprived them, by murdering the people on whom he has obtruded them: thus paying off former crimes committed against the liberties of one people, with crimes he urges them to commit against the lives of another. (Jefferson 2002, 973)

## THE RECONFIGURATION OF RACE

For America, moving beyond the labels "black," "white," and "minority" means engaging in a process of the reconfiguration of race and ethnicity. Educators have a potentially significant role to play in choosing curricular materials and weaving them into the everyday treatment of subject matter in science, social science, and the humanities. In the twenty-first century token representation of America's colorful minorities in the classroom and textbooks is no longer viable. At present tokenism is at its maximum during day-long or week-long celebrations of Martin Luther King Jr.'s birthday, held annually in January to meet a school's diversity goals or requirements. Continual replaying of King's "I Have a Dream" speech is a meager substitute for the sustained hard work that is required for racial learning, healing, and reconciliation. Likewise, a "colors of the rainbow" approach, viewed as appropriate to elementary schooling, does not prepare children for the racial divide that they will likely experience beginning in middle school.

Middle and high school educators would better serve their students through the use of racially and ethnically balanced curricular materials, combined with frank discussions about racial subjects in a safe environment created in the classroom by the teacher. A safe environment is one in which issues and stereotypes involving race as well as barriers to relationships can be confronted without any student feeling out of the conversation through a sense of shame or blame. The importance of understanding white privilege and historical black anger, or Latino and immigrant fears about assimilation to U.S. culture, for example, can be explored when students come to trust their fellow students and the teacher-facilitator and realize that they will gain and not be harmed by the discussions. These should be academically informed sessions to avoid the personal and to focus on issues. A creative, committed group of students and their teacher can devise their own methods to create this needed educational environment.

The media potentially can play a major role. Media coverage of inner-city crime and violence might be curtailed or balanced with stories of white-collar crime in suburban areas. Television news might balance coverage of comparable tragedies of missing or abducted children or young women across racial and ethnic lines, and not dwell on the cases involving white children or women, which are currently more likely to be aired on shows such as "America's Most Wanted." Entertainment shows might freely mix performers of all racial and ethnic backgrounds, not in a mechanistic "bean-counting" manner, but in a more natural way, whereby race both does and does not matter among friends. The hugely popular show "Friends" featured a core group of only white friends with few stories featuring the "minorities" whose presence in New York City is well known. The NAACP and other racialist advocacy groups have repeatedly complained about the lack of shows with minorities or about minorities.

## NECESSARY PARTS OF A NATIONAL DIALOGUE ON RACE EMPHASIZING "TRUTH AND RECONCILIATION"

### Acknowledging That the United States Is Still a Segregated Society

Interracial dialogue, if it is to succeed, must find a way to overcome the fundamental racial segregation of the society. The last U.S. Census in 2000 showed that blacks and whites are still geographically and residentially segregated. Whites remain concentrated in counties in the North and blacks are concentrated in counties in the South. The proportion of whites to minorities has dropped to 77 percent of the total 281.4 million people in the United States, and whites are predicted to drop to less than 50 percent after the 2020 Census (Ling 2001). Currently the only state with a white minority population is Hawaii—whites were counted in the last census by self-reporting and included white Latinos, who checked both "Hispanic" and "white." Blacks are concentrated in southern states, reversing a trend that witnessed massive black migration from the South to the North up until 1990. With the new option on the census of checking

more than one race, youth were more likely than adults to report multiracial heritage.

Despite school "desegregation" in 1955, more than 70 percent of blacks
and Latinos attend predominantly minority schools in the United States.
The segregation of whites in separate schools is so strong that even in
predominantly minority communities, such as Washington, DC, where
whites are outnumbered twenty to one, whites attend schools with a
white majority (Fears 2001). Fifty years later whites and minorities still
live, study, pray, and work far apart from one another.

Predictably, stereotyping and fear result in a credibility attached to
racial profiling—driving or shopping while black; flying while Arab—
that many whites neither perceive as racist nor understand when these
minorities take offense. Post-9/11 national security or defense of the
homeland has blunted criticism of the racial profiling of Arabs or Arab-
looking individuals (e.g., turban and beard; many Indian Sikhs have been
wrongly harassed or arrested for fitting the profile). Individuals with
Muslim names, irrespective of outward appearance, have been religiously
profiled.

Fear of blacks in enclosed places—such as white women clutching their
purses when a black man enters an elevator, or the fear of being confined
with a black in an ATM enclosure—is so common that it has been analyzed as "reasonable racism," and even employed as a defense of the
actions of whites, better known as the Bernhard Goetz defense. Bernhard
Goetz opened fire when accosted by a group of black youths on a New
York subway in 1986, and he was acquitted of murder on the grounds
of the "reasonable" fear he had as a white when confronted by young
blacks.

### Denial about Race in a "Color-Blind" Society Makes the Dialogue on Race a Nonstarter

In the United States race-evasive idioms, such as "multiculturalism,"
highlight culture or class over race, giving white working-class people
privilege over racial minorities. Conservatives tend to acknowledge the
existence of race and racism only when there are charges of whites being
victimized by "reverse racism" emanating from government policies and
racial minorities' insistence on "making race an issue"; thus, conservatives ignore the continuing racism still experienced by middle- and even
upper-class blacks (Harrison 2002, 154).

The inability of America to confront its history of slavery and its legacy
is an example of American denial of the centrality of race. Today more
than twenty museums are in existence or planning devoted to African
American history, not the least of which is a proposed National Museum
of Slavery conceived by former Virginia governor Doug Wilder, who is a

descendant of enslaved Americans. His concept is that the real story needs to be told, not sugar coated; however, most white Americans are probably not as yet prepared to pay admission and visit a museum that details the brutality of the slave trade and plantation conditions. The living historical exhibits at Colonial Williamsburg experimented with reenactments of the sale of slaves and the realities of everyday life for enslaved persons. Among the unintended consequences was the burnout experienced by African American actors portraying these painful roles and the protest organized by the Virginian coordinator of the NAACP (National Association for the Advancement of Colored People), who complained that the exhibit turned historical pain into entertainment. A more successful model for what is palatable or acceptable for America at this moment in its history is the recently opened Freedom Center in Cincinnati, which chronicles and celebrates the Underground Railroad, a rare but important example of white and black collaboration that freed perhaps one hundred thousand of the estimated four million slaves in the United States around the time of the Civil War. This museum allows visitors to speak about slavery, but in a way that is more constructive than the other examples.

Continuing difficulty in discussing frankly this central theme in American history underscores the underlying denial, and the subject will likely remain a sensitive one for educators until creative teachers and texts develop a new approach. One middle school teacher in Rhode Island who is African American teaches with honesty and creativity about the slave trade to mainly white students. For one exercise he has his middle schoolers lie on the floor imitating the "tight pack" and "loose pack" strategies of the slave ship entrepreneurs and their captains. In "tight pack" they lie cramped together while learning that a certain percentage of slaves were calculated to die in these conditions in the notorious Middle Passage, while "loose pack" is less cramped and was calculated to produce a greater survival rate. What is notable about this teacher is how he is remembered by many former students of his whom I have had as college students, and that he considers the truth about the slave trade and its many social expressions as suitable and important material for his sixth- and seventh-graders.

The issue of slavery and reparations is probably still too sensitive to discuss dispassionately, for it raises the twin issues of white fear—over whites' perceived accountability for slavery and their resulting privilege—and black anger, along with blacks' perceived enrichment of white society and an attendant sense of entitlement to compensation. Whites fear this right to compensation and may trivialize reparations as writing a check to individual blacks, while black advocates of reparations talk about repairing the historical record and expanded economic and political opportunities. Reparations for American Indians may be coming in the form of lucrative casino concessions on reservation lands, with one of the largest success stories being that of Foxwoods in Connecticut, which rose from the nearly entirely deracinated Pequot nation, the first to experience European genocide in 1636. With some of its profits the Pequot nation opened a state-of-the-art museum telling its own story; it supports a full-time lobbyist for American Indian causes in Washington; and it sponsors a national gathering of Indian people, Skemitzon (First Corn festival), annually in August.

### "Mutual Cluelessness"

"Mutual Cluelessness" was the title of a newspaper article by Todd Gitlin and Earl Ofari Hutchinson in the *Philadelphia Inquirer* that summarized a Kaiser/Harvard/*Washington Post* study of 1,709 randomly selected adults in 2001. The study reveals staggering ignorance among whites of the lives lived in America by blacks and other minorities. Examples of widely held beliefs as contrasted with the social facts are given here:

1) Between 42 and 50 percent of whites believe blacks have achieved economic equality.
   **Fact:** Blacks are twice as likely to be unemployed or poor as whites; one-third of whites have professional or managerial jobs as compared with one-fifth of blacks.
2) Sixty-one percent of whites believe that blacks have equal access to health care.
   **Fact**: Blacks' access to health insurance is half that of whites.
3) About 50 percent of whites believe blacks and whites have equal access to education.
   **Fact:** Only 17 percent of blacks have completed college, compared with 28 percent of whites. (*Race and Ethnicity in 2001*, 2001)

The most benign explanation of the disparities is the wishful thinking on the part of many whites that racism is over. Whites suffer from delusion and ignorance, and especially in their experiences with blacks (Gitlin and Ofari Hutchinson 2001). A black take on this ignorance is that whites are hopelessly racist, but the reality is that since legal segregation has ended many whites really believe that racism is over. They see blacks on TV, the success of Oprah, Michael Jordan, and Bill Cosby, and they believe equal opportunity is real. Believing in the American dream, they are also puzzled as to why suburban, middle-class, white youths bring guns into their schools and kill teachers and fellow students. In the main whites may be angriest about government policies and the lack of control in their lives. Counter to the stereotype held among blacks that all whites are financially privileged, millions of whites are trapped in poverty. Many whites sense that they are losing ground, which shapes their thinking on affirmative action, while the truth is that much white anger is fueled by economic uncertainty, political cynicism, and personal alienation, not racial hatred.

These facts, if discussed, present a good common base from which to begin, but the discussion has to be sustained and it has to be local, regional, and national. An engaged and constructive media could play a vital community role in the needed dialogue about black anger and white fear.

Americans have the ability and goodwill to "get along." In New York after 9/11, for the first time in fourteen years, a majority of all races (53 percent of blacks, 56 percent of Hispanics, and 69 percent of whites) said race relations in the city were generally good (Murphy and Halbfinger 2002).

## White Fear and Black Anger

White fear and black anger are the two sides of the American racial coin. Whites' fear stems from the perhaps unconscious or subconscious recognition of their privilege at the expense of nonwhites; black anger, despite the window dressing of black advance and affirmative action, reveals the persistence of racism and maintenance of the status quo. Because of the American assertions of a "color-blind" society and the rhetoric given to equal opportunity, neither truthful black anger nor white fear is permitted to be discussed. Both are taboo until a racial crisis explodes and these sentiments are called up to explain events, such as black rage at the consistent failure of the Los Angeles Police Department to sanction or penalize, much less fire, racist police. Black rage exploded in Providence over the killing of a young black officer (among the few black officers on the force there; his father was the only colonel of color) in plain clothes who was mistaken by his fellow officers for a suspect. Black rage was dispelled temporarily by a large, city-sponsored funeral and by denials that the case of mistaken identity had had anything to do with race. Black anger erupted again when no criminal action was undertaken against the white officers, and the civil suit was thrown out by the judge. White flight from the inner cities is justified by the "reasonable racism" of the perceived lack of safety of living in black and Latino neighborhoods and the allied problem of poor public schools. Instead of whites unifying with neighbors of color and fighting, along with their fellow citizens, to improve neighborhood safety and public education, they have fled in vast numbers to the suburbs, making metropolitan areas such as Atlanta, Detroit, Newark, Philadelphia, and Baltimore essentially black cities. Downtown areas where suburban whites earn their income are improved for daytime business, but whites return to their bedroom communities daily in apartheidlike fashion. Urban housing for blacks and Latinos is so depressed and substandard that an outsider may think that the city has been bombed during a war, thus fueling more black rage at the two Americas in which they live.

### Ten Reasons Why America Can't Talk about Race

The following was generated by students in my Critical Race Theory seminar at Rhode Island College in 2001 in response to an ad placed in the student newspapers of major universities by conservative David Horowitz: "Ten Reasons Why Reparations for Slavery Are a Bad Idea for Blacks—and Racist Too." The ad caused dissention and polarization on the campus of Brown University, such that "dialogue" between black and white students became impossible. This prompted our students to reflect on why Americans can't discuss race. Seminar participants Christopher Souza, Joyce Stevos, Richard Martin, Hannah Resseger, Stephanie Santos, and others developed the following points:

1. America is in denial about race. Racism is everywhere, yet nobody thinks that they are racist.
2. America only talks about race in times of crisis, the worst times to talk about race. Race is a taboo subject even though it is central to understanding America.
3. America is still a largely segregated society in which we do not know one another.
4. America's inability to define race leads to confusion as to whether race is a biological or sociological phenomenon.
5. There is little common ground where it is safe to talk about race. The deep and unfounded beliefs that are held about the superiority and inferiority of peoples need to be critically discussed.
6. When people talk about race it is often in terms of "winners" and "losers," "victims" and "victimizers," "oppressors" and "oppressed." Those who are privileged by race have no idea why they are privileged, or have no incentive to talk about race or white privilege.
7. Race and non-Western cultures are not taught in schools. Diversity is for everybody, including whites. The dialogue on race in school is often silenced or marginalized instead of being encouraged and protected.
8. Where are our leaders? Who will come forward to be our moderator(s) in a national forum on race?
9. People can't talk about race because they have fears of being labeled

racist. This fear comes from being uneducated about race and racism, and perpetuates the cycle of misunderstanding among peoples of different backgrounds.

10. America is unwilling to pay what it would cost to build an equitable society. There is no financial payoff for solving America's race problem, while the true wealth of America lies in its diversity. (printed in Rhode Island College student paper, the *Anchor*, April 10, 2001; reprinted in the *Providence Journal* and *Providence American*)

## The Black-White Binary and the Asian Model Minority

Americans are conditioned to think in terms of a black-white binary, with other populations that have historically experienced discrimination referred to as "minorities." These "minorities" are growing so fast that one—Latinos, the rubric for all Spanish-speaking Americans—has increased to a larger percentage of the population than African Americans in the 2000 Census.

Asian Americans are also expanding their numerical base. Dubbed the "model minority" they occupy a special status of being the acceptable, nonthreatening minority for the white majority. The relatively high number of Asians in higher education has caused them to be dropped from some affirmative action programs even before such programs were officially outlawed, such as in the state of California. A new racialist stereotype has emerged, suggesting that Asians are naturally smarter than whites and blacks. In the 1994 book *The Bell Curve* Asians are put in first place, ahead of whites, in intelligence and achievement, reflecting or perhaps contributing to the new stereotype.

Despite this special consideration of Asian Americans, a poll conducted by a Chinese American group, the Committee of 100, discovered that 25 percent of those polled would feel uncomfortable voting for an Asian American to be president or if an Asian married into their family. Cases of overt racism are still in evidence for America's model minority. Japanese Americans were incarcerated in camps on the West Coast during World War II due to the widespread belief that they would be disloyal Americans and assist the Japanese enemy. Recently, physicist Wen Ho Lee was alleged to have conducted nuclear espionage on behalf of the Chinese government, primarily because he is a Chinese American and therefore "naturally" sympathetic to China. He was imprisoned and ultimately vindicated. Few major Asian American political figures can be found in the country, with governor Gary Locke of Washington the only major elected official and the only Asian mentioned as a potential candidate for national exposure at the presidential level (Pike 2001).

## Issues That Remain Unprocessed

Slavery and the related issue of reparations have been placed on the American agenda, but remain unprocessed and unresolved. The Holocaust that occurred in Europe, however, is much discussed and covered in American curricula. The other holocausts remain unprocessed in American and Western culture and society—the genocide against Indians in North and South America and the Caribbean, and the four centuries of the Atlantic slave trade, preying on tens of millions of innocent Africans between the fifteenth and nineteenth centuries.

Likewise, the history of brutality and terror perpetrated by the terrorist organization, the Ku Klux Klan, has not been adequately confronted. For example, it was not until nearly forty years after the 1963 bombing of the Sixteenth Street Baptist Church in Birmingham, Alabama, which killed four small girls, that the last of the perpetrators, Bobby Frank Cherry, was successfully prosecuted in 2002.

The painful subject of lynching—beginning in the post–Civil War period and lasting until the 1950s, with the brutal lynching of Emmett Till—is likewise not processed in the American psyche or in the history books.

Hate speech is protected as free speech, while hate speech websites proliferate. Stories such as that of a Boston couple tried in 2002 who planned to bomb the African American Museum or the Holocaust Museum are still to be found in the daily news. The couple was tied to World Church of the Creator, a Christian sect devoted to the "survival, expansion and advancement of the white race exclusively" (*Providence Journal* 2002).

## Undoing White Privilege: What Whites Have to Contribute to the Dialogue on Race

Solving the problems of racism is often left to the victims, who are expected to fight for their rights. The active involvement of whites in discussing and influencing policies relevant to the legacy of racism and its attendant white privilege are key parts of the national racial healing needed to advance from civil rights to full human rights in the new millennium.

Peggy McIntosh's pioneering and widely reprinted "White Privilege: Unpacking the Invisible Knapsack" (1988) is probably the best place to start this dialogue in the classroom. The article details the everyday benefits of white privilege and how it inoculates whites from responsibility for racism or the need to be a part of the solution.

Also, Paul Kivel's 1996 *Uprooting Racism: How White People Can Work for Racial Justice* offers examples of the myriad everyday interactions in which whites do not have to consider their race, from blatant examples of shopping and driving while black, to moving about freely in every corner of society, to living where you please and marrying whom you please. He notes that the United States talks about race at the worst times, when there is a crisis, a racial uprising, a horrible new racist crime against humanity. Typically, such discussions become polarized as black anger and white denial of the racial basis of the act overwhelm any constructive dialogue; shame, fear, and outrage overflow at such times.

The necessity is underscored of enabling and encouraging familiarity across races in every social institution—housing, schools, places of worship, the workplace—but especially in places where people can be themselves and express their humanity to one another. People would probably work out their racial differences on their own if it were not for the vested interest of powerful political and business institutions to keep race performing its historic and unchanged role of keeping people divided and focused away from more basic class divisions.

## Best Practices That Are Simple to Emulate: Rhode Island College Unity Players

In 2004 the Unity Players of Rhode Island College (RIC) celebrated their fifth year as a multiracial volunteer group of students devoted to educating young people about race and diversity through skits, rap, musical performance, and, most importantly, dialogue. Several "generations" of students have worked with the Unity Players since their first performance in May 1999 for fifth- and sixth-graders at the Henry Barnard Lab School on campus after being recruited from my Anthropology of Race and Racism class. Since then they have performed at local colleges and universities, at high schools, and at various community events. In 2001 they were the recipients of the Greater Providence NAACP's Community Service Award. Individual members of the Unity Players have spoken in RIC classes about their role in diversity education. Veteran player Chris Souza plans a career in education, while hip-hop artist Hannah Resseger has frequently performed her own work in classes on subjects from "American History: The Real Story" to affirmative action and white privilege. Other former members of the Unity Players have gone on to professional activist and acting careers, such as Ghislaine Jean, who has performed with the Black Repertory Company and performs for community service groups.

Perhaps the best way to describe the focused improvisational style of the skits that the Unity Players perform is to quote from an article about them that was published in the *Providence Journal* describing that early performance at the Henry Barnard Lab School.

Figure 8.1.   Rhode Island College Unity Players, 2001. Courtesy of the author.

*Scene One*

Children fight over a toy in the playground. One boy, who is white, yells to his black friend, "Why don't you just go back to where you came from?" The black boy retorts, "You brought us here."

*Scene Two*

At a basketball court at school, two youths push aside two Asian girls trying to join in. "Aren't you Chinese too smart for basketball?" one of the boys says sarcastically. "We're Cambodian, not Chinese," one girl corrects. Her answer doesn't make a difference to this boy, who continues with his these-people-are-too-smart theme. "Why don't you ask your principal if you can go to school seven days a week? On second thought, we'll let you come back and play, if you bring back two egg rolls and fried rice."

**Figure 8.2.   Rhode Island College Unity Players, 2004. Courtesy of the author.**

*Scene Three*

A boy and a girl, both French speakers, encounter each other at school and begin conversing in French. Another boy, looking up from his book, finds it irritating. "Excuse me," he says, "speak English." "What's your problem?" the girl asks. "This is the language we speak in our country. This is America and over here we speak English. You're just speaking mumbo jumbo."

*Scene Four*

An elementary schoolgirl who is white informs her father that she intends to sleep over at the home of her friend Tenika. "Tenika?" he says. "That sounds like a black name." "Well, Tenika is black, and she's my friend." "So you're friendly with a black person? Why did you do this? Don't you know that black people are not as good as you? No, you can't sleep over." They change plans and decide to sleep over at Mary Beth's home.

At Tenika's home, Tenika runs into a similar problem. Her parents, who are black, express concern about their daughter's plan. "Where does Mary Beth live, anyway?" the father asks. "Barrington [white suburbs]. I'm not going to let you go," the father says. "They're not used to black people over there. They will stare at you and call you names."

*Scene Five*

A more complex problem regarding another sleepover in a predominantly black neighborhood emerges at the home of a girl whose parents are interracial. Her black father sees no problem with the sleepover, but her white mother is horrified. "You can't go there," she exclaims, "there's so much crime." "What's wrong with that neighborhood?" the father asks. "That's where I grew up—look, it was safe enough for me and it is safe enough for my daughter." "No, it's a terrible place, I won't let her go," the mother insists. (Extracted from *Providence Journal* 1999.)

For college-level audiences the Unity Players have performed skits about the word "nig—r" and critiqued and contextualized its frequent use in rap and hip-hop lyrics. They have condemned the word "mulatto" for its origins and misuse. "Mulatto" comes from the word "mule," the sterile offspring of a horse and a donkey, and should not be applied to humans, they argue. Their skit "Cream in Your Coffee" delves into problems of interracial dating and the problem of black and white female rivalry over dating black athletes at predominantly white private schools.

Other relevant skits deal with the dynamics of driving or shopping while black or brown and often have a sharp-edged twist. In one, black college student drivers are stopped in a predominantly white neighborhood when they are returning from an intercollegiate basketball game. A white friend is sitting in the back, and they are having fun singing the lyrics of a song on the radio when the police stop the car. Experienced with such stops the black student driver displays his college ID along with his driver's license. The police demand a search for drugs, to which all of the passengers object, but the police separate the blacks and the white student—telling her that she has no business being with this crowd. A sharp exchange over potential civil rights violations ensues, and the black students are arrested, leaving the white student "free" to drive the car back to the college. This ending, with the white student shocked at the treatment of her friends, sparks a dialogue with the audience, which is always rich.

In another skit, black and brown shoppers are subject to surveillance by black and white clerks. They are closely and comically shadowed, while a white male shoplifter openly stuffs clothing and jewelry into a backpack and then exits the store. As beepers sound the staff attempts to prevent the black customers from exiting the store. Sometimes the skits are pur-posely overdrawn, but the tactic is effective as it often provokes audience reaction and participation from multiple racial and ethnic perspectives. White counterculture youth speak of their being profiled—perhaps for their dress, hairstyle, or attitude—nearly every male of color has one or multiple variations of the story to tell. Young women are increasingly scrutinized as potential shoplifters, but candid white women often reveal that they are able to shop without the "inconvenience" of racial or gender profiling.

The Unity Players always remind their audiences that creating such groups in their schools or universities is easy and fun. The sense of mis-sion is most often what attracts the volunteers initially, but the fun of per-forming and becoming close with a multiracial group of friends is a significant by-product.

## FINAL REMARKS

Education and increasing familiarity across racial lines are key to a funda-mental alteration of American racial practices. The persistence of de facto segregation means that most Americans miss having opportunities to know and understand members of racial groups different from their own. How many white students from America's suburbs come to know their first African Americans and Latinos in college? The important task of demythologizing race—from kindergarten through secondary and higher education—is best complemented with sustained, intensive interactions among children of varying racial backgrounds. It is important to explain racial difference practically and scientifically at an early age. Answering questions children have about differences in skin color or hair form can easily lead to the more difficult task of tackling racial stereotypes, such as the "natural" rhythm or athleticism of blacks, or the "innate" intelligence of Asians, or the violence of "hot-tempered" Latinos. A reflective teacher will explore with her or his students the fact that there are few if any "nat-ural" stereotypes of whites, who are offered a full range of their humanity in society. For example, Timothy McVeigh can bomb the Murra Federal Building in Oklahoma City without the accusation being leveled that all whites are terrorists, as has been alleged of Arabs and Muslims.

I could not end this book with a better quote than that of pioneering anthropologist Anténor Firmin, who concluded his great 1885 tome, *The Equality of the Human Races*, with the exhortation to humans, irrespective of race and of its often brutal history, simply to love one another.

**Figure 8.3.    Inspirational message, New York City, 1993. Courtesy of Jane Feldman.**

## REFERENCES

Burger, Frederick. 2002. "The Ghosts of Alabama." *Newsweek*, May 27.
Fears, Darryl. 2001. "Despite Desegregation, Whites, Minorities Still Far Apart." *Providence Journal*, July 19, A2.
Gitlin, Todd, and Earl Ofari Hutchinson. 2001. "Mutual Cluelessness." *Philadelphia Inquirer*.
Harrison, Faye V. 2002. "Unraveling 'Race' for the Twenty-first Century." In *Exotic No More: Anthropology on the Front Lines*, edited by Jeremy MacClancy, 145–66. Chicago: University of Chicago Press.
———. 1995. "The Persistent Power of 'Race' in the Culture and Political Economy of Racism." *Annual Review of Anthropology* 24:47–74.
Ignatiev, Noel. 1996. *How the Irish Became White*. New York: Routledge.
Jefferson, Thomas. 1787. "Notes on the State of Virginia." In *The Heath Anthology of American Literature*, 4th ed. Repr., Boston: Houghton Mifflin, 2002.
Kivel, Paul. 1996. *Uprooting Racism: How White People Can Work for Racial Justice*. Gabriola Island, Canada: New Society Publishers.
Ling, Christina. 2001. "Blacks, Whites Still Geographically Divided, Data Show." *Philadelphia Inquirer*, August 13, A2.
McIntosh, Peggy. 1988. "White Privilege: Unpacking the Invisible Knapsack." Abstracted from "White Privilege and Male Privilege: A Personal Account of Coming to See Correspondences through Work in Women's Studies," all rights reserved. Wellesley College Center for Research on Women, Wellesley, MA.

Murphy, Dean E., and David M. Halbfinger. 2002. "9/11 Aftermath Bridged Racial Divide, New Yorkers Say, Gingerly." *New York Times*, June 16, 21.

Pike, Douglas. 2001. "A Presidential Bid Might Raise Views on Asian Americans." *Philadelphia Inquirer*, August 15, A23.

*Providence Journal*. 1999. "RIC Students Act Out Many Signs of Racism for Classes at Barnard," May 10.

———. 2002. "Alleged Plotters of 'Racial Holy War' on Trial," July 9, A2.

*Race and Ethnicity in 2001: Attitudes, Perceptions and Experiences*. 2001. Washington Post/Kaiser/Harvard University Survey Project. Washington, DC: Kaiser Foundation.

Sacks, Karen Brodkin. 1994. "How the Jews Became White Folks." In *Race*, edited by Steven Gregory and Roger Sanjek, 78–102. New Brunswick, NJ: Rutgers University Press.

Shanklin, Eugenia. 1998. "The Profession of the Color Blind: Sociocultural Anthropology and Racism in the 21st Century." *American Anthropologist* 100, no. 3:669–79.

# Index

# About the Author

Carolyn Fluehr-Lobban, PhD, is professor of anthropology at Rhode Island College, where she teaches courses in anthropology and African and Afro-American studies. At Rhode Island College she has received both the Award for Distinguished Teaching in 1990 and the Award for Distinguished Scholar in 1998. Since 1976 she has taught Anthropology of Race and Racism at Rhode Island College.

She is the author or editor of eleven books, among them *Islamic Societies in Practice* (1994; second edition, 2004) and *Islamic Law and Society in the Sudan* (1987; second edition, 2004), which has been translated into Arabic. She also edited *Ethics and the Profession of Anthropology: Dialogue for a New Era* (1990; second edition, 2003), and with Haitian collaborator Asselin Charles she published in 2000 the first major work of anthropology by a scholar of African descent, Anténor Firmin's *The Equality of the Human Races*, originally published in French as *De L'égalité des Races Humaines* in 1885. Recently she coedited *Race and Identity in the Nile Valley: Ancient and Contemporary Perspectives* (2004).